"BENEATH IËRNE'S BANNERS"

"BENEATH IËRNE'S BANNERS"

Irish Protestant Drama of the Restoration and Eighteenth Century

Christopher J. Wheatley

UNIVERSITY OF NOTRE DAME PRESS

Notre Dame, Indiana

Library of Congress Cataloging-in-Publication Data

Wheatley, Christopher J., 1955–

Beneath Ïerne's banners : Irish protestant drama of the

Restoration and eighteenth century / Christopher J. Wheatley.

p.   cm.

Includes bibliographical references and index.

ISBN 0-268-02158-9 (cloth : alk. paper)

1. English drama—Irish authors—History and criticism.

2. English drama—Restoration, 1660-1700—History and criticism.

3. English drama—Protestant authors—History and criticism.

4. Protestantism and literature—History—17th century.

5. Protestantism and literature—History—18th century.   6. English

drama—18th century—History and criticism.   7. Theater—Ireland—

Dublin—History—17th century.   8.   Theater—Ireland—Dublin—

History—18th century.   9. Christianity and literature—Ireland—

History.   10. Protestants—Ireland—History—17th century.

11. Protestants—Ireland—History—18th century.   I. Title.

PR8785.W48   2000

822′.4099417—dc21   99-35477

CONTENTS

ACKNOWLEDGMENTS

ix

INTRODUCTION

*Originality and Derivation in Seventeenth- and Eighteenth-
Century Irish Drama*   1

1.

Dublin as Utopia: Symbolic Construction in Richard Head's
Hic et Ubique; or, the Humours of Dublin   15

2.

*"I've saved your Country, and would gain your Love":
Conquest and Conciliation in the Plays of Charles Shadwell*   29

3.

*"And mix their Blood with ours; one People grow": The
Ambivalent Nationalism of William Philips's* Hibernia Freed   49

4.

Robert Ashton's Heroic Palimpsest, The Battle of Aughrim   63

5.

*"Our own good, plain, old Irish English": Charles Macklin
(Cathal McLaughlin) and Protestant Convert Accommodations*   85

Contents

6.

"Beneath Ïerne's banners here I stand": Francis Dobbs,
Gorges Edmond Howard, and Irish Drama of the *1770s*   101

EPILOGUE

123

NOTES

133

BIBLIOGRAPHY

151

INDEX

161

ACKNOWLEDGMENTS

Research for this book was largely conducted on a Fulbright grant, for which I thank the Council for the International Exchange of Scholars and University College Galway. I am also grateful for the help and advice of the members of the English Department at Galway, and especially to Kevin Barry, department chair, and to Séamus Ó Maoláin for his wizardry at guessing what eighteenth-century phonetic renderings of spoken Irish in English orthography might have meant. Christopher Morash read the entire manuscript and made helpful suggestions, and provided authorial identifications on anonymous publications. Further research was done at the Linen Hall Library and Queen's University, Belfast, on a grant from the British Council, with financial aid from the Foley Fund of the English Department of the Catholic University of America; I am grateful for their support.

At various times, Irish historians have pointed me in the direction of archival and secondary materials, answered idiotic questions, and read chapters, with a patience and generosity that indicate *saint* and *scholar* are practically synonyms in Ireland. Nicholas Canny gave me the okay to call these playwrights Irish, the dashing and erudite Niall Ó Ciosáin allowed me to see his work on *The Battle of Aughrim* prior to its publication, Dáibhí Ó Cróinín answered numerous questions about seventeenth- and eighteenth-century Irish-language-histories, Kevin Whelan handed me many references I would never have found for myself, and David Hayton dissected two chapters and provided information about William Philips that, once more, I would never have found on my own. Above all, Thomas Bartlett was a fountain of information and direction on the eighteenth century, particularly at regular Saturday afternoon tutorials at Taylor's in Galway.

In Ireland, Eileen Wheatley and Bill Mackay, Paul Moloney and Pauline Wheatley, and Jane and Aidan Hanratty were my sources for information on Dublin social life, just as Patrick and Reena Burke and Michael and Margaret Donnellan supplied information on Irish rural life. Mary Keane and Barbara Cahalane of the Law Society helped with Irish legal history and excavations of Leeson Street. Danny and Alice Carr not merely taught me about Irish cuisine but embodied the virtues of Irish hospitality. Jane Leonard and Caroline Windrum of the Institute for Irish Studies in Belfast instructed me in the history of eminent Belfast establishments, such as the Crown. Martin Burke supplied intellectually stout discussion, while my great-uncle Martin Burke (no relation to the above) was a constant source of wisdom.

Stateside, Helen Burke and John Greene have been participants in many con-

versations on Irish drama, regular copanelists at eighteenth-century confer-
ences, and morale builders while this book was being written: I have borrowed ideas from them shamelessly. Kirk Combe clarified my thinking on
Charles Shadwell. Kevin Donovan explained the relationship between various texts slowly and carefully, which is the only way I could follow them, and
made detailed comments on a draft of this book. At my own university, Mark
Scowcroft was my source for information on the Irish language. Work-study
student Joanne Macguire cheerfully typed and went to the library. Barbara
Talbot read most of this book and made helpful suggestions, as did my father,
John Wheatley. Of course, conversation with Ernest Suarez always provides
intellectual fermentation, and he remains adept at distilling insight out of it.

Further, I am indebted to the library staffs at University College Galway, the
Royal Irish Academy, the National Library of Ireland, Dublin City Library,
Trinity College Library, Queen's University Belfast Library, the Linen Hall
Library, Cambridge University Library, the Library of Congress, the Folger
Shakespeare Library, and the Catholic University of America. I must also
thank Peter Holland of Trinity Hall at Cambridge for allowing me a room
while I was doing research there, and Margo Shearman for copyediting the
manuscript for Notre Dame.

I would like to blame any remaining absurdities on the Arthur Guinness
Company but, after the aid detailed above, can only attribute them to uncon-
querable ignorance.

Originality and Derivation in Seventeenth- and Eighteenth-Century Irish Drama

Some readers will assume this book is mistitled, on the grounds that there was no Irish drama in the seventeenth and eighteenth centuries. Vivian Mercier states flatly that "Anglo-Irish literature began to separate itself decisively from English literature with the publication of *Castle Rackrent* in 1800—I offer no apology for so hackneyed a view."[1] J. C. Beckett claims that literature in general and drama in particular in Dublin in the eighteenth century was derivative of English drama: "In the drama, as in other branches of literature, the influence of London was predominant: Dublin audiences wanted to see the plays that London was talking about; and the Irish dramatist who had made his first success in Dublin wanted, as soon as possible, to repeat and extend it in London."[2] In Beckett's view, Irish writers were dependent financially on the London market; moreover, there was no independent Anglo-Irish culture upon which they could draw for cultural sustenance. Roger McHugh and Maurice Harmon claim that Dublin theaters "performed the function of provincial theaters, offering the same fare as English theaters or providing premises for touring English companies which, increasingly in the eighteenth century, toured the Irish provincial towns."[3] Seamus Deane concurs in stating that the Dublin theater was "little more than a reflection of the London theatres, Drury Lane and Covent Garden, governed by what was fashionable and successful there, especially in the field of light entertainment."[4]

The consequence of this widespread agreement about the nonexistence of Irish drama prior to the twentieth century is that in the *Field Day Anthology of Irish Literature* (1991), the ambitious attempt to establish a canon for Irish literary history, Christopher Murray (the editor of the eighteenth-century drama section) selects a group of plays that largely demonstrates the proposition. With the exception of Thomas Sheridan's *The Brave Irishman* (1743), and selections from Charles Macklin's *The True-Born Irishman* (1762) and John O'Keeffe's *The Poor Soldier* (1783), Murray's choices are difficult to distinguish from contemporary English drama. By this I mean that if one did not know where Farquhar was born and bred, one would probably not guess it from *The Beaux Stratagem* (1707), any more than one would guess Hugh Kelly was from Ireland from *The School for Wives* (1773). Farquhar is clearly influenced by both Vanbrugh and Cibber, and Kelly's work is very similar to that of, among others, Hannah Cowley.

While I would like to avoid the sort of historical one-upmanship that Gerard O'Brien identifies in analysis of the decay of the Irish language[5]—I am not attempting to push back the date of Irish literary nationalism beyond the 1770s—whether the playwrights writing in Ireland were essentially derivative of the English stage seems to me to be a much more complex question than the unanimity of historical and critical authorities claiming it was would suggest. That the vast majority of the plays presented in Ireland were written in England is clear.[6] Moreover, eighteenth-century critics also commented on the limited quantity of original Irish drama. An anonymous commentator, in an undated epistle probably from 1758, complains that the Irish stage suffers from poor acting and that

> to this capital Defect, another may be added:— the Sterility of the *Irish* Stage with respect to new Pieces. True it is, that in *London* our Countrymen have wiped off the Reproach under which we long laboured, and have furnished Pieces for the Theatre that are deservedly considered an Ornament to it: Nay, they seem to have obtained an exclusive Possession of it, and to have united in sharing its Emoluments and Fame.[7]

The English encourage playwrights, while Irish stage managers, the critic goes on to say, cannot even be bothered to read the plays that are submitted to them. However, both in terms of subject matter and generic conventions, Irish dramatists in Ireland wrote plays distinctly different from those produced in London, and I think these plays have been overlooked because of dubious assumptions about dramatic innovation and cultural nationalism.

Tragicomedy in Dublin, for instance, does not resemble the English variety. Henry Burnell's *Landgartha* (premiered in Dublin 17 March 1639)[8] ends with Landgartha unreconciled to her husband, Reyner, whom she has rescued from his rebellious Danish subjects, despite the fact that he has been unfaithful with the Swedish Vraca. Love and magnanimity require her noble rescue of Reyner, but she returns to Norway indicating that she will not allow him to return to the bed that he has polluted, despite the pleas not only of Reyner's advisers but of her own amazons. The printed version of Burnell's play ends with this justification:

> Some (but not of the best judgements) were offended at the Conclusion of this Play, in regard Landgartha tooke not then, what she was perswaded to by so many, the Kings kind night-imbraces. To which kinde of people (that know not what they say) I answer (omitting all other reasons:) that a Tragi-Comedy sho'd neither end Comically or Tragically, but betwixt both: which Decorum I did my best to

observe, not to goe against Art, to please the over-amorous. To the rest of the
bablers, I despise any answer.[9]

No one familiar with English tragicomedy is going to recognize this formulation. John Fletcher, regarded as the chief practitioner of English tragicomedy
as the term is usually understood, described it as a play in which the main
characters are brought near to death but do not die: "a tragie-comedy is not so
called in respect of mirth and killing, but in respect it wants death, which is
inough to make it no tragedie, yet brings some neere it, which is inough to
make it no comedie."[10] Fletcher's plays have happy endings; indeterminacy is
no part of English tragicomedy.[11] If *Landgartha* had been produced in London,
Landgartha and Reyner would have been reconciled.

Moreover, the entire tone of the passage is not of some modest imitator but
of a confident artist, and John Bermingham's epistle dedicatory to *Landgartha*
also indicates a high degree of regard:

> (Let others boast of their owne faculties,
> Or being Sonne to Johnson) I dare say
> That thou art farre more like to Ben; than they
> That lay clayme as heires to him wrongfully:
> . . . .
> Nay, I can more affirme (and truly) that
> In some things thou do'st passe him: being more sweet,
> More modest, mylde, lesse tedious: Thy owne feet
> Goe thou on stoutly then: if thou proceed,
> Him (though't be much) in all points thou'lt exceed.

With the benefit of 350 years of hindsight, we can see that the comparison is
absurd, but aesthetic batting averages were still fluid then.[12] In any case, when
Bermingham unapologetically claims Burnell is in some things better and
likely to surpass Ben in all, his rhetoric of praise only makes sense if he believes
some readers are likely to agree with him.

Also, that Burnell is identified as a son of Ben when Burnell is writing tragicomedy—Jonson did not—again shows a gap between what Burnell and
Bermingham thought of dramatic practice and what English playwrights and
critics thought; whether or not the late twentieth century finds the comparison
believable is irrelevant. Catharine Shaw argues compellingly that Burnell's play
is a complex political allegory pleading with Charles I (Reyner) to be faithful to
the Old English (Landgartha) instead of the Protestant New English (Vraca);
this would clearly make the play more interesting to a Dublin audience than to
an English one.[13] But even if one denies the play's political subtext, we clearly
have a play that is not best understood in terms of English models. Burnell,
who became a member of the Catholic Confederacy, is not slavishly following
English assumptions of dramatic forms.

Nor is Burnell's character of Marfisa typical of the English stage.[14] A comical Irish figure—she is introduced wearing "an Irish Gowne tuck'd up to mid-

legge, with a broad basket-hilt Sword on, hanging in a great Belt, Broags on her feet, her hayre dishevell'd, and a pair of long neck'd big rowell'd Spurs on her heels" (20)—she is nevertheless "Cossen-german to th' Lady *Fatyma*," one of Landgartha's Norwegian and, in Shaw's analysis, Old English amazons. The implicit threat in Burnell's play is that the native Irish are more likely to aid the Old English than the New English in the complicated political position of the late 1630s, a threat that turned out to be more or less true in the 1640s. More importantly, Burnell acknowledges that some of the Old English are in fact related to the native population, something an Old English playwright would, perhaps, not have mentioned to an English audience, from whom one might wish to conceal family indiscretions; the English mostly thought the Irish were savages.

Just as *Landgartha* differs significantly from English tragicomedy, eighteenth-century Irish tragedies tend to diverge from English practice in the matter of the death of the protagonist. While it is true that Aristotle defines tragedy as the imitation of a significant action, which obviously implies a rising action is as possible as a falling one, and French tragedians of the seventeenth century, notably Pierre Corneille, leave noble protagonists alive at the end of the play, the standard English practice is that somebody other than just the villain must die. Whether it is the title character in Addison's *Cato* (1713), Rowe's *Jane Shore* (1714), Samuel Johnson's *Irene* (1749), John Home's *Douglas* (1756), or George Barnwell in Lillo's *The London Merchant* (1731), a sympathetic though erring or flawed protagonist must die for tragic effect.

However, in Irish tragedies of the eighteenth-century, such as Charles Shadwell's *Rotherick O'Connor* (1719), William Philips's *Hibernia Freed* (1722), Francis Dobbs's *The Patriot King* (1773), and Gorges Edmond Howard's *The Siege of Tamor* (1773), only the villains die. In each case, the hero or heroes, Strongbow, O'Brien, Ceallachan, and Malsechlin respectively, live happily ever after. Whether one wishes to attribute this to French influence on the Irish stage, theories of poetic justice, or a complex fear upon the part of the Anglo-Irish as a minority in catholic Ireland (and, consequently, unwilling to contemplate utter catastrophe), the fact remains that Irish tragedy does not look like most of English tragedy.

Although these plays represent dramatic forms that are not simple imitations of the English theater, when there are overlaps between drama in England and Ireland, the similarity between plays may be a function of genre rather than an indication of subordination. By this I mean that in the European dramatic tradition the number of playwrights who have produced something that is genuinely *sui generis* or that initiates an entirely new view of drama are few and far between. Marlowe may drag the English stage "from jigging veins of rhyming mother wits" in *Tamburlaine* to the "high astounding terms" of blank verse tragedy, but it is not long before Shakespeare arrives to do it better. And some kinds of dramatic ideas just seem to be ripe at a particular time. Thus Brecht and Wilder for wholly different reasons assault the fourth wall at about the same time in the late 1920s; subsequently they knew and admired each other's stagecraft (while obviously having nothing in common politically), but there is simply no way to ascribe "influence" to one over the other. The position is analogous to the debate over the discovery/invention of calculus. Newton may have beaten Leibnitz to the punch, but there is no reason to doubt that Leibnitz developed calculus independently, and if neither of them had, somebody else would have to answer the kind of questions that were being asked at the end of the seventeenth century.

Thus in Charles Shadwell's *Rotherick O'Connor* (produced in Dublin in 1719)[15] the son of Dermod who becomes the tragic scapegoat is the characteristically noble and doomed sentimental youth who appears in much of the drama of this period in England (such as Marcus in Addison's *Cato*).[16] Strongbow is victorious and O'Connor is too villainous, so someone else had to bear the weight of the catharsis: the formulaic nature of the son is apparent in his name; named Cothurne in Sir Richard Cox's *History of Ireland*, Shadwell's probable source, he becomes in Shadwell's play Cothurnus, which simply means the tragic buskin, emblem of the genre tragedy. Nevertheless, the subject of the play is from Irish history, the Norman victory over the native Gaelic population. And while the play exploits an immediate topical application in terms of anti-Jacobite fears in England and Ireland, there is no getting around the fact that Strongbow is also Catholic; neither side, native Irish or Old English, is identical with the Protestant audience watching the play in Smock Alley. Some kind of Irish history that cannot be subsumed in English history is present here. When Eva, daughter of Dermod, says about the Normans, "But when they have conquered all our Enemy's,/Perhaps they'll then attack my Father's Friends,/And so in Time make slaves of all this Island,"[17] Shadwell, son of the Whig poet laureate Thomas Shadwell, presumably intends to show she's mistaken over the course of the play; the Irish will be better off with the English, as the prologue makes clear:

> He brings to View, five hundred Years ago,
> *Heroes* nursed up in Slaughter, Blood and Woe:
> Kings, that Governed with an Arbitrary Sway,
> And slavish Subjects, born but to Obey.
> When *Brehon* Laws cou'd reach the Subjects Life,
> And none but great Ones, dare support the Strife.
> (2,267, italics reversed)

Rotherick becomes an analogue for James II or James III (the old Pretender), and Strongbow of course represents either William III or George I; Rotherick symbolizes the arbitrary power Whigs perceived in Stuart monarchy, and Strongbow, bizarrely, signifies a lawful, constitutionally bound monarch like William III. But Shadwell, as the prologue also says, "tries by Different Ways to please,/And shews you Kings, That never cross'd the seas" (267). The fact that characters such as Regan, Cothurnus, and Eva, none of whom receive any development in Cox, are sympathetic inevitably distinguishes them from the stage Irishmen current at Covent Garden and Drury Lane, where the Irish servant is allowed to be good-hearted although inept. And even though Eva is shown to be mistaken about the English, Shadwell has to give her a voice, if only so that she can be refuted. In short, although the form of *Rotherick O'Connor* is not inherently distinct from English tragedy, the subject and characters, while appropriated to English political concerns, remain recognizably not English (whether one would want to call them Irish is an issue that, if not separate, is at least separable).

Similarly, Mary O'Brien's *The Fallen Patriot* (1790) possesses the recognizable elements of some late eighteenth-century comedy: a witty heroine, Harriet; a sentimental heroine, Eliza; a witty hero, Major McCarthy; a sentimental hero, Freeport; and a sudden discovery of a long-lost father to save the day at the end. Still, the dominance of "sentimental comedy" in the period has been overstated,[18] and what really matters in the play is the political satire; the noble Freeport enters "dressed as a Volunteer," and Sir Richard Greyley is the comic butt because "I have barter'd—my country's rights for a title, and am dubb'd a Knight, forsooth, to please my simple helpmate."[19] The political issues of the play are issues concerning Ireland, not England, and *The Fallen Patriot* acknowledges its ties to a heritage absent from the English stage. Eliza says, "Aunt Madge never made a better confession to a Franciscan Friar in the warmest fit of devotion than I have done to Dame Reason" (16). Aunt Madge may have been either Old English or Gaelic, but the heroine acknowledges relatives who are not members of the Protestant ascendancy.

Just as an eighteenth-century Irish comedy is likely to share some generic characteristics with an English (or French) comedy, so too eighteenth-century Irish tragedy reveals some similarities with English (and Scottish) tragedy. In Gorges Edmond Howard's *The Siege of Tamor* (1773), the hero, Niall, declaims,

> Never, O! never, may Iërne yield!
> Ne'er be a vassal to a foreign yoke!
> Behold the stag, that haunts the vast desert!
> Free and delighted 'midst its wastes he roams,
> Nor fears the hunter's wiles. High o'er the cliff,
> Whose awful brow o'ershades the foamy deep,
> Mark how the tow'ring eagle builds his nest.[20]

The language of extended metaphors and the invocation of the sublime coming from a disguised hero recall John Home's hit *Douglas* (1757). But the rest of Niall's speech is entirely late-eighteenth-century Irish Protestant nationalism:

> All, all of earth, of air aloud proclaim,
> That liberty, though join'd with toil, with want,
> And peril imminent, is nature's charter.

(1,205)

Influence of various sorts is clearly apparent here, but artistically the influence runs from Scotland to Dublin, and politically from North America to Dublin.

William Philips's *Hibernia Freed* (first staged in London in 1722)[21] is, I believe, an oblique response to Swift's *Proposal for the Universal Use of Irish Manu-facture* (1720). Swift writes, "The Scripture tells us, that *Oppression makes a wise Man mad*; Therefore, consequently speaking, the Reason why some men are not *Mad*, is because they are not *Wise:* However, it were to be wish'd that Oppression wou'd in time teach a little *Wisdom* to *Fools*."[22] An anonymous re-spondent is frightened of the consequences of Swift's polemic: "He [Swift] stimulates them with an Aggravation of their Wrongs, and instead of Oyl pours Vinegar in to their wounds. . . . Wise-men more frequently make Op-pression light by bearing it."[23] The endurance of political subjugation recurs throughout Philips's play as the noble O'Brien bears with Turgesius' oppres-sion:

> The loss of Empire and the Loss of Pow'r
> We may support, while Reason is our Guide.
> Better be subject to the Danes, than as
> This Dane, to ev'ry Passion be a Slave.[24]

The theme of patient acceptance of foreign rule is here embodied for a London audience and a restless Irish Protestant readership unhappy with restrictions on Irish trade. Stoic patience is better than Swiftian madness.

But what the play shows is O'Brien and O'Neill defeating the Danes. When the libidinous Danes call for women, O'Neill and a chosen few show up as cross-dressers and stab the Danes to death. Whatever Philips sets out to preach (and at the end of the play the bard Eugenius foretells that the English will come benignly to conquer and civilize the Irish), the play shows successful violent resistance to a foreign power. The theme of the play, then, is that the Irish should endure rather than rebel, but the administration had best beware pushing nascent Irish nationalists too far. Granted the Declaratory Act of 1720, which asserted the authority of the English Parliament over Ireland, it is hard to see why an English playwright would dramatize this sentiment, since the English presumably regarded the issue as settled.

Attempts to find an Irish sensibility informing plays that share generic characteristics with plays on the English stage will inevitably lead one to draw blurry lines. Thus *Love à la Mode*, by Charles Macklin (born Cathal McLaughlin), which premiered in Drury Lane in 1759, seems like a fairly or-dinary English farce, despite the nobility of the successful suitor, Sir Callaghan O'Brallaghan.[25] Likable but comical Irishman were becoming increasingly popular on the London stage at the time,[26] and even George II was pleased that the Irishman triumphed over a group of rivals made up of a Jew, a Scotsman, and an English country bumpkin.[27] Macklin's exceptionally good political com-edy *The Man of the World* does not seem to possess any Irish referent whatso-ever, as the object of satire is a Scotsman in the English administration.

But *The Man of the World* originally premiered in Dublin in 1764 as *The True-Born Scotchman*; only after being rejected in 1770 and 1779, and signifi-cantly toned down, was it accepted for the English stage in 1781.[28] In 1785 the full-length play with Macklin in the lead was the toast of Dublin. Partially this can be explained by the applicability of patriot satire on maladministration to either Dublin or London, but Macklin's Irish identity also partially accounts for the play's Dublin success, as an early biographer points out:

> He had likewise other qualifications to ingratiate himself with the people of Ireland; he was their countryman, and had acquired a long celebrity from his professional talents, and even from his longevity; he was, besides this, what he used to call himself—a *College man,* (being originally a badge-man to the College,) and from this situation could remember the ancestors of most of the people of distinction in and about Dublin.[29]

Class and race are transcended by an Irish identity in a star performer like Macklin (after Garrick, possibly the most influential of the century because of his portrayal of Shylock). In a real sense the play belongs to Ireland because of its inception, early success, and Irish author.

While *The Man of the World* is Irish by origin, Macklin's *The True-Born Irishman* is unmistakably Irish because of its subject, despite its conventional farcical structure. Popular in its Dublin premiere at Crow Street in 1762, it bombed as *The Irish Fine Lady* before English audiences in 1767.[30] This is not surprising; the chief requirement of the title character when he reconciles with his wife is that she cease to anglicize his name to Diggerty:

> O'Dogherty!—there's a sound for you—why they have not such a name in all England as O'Dogherty—nor any of our fine sounding Milesian names—what are your Jones and your Stones, your Rice and your Price, your Heads and Foots, and Hands, and your Wills, and Hills and Mills, and Sands, and a parcel of little pimping names that a man would not pick out of the street, compared to the O'Donovans, O'Callaghans, O'Sullivans, O'Brallaghans, O'Shagnesses, O'Flaherty's, O'Gallaghers, and O'Dogherty's—Ogh, they have courage in the very sound of them, for they come out of the mouth like a storm.[31]

In contrast to one-syllable English names that describe geological phenomena, body parts, and commodities, Macklin offers the names of the ancient Irish aristocracy—many of whom he claimed as relatives, and whose descendants, as converts, were sitting in the audience. Yet another early Macklin biographer explained the failure of *The Irish Fine Lady* in terms of its Irish orientation; it was "rather too long, and calculated only for the meridian of Dublin."[32] Unapologetic and intelligent Irishmen who satirize a prosaic English character succeed in the Irish theater, not the English.

Even to make English victory noble, the defeated Irish must be a worthy opponent; this is a creative principle going back to the *Iliad,* and Robert Ashton in his 1728 tragedy *The Battle of Aughrim and the Fall of St. Ruth* specifically invokes that comparison:

> Never did *Cæsar* do an action bolder,
> And was our Author but a little Older,
> Not *Pompey*'s Triumphs nor great *Scipio*'s Fame,

Could once compare with glorious *William*'s Name:
'Tis True, the *Irish* found it to their Cost,
They fought the Battle bravely which they lost,
Even like *Hectors* as for a Time they stood,
And e're they run, they dy'd the field in Blood;
Not great *Pharsalia*, nor the *Africk* Coast,
Could ever so great a Wonder Boast.[33]

If De Gincle is to be Achilles, then Sarsfield has to be Hector; there is no merit in victory against an easy foe. But the literary allusions in Ashton's speech complicate the picture even more. The reference to Pharsalia, while explicitly mentioning Pompey, leaves out Cato, the defender of Roman liberty against the tyrannical usurper Caesar in Addison's popular tragedy; Pharsalia is a great victory for the Roman empire but the *coup de grâce* for the Roman republic. Caesar is a great conqueror in the theatrical imagination of the early eighteenth century, but Cato, and consequently Sarsfield, are the sympathetic patriots.

Carleton in his autobiography mentions that in his youth in Ulster, Protestants would perform *The Battle of Aughrim* in a barn with a religiously mixed audience and cast.[34] There is an eerie symbolism in Catholics' repeatedly enacting defeat, but it also shows the surprising complexity of Ashton's play. With the exception of an occasional outburst from St. Ruth about instituting the Inquisition in Ireland after a victory, the play presents all the players as patriotic and brave. And if the play reaffirms Catholic defeat, it also dramatizes Catholic defiance—which may be why I have found no record of performance in the official theaters, although the play went through at least twenty-five editions between 1770 and 1840.[35]

The question I have avoided to this point is whether these plays should be called Irish drama. My own predilection is to oversimplify and say that plays written or produced in Ireland, or on Irish subjects by someone born and raised in Ireland (i.e., Philips), should probably be called Irish because it is not clear what else one would want to call them. Or to put it another way, in the most radical case, Charles Shadwell, born and bred in England, and son of the Whig poet laureate, is difficult to describe as Irish (although there are Irish connections—his grandfather was recorder of Galway, and his father was described by Dryden in *MacFlecknoe* as having an Irish wit). But Shadwell was the equivalent of playwright-in-residence at Smock Alley from 1715 to 1720. In *Irish Hospitality* (c. 1717-18) he writes what one might wish to describe as a typically English sentimental comedy, where the rakish son of the landlord reforms to marry the penniless but virtuous daughter of one of the tenants. But although the daughter's name is Winnifred, her mother is named Shela Dermott, implying a Gaelic connection, and the play is set in Fingall.[36] The marriage of New English and native Irish takes place at *finis galliae*, the end of the pale, and traditional Irish hospitality is incorporated in a new culture that is no longer simply English.[37] If Shadwell does not count as Irish literature, does Joseph Conrad's work not count as English literature, or Vladimir Nabokov's novels in English as American literature?

And the other playwrights represent much more complex cases than Shadwell (that is when we know anything about them). Burnell was from a family prominent in Dublin politics as early as the thirteenth century: they were not Gaelic, but assuredly not English, as the Normans of Ireland had long ceased to have much in common with Anglo-Normans. William Philips was the son of the governor of Derry; he says in his dedication to *Hibernia Freed* to the earl of Thomond, "Love of my Country induced me to lay the Scene of a Play there." And the choice as dedicatee of Henry O'Brien, earl of Thomond and a member of the Irish Privy Council, is particularly instructive for an understanding of Philips. As he points out, "None are ignorant that Your Lordship is lineally descended from the Monarchs of [Ireland]." Some Gaels might not have been happy with O'Brien, as his grandfather had converted to Protestantism, but that did not alter the fact that his family predated any English arrivals. And Philips is clearly laying claim to an Irish heritage in his choice of subjects. Sir Richard Cox claims that there is no Irish history prior to the Norman invasion; Keating and the Four Masters are simply writing fables.[38] In recapturing Irish history prior to the Norman conquest for dramatic purposes, Philips asserts a cultural identity independent of England.

Where Philips differs culturally from the English, Mary O'Brien differs politically; although little is known of her life, her politics are clear from her work, and show a dedicated Irish Whig. During the Regency crisis of 1789, she praises the Irish Parliament for sending a committee to ask the prince of Wales to assume the Regency, and blasts Pitt for his attempt to impose conditions:

> Arrah, then, my dear Billy,
>   It might prove in the pull,
> Paddy's not quite so silly
>   As your Jacky Bull.[39]

One of the villains of *The Fallen Patriot*, Captain Puff, is the son of a butler and an English lady. Since he pretends to be a gentleman, he is consequently a threat to the Irish heiress Harriet. Just as in the above verse the English bull turns out to be more silly than the Irish, O'Brien in her play reverses the conventional stereotype of the Irish fortune hunter by supplying an English cad; Puff attempts to prey on Irish women. On a larger level, and more dangerously, the English administration preys on Ireland herself.

John O'Keeffe, whom I shall discuss later (author of *The Poor Soldier* [1782] and *The Wicklow Mountains* [1796]), is clearly Irish by anyone's definition, although his biggest successes occurred in England, but most of these other playwrights exist in a shady area. The Irish have ignored them, but the English did not and do not regard them as English. In other words, we are not really in the situation of Eliot and Auden, where the English and Americans are inclined to claim both for themselves.

At this point I would like to flourish Occam's razor. No one would ever re-gard Kipling as part of an Indian literary tradition, despite the fact that he was born and raised in India, apparently loved the country (and I do not mean that ironically), and most of his best works are set there, because Kipling never thought of himself as anything but British. The definition of Irishness that most of the authors I have discussed would claim is exclusionary; they were for the most part members of what would come to be called the Anglo-Irish ascendancy. Nevertheless, if playwrights claim Irishness, and nobody else wants them, they should probably be described as such posthumously, whether or not they were so pluralistic themselves. What the plays I have discussed share is an interest in the events and history of Ireland, something that, with the exception of *Hibernia Freed*, the English stage could not have cared less about. Francis Dobbs I think speaks for all these playwrights in the prologue to *The Patriot King* (1773):

> To hold forth Nature, once the stage was meant:
> 'Tis strangely alter'd from its first intent.
> Were we by it to judge Ierne's sons,
> They all are honest—but they all are clowns.
> Yet truth has said, and I shall take her word,
> That some have grac'd a court—and some a cord.[40]

Dobbs's contempt for brogue, mentioned earlier in the prologue in connec-tion with "honest Teague," shows his contempt for the stage Irishman, even when that character is relatively benign. Dobbs is claiming a more complex history for Ierne's sons. He remains unconsciously exclusionary. The English audience's error is to "think a Porter's, is a nation's phrase." The "real" nation is the ruling elite of which Dobbs is a part. But the play shows an Irish hero, Ceallachan, drawn from Irish Catholic historical sources. The answer to the question "what ish my nation" for his play is larger than just his religious and social group, and reveals a dramatic syncretism not present at Drury Lane or Covent Garden. Nor should this be surprising. After all, Dobbs is a product of the European Enlightenment. Although he admired the politically conservative Samuel Johnson, he also admired Sterne, regarded Voltaire as a "universal gen-ius," and, at least by 1800, thought "that Germany now takes the lead in dra-matic performances."[41] Dobbs's recognition of the superiority of Goethe and Lessing to their English contemporaries shows good taste, but even more it shows a cosmopolitan erudition that cannot be reduced to "West British."

Peter Sequin's prologue for Howard's *The Siege of Tamor* asks for an audience that will incorporate both the sorrows and triumphs of Ireland's history into an Anglo-Irish bosom:

> Oh shame! not now to feel, not now to melt
> At woes, that whilom your fam'd country felt;
> Let your swol'n breasts, with kindred ardours glow!
> Let your swol'n eyes with kindred passions flow!

> So shall the treasure that alone endures,
> And all the worth of ancient times—be yours!
>
> (1,168)

Sequin's conclusion is striking: emotional empathy creates national identity. Religious and ethnic difference is subsumed by a conscious appropriation of an Irish heritage through the audience's response to a play. As Joseph Leerssen states about *The Siege of Tamor* as a whole, "The Dublin audiences thus effectively identify with the Milesian Gaels, and in this fact lies a basic difference from the London audiences whom Stage Irishmen served to confirm in their Englishness."[42] Howard's dramatic theory supports this identification. In his poem "On Seeing Mrs. Fitzhenry Play the Part of Jane Shore" he writes,

> With sympathetic pow'rs supremely strong
> The priestess thus arrests the list'ning throng;
> Informs their joys and griefs, their hopes and fears;
> And they in fact become, what she appears.[43]

The importance of drama from an eighteenth-century perspective is not merely its re-enactment of events but its creation of community. A well-acted play can turn an audience into mourners or fellow countrymen.

The few critics who have looked at eighteenth-century Irish drama seem to do so with critical blinkers. Thus Heinz Kosok dismisses John O'Keeffe's own claim that he was an "Irish" playwright and asserts that "O'Keeffe and his works belong predominantly to an English tradition of drama."[44] In an earlier and much better article not cited by Kosok, Karen J. Harvey and Kevin B. Pry have shown that O'Keeffe's plays depict "a poor agrarian country, plagued by sectarian differences, and suffering in large part from its uncaring and indifferent attitude on the part of its landowning elite who have, in the playwright's judgment, been shirking their responsibilities."[45] One could easily apply this description to Padraic Colum's *The Land*.

The difficulty is that Kosok, for instance, sees O'Keeffe as a supporter of the English monarchy; as a conservative unionist, O'Keeffe ceases to be an Irish writer. As it happens, St. John Ervine was also a conservative unionist. Yet Irish Catholics in the latter half of the eighteenth century tended to be royalists because the English monarchy was more sympathetic than the Irish Parliament. By twentieth-century standards, the authors of the plays I have discussed (with the exception of Dobbs) are "conservative"; so was almost everyone else in Ireland except the United Irishmen, and a fair number of them were interested in parliamentary reform rather than in a French-style revolution. In other words, Irish separatism is not very useful as an indication of whether or not someone was an Irish playwright.

These playwrights did not write in Irish, some did not have Gaelic names, they were not, for the most part, Catholic, and their plays are not examples of an indigenous literary tradition. But literary history is as much involved with discontinuities as it is with great traditions. *Beowulf*, *The Canterbury Tales*, and

Paradise Lost have not a great deal to do with each other, and all are heavily indebted to Continental sources; they are nevertheless important works in the canon of English literature and are of interest as historical documents. There is an eighteenth-century Irish drama, and it tells us a great deal about the developing notion of what it meant to be Irish in the eighteenth century, precisely because dramatists write for an audience. Lyric poets need not concern themselves with what their readers or auditors will or will not accept as "Irish." A playwright, on the other hand, hoping for not just approbation but the coin of the realm, is inherently engaged in a complex negotiation between his ideas and what the audience will accept. Ashton's *The Battle of Aughrim* is an example of a play that does not merely celebrate Protestant victory, but helps to define for Catholics their nobility in defeat. In the absence of controversy (e.g., the premiere of *Waiting for Godot*) one can assume that a play speaks for at least some segment of its audience.

I have chosen in this book to focus on the Protestant playwrights, partially because O'Keeffe and Burnell have already been the subject of fine articles, and partially because Catholic playwrights were shaped by different assumptions and experiences than were the Protestants; in other words, when I call the Protestant playwrights "Irish," I am by no means claiming that one definition fits all who would claim that heritage. As I shall show, Protestant Ireland, even excluding the Dissenters, was by no means a homogeneous group. Recent arrivals, Tory and Whig politicans, Catholic converts, and political reformers agreed on little except that their own group probably best represented moral rectitude and/or the real Irish nation. Thus this book is not an attempt to capture the elusive essence of Protestant Irish identity. On the contrary, each of the playwrights in this book defines Irishness in terms shaped by his or her own immediate circumstances. When I claim that this is a book about Irish playwrights, I mean only that these playwrights are best understood through reference to an Irish context, rather than as mere imitators of the English stage. My method throughout, then, is what some would deride as the "Old Historicism." That is, I have assumed the primacy of the author and play, and have attempted to illustrate the play by reference to a broader context, rather than by assuming that the context (and in particular the economic modes of production) determines the play (i.e., the "New Historicism").

The obvious question this book provokes is, why bother to examine these historical losers? One thinks, for instance, of Daniel Corkery's dismissal of what many of the Anglo-Irish would have regarded as their greatest achievement—parliamentary independence in 1782: "that noisy side-show, so bizarre in its lineaments and so tragi-comic in its fate."[46] After all, not merely did the Anglo-Irish fail to achieve Irish independence, after 1800 and the Act of Union they slowly dwindled to political insignificance. Moreover, the Irish Protestants of the seventeenth and early eighteenth centuries participated, actively or tacitly, in the attempts to erase the Gaelic culture they had displaced; a kind of cosmic irony attends their own erasure from consideration through much of the twentieth century. Corkery's dismissal of the Anglo-Irish and their literary creations has an odd parallel in Sean O'Faolain's dismissal of the Irish-language poets of the seventeenth and eighteenth centuries as having nothing to say to the majority of the Irish people about their real political and social conditions.[47] Between Corkery and O'Faolain, there seems little point in looking at literature in Ireland in the period at all.

Nevertheless, as Mary Helen Thuente has shown, the eighteenth-century background is important to understanding the United Irishmen's literary nationalism.[48] If the movement toward Irish independence is the unifying thread of the history of nineteenth- and early twentieth-century Ireland, then the writers who helped to prepare the material are worth considering. Even in the Restoration and the eighteenth century, I find it difficult to believe in a firewall between Gaelic and Saxon culture. An Irish epigram, possibly by Dáibhí Ó Bruadair, complains about the attempts of the Irish to speak English:

> Is it not strange how most of the men of Ireland
> have swelled of late with ostentatious pride?
> Though slack their grasp of the foreign scholars' writings
> they'll speak no tongue but the ghost of a clumsy English.[49]

English was the language of political and economic power. At least some of the Irish read or saw these plays and understood Irish history through them.

Finally, something is gained by recognizing that Irish culture is a complex tapestry, not merely a series of oppositional units: Catholic versus Protestant, colonizers and oppressed, aristocrats and peasants, rich and poor. When the only available models for social interaction are adversarial, conflict becomes unavoidable. The English attempt to colonize Ireland ultimately failed, even in Northern Ireland, whose citizens, whether Protestant or Catholic, are recognizably no more English than the Welsh or Scots. Still, traces of that attempt are present in contemporary Irish society, in law, architecture, and literature. What follows is, again, not an attempt to describe Protestant Ireland in the eighteenth century. Rather, it is an attempt to explain how some of the Protestants may have thought about the world to write the plays that they did. Their drama shows the mingling of English and Irish culture, and that, I hope, will be of interest to the Irish and their descendants today.

ONE

Dublin as Utopia

Symbolic Construction in Richard Head's
Hic et Ubique; or, the Humours of Dublin

For you spoil and corrupt the play that is in hand when you mix it with
things of an opposite nature, even though they are much better. Therefore
go through with the play that is acting the best you can, and do not confound
it because another that is pleasanter comes into your thoughts.

—Thomas More, *Utopia*[1]

Richard Head's *Hic et Ubique; or, the Humours of Dublin* (1663) has been virtually ignored by modern critics. This is partially a function of the absence of a
production history for the play; the title page says only that it was "acted privately, with general Applause."[2] However, it is also a consequence of the play's
odd geopolitical position. The standard histories of English drama do not discuss the play, and critics of Irish literature pass over it swiftly. J. O. Bartley
makes the interesting and accurate comment that "all the Irish characters but
one are of the Pale and unnationalized," but he does not develop the implications of that insight.[3] What would it mean to be "Irish" and unnationalized?
Joseph T. Leerssen writes, "A few comedies were produced in Dublin which,
though in no way dissimilar to their English counterparts, make use of (or
rather, reference to) a Dublin setting"; *Hic et Ubique* is in this list.[4] If by "in
no way dissimilar" Leerssen means the play's genre—i.e., Jonsonian humours
comedy—he is quite right; the London stage immediately after the Restoration
was divided between Jonsonian city comedy and Fletcherian romance.[5] However, the use of London stage conventions "in reference to a Dublin setting"
and the occasional speeches in Irish make the play entirely unlike comparable
London drama and underline the "unnationalized" nature of the play, as does
the title itself: the play takes place "here and everywhere," and, consequently,

nowhere: hence the importance of the distinction between reference and use in Leersen's comment.

Hic et Ubique presents Dublin as a utopian landscape for English emigrés, a neutral space in which to act and a blank page upon which to write a meaning, superior to "present" and therefore intractable London. However, Head satirizes this English fantasy with persistent reminders of "present" Dublin, a crowded landscape peopled with inconvenient relics of a messy history who decline to be written out of the story. Ultimately, the New English are required to adapt and begin the uneasy movement from nationless utopia toward an Irish identity. The latter event does not occur in the play but is created as a possibility of the play of utopic space.

According to Louis Marin,

> Utopia is first and foremost a text, a narrative that frames a description to which it ascribes conditions of possibility. It is a text that points to a gap or difference that is active within historical and geographic reality: between England and America, the Old and New Worlds, misery and happiness, political analysis and travel journal.[6]

That is, the utopic text describes a geographic location through discursive practice. The utopia not merely does not exist, but cannot exist, as its position of neutrality lies between kinds of real or constructed presence. Utopia can be created on a blank page but not on a real landscape, where geographical, historical, and social entities inevitably tie the neutral to a particular ideological position. In a sense, the private stage of Head's *Hic et Ubique* is also blank, in that it is not the space of the public theaters, licensed by Charles II, but a private room, free, at least, of theatrical landmarks. Moreover, the "Dublin" that some of the characters move around in and that contemporary English figures eyed speculatively was equally blank, a fictional construct with no connection to reality; indeed, it *was* between the Old World and the New, not so much literally but figuratively, where new money was to be made but by old means.

Historically, utopian literature, Marin argues, arises in the early modern period "when the material possibilities for the existence of bourgeois conditions of production are ripe within 'old feudal society'" (198). The neutrality of the utopic is dynamic:

> With respect to the two parts of the whole that are both in conflict, the center occupies a position of potential reference. Through and because of its absent presence the conflict stops being a strict face-off and acquires the empty possibility of opening up. This position of potential reference is related to the contrary and reciprocal neutralizing elements in a state of tension: a real zero of opposition. The position of the third term as neutral (neither one nor the other) is thus the projection of the dynamic neutrality of conflicting forces, of opposing values and sizes. It indicates the equilibrium of tension between forces and receives from the forces its own force. (16)

Thus the utopic landscape is neither feudal nor bourgeois, but the zero point where both are in play, and that neutral space is alive with the tension between a hierarchical, *ancien régime* society and an emergent mercantilist society where social position is flexible. In other words, utopic space allows a vantage point from which neither the traditional interpretation of Ireland as colonized victim, nor the revisionist view of Ireland as simple reflection of the larger European aristocratic society, is excluded; rather, the interplay between the positions is dramatized.

Head represents himself as a displaced person in the introduction to *The English Rogue*: "There is no fear that *England* and *Ireland* will after my decease, contend about my Nativity, as several Countreys did about *Homer*."[7] This is partially a comic recognition of the worthlessness of Head's life as gambler and con man, but it also reveals the ambiguity of his nationality. He was born at Carrickfergus around 1637; his father was killed in the rising of 1641. Head's mother escaped with her two sons and two servants. Captured by the Irish, Head's brother and one of the servants were killed: "The surviving servant who carried me, declared that he was a Roman Catholick, and imploring their mercy with his howling *Chram a Cress,* for St. *Patrick a gra*, procured my Mothers, his own, and my safety" (*Rogue,* 8–9). The servant establishes Irish identity through language and religion, but he does so to protect the English: "By break of day we were at *Belfast*; about entering the skirts of the Town, this honest and grateful servant (which is much in an Irish man) being then assured of our safety, took his leave of us and returned to the Rebels" (*Rogue,* 10). The servant is simultaneously both a member of the rebels and hence entirely other, and a member of Head's household, demonstrating feudal loyalty for past kindness.

Head sums up the Irish rising against English government as a civil conflict: "All bonds of Faith and Friendship now fractur'd, Irish landlords now prey'd on their English Tenants; Irish Tenants and Servants, made a Sacrifice of their English Landlords and Masters, one Neighbor murthering another" (*Rogue,* 15). The normal economic bonds (landlord and tenant) are displaced by ethnic identity (Irish and English), and the result is crime against the entire social structure: neighbors murder each other. On every level, Ireland ceases to be a part of the known or civilized world, since the methods by which the world organizes itself no longer obtain. Thus, the rising of 1641 is a "civil war," rather than a rebellion by a subject people, in that the religious and ethnic divisions displace the "natural" organizing principles of society, economic, hierarchical, and divine. In such circumstances, the servant who saves Head is Head's countryman in that only personal loyalty, personal allegiances have any meaning.

Head presumably regards himself as English, even though he returns to Ireland when broke in the early 1660s. He is, for instance, open about his limited grasp of Irish. About an attempt to seduce an Irish countrywoman, Head says,

"Then did I make use of that little *Irish* I had learned, which were some frag-
ments of lecherous expressions, to which she replied, but I understood her not"
(*Rogue*, 230). Still, he frequently alludes to Ireland in his writing for examples
of universal human characteristics. Thus, in *Proteus Redivivus*, a good confidence man employs civil language:

> The *French* have a significant Proverb to this purpose, *Parleʒ bien, or parleʒ rien*,
> speak well or dont speak at all; which is somewhat like the *Irish, Aber began, aber
> ghemah* [abair beagán, abair go maith]; Speak a little, and speak it well.[8]

The Irish, therefore, are not the savages the English suppose, but participants
in the arts of civilization, such as fraud.

Moreover, the faults of the Irish are not unique to them. An English gentleman ruins his son rather than allow him to go into trade:

> [H]e hates with the *Irish-man*, that his Son should be a Tradesman, for fear of
> murdering his gentility, and yet never thinks, that after his decease the Gentleman
> must be converted into a Serving-man, and it is well if it be no worse; so that the
> Pride of his house hath undone him. (*Proteus*, 161)

The English typically mocked Irish genealogical hubris.[9] Head sees it as a universal failing. Thus, that which makes the Irish strange makes them familiar.
They are consequently suitable inhabitants of a utopia in that they are the other
that reflects and defines one's own identity.

Instability throughout the century caused large-scale immigration to and
emigration from Ireland in the seventeenth century.[10] When Head returns to
Ireland he does so to escape English debts; he participates in the attempts to
repair English disasters through Irish property. Cromwell's soldiers, English
merchant adventurers, cronies of Charles II, and the Catholics who could
prove themselves innocent of rebellion all expected to have land either restored
or awarded to them, and the English did not seem to understand that there
might not be enough to go around. For example, one anonymous author argues
that Ireland can easily afford to pay for the necessary standing army out of
newly arrived English immigrants who should be encouraged, "since *Ireland* is
under-peopled in the whole, and since the Government there can never be safe
without chargeable Armies, until the major part of the inhabitants be English,
whether by carrying over there, or drawing the other."[11] More aware of how
many people actually expected land, the duke of Ormond famously remarked,
"There must bee new discoverys made of a new Ireland for the old will not
serve to satisfy these arrangements."[12]

For the most part, of course, adventurers were interested in wealth (land)
and were sometimes criticized for their greed accordingly. One commentator
attacks English policy on both religious and humanitarian grounds. This writer
claims that no attempt is being made to convert the Irish: "It is sad [to] observe
how Garrisons are placed in every quarter where the Irish inhabit, Ministers
in none; as if our business in *Ireland* was onely to set up our own interests, and

not Christs." Under such circumstances, the rapaciousness of the English administration forces the Irish into behavior destructive to both sides: "The Tax sweeps away their whole Subsistence: Necessities makes them turn Theeves and *Tories,* and then they are prosecuted with fire and sword for being so. If they discover not *Tories,* the English hang them, if they do the Irish kill them." This is, moreover, entirely counterproductive, since the Irish "being mixed with, they are likelyer to be swallowed up by the English, and incorporated into them; so that a few Centuries will know no different present, fear none to come, and scarce believe what were pass'd."[13] Unconsciously, this commentator highlights the danger that seventeenth-century utopic dreamers sought to obviate. Henry Neville's *The Isle of the Pines* (1668) proposes a utopia based on sharply delineated categories of race and nationality precisely because he perceived those categories to be in jeopardy.[14]

The reasons for the post-Restoration land grab were sometimes explicitly utopic, rather than simply statements of self-interest, and such justifications were sometimes even more dangerous than naked greed, perhaps because of their quasi-scientific justification.[15] Earlier in the seventeenth century Robert Burton had suggested that Ireland and Virginia would be good places to establish utopias free from the effects of political and personal melancholy. Burton's model is explicitly imperial: Rome.[16] Samuel Hartlib is an example of an Englishman looking into blank space and seeing a preferable model to contemporary society:

> Hartlib had a vision of a reformed society, a utopia which he called "macaria," and throughout his life he lobbied for its creation. In the perfect macaria there would be generous provision for the advancement of learning. Until macaria itself was realized, Hartlib worked for the establishment of its parts. In particular he pinned his hopes on an office of address, or foreign correspondency. . . . Such a correspondency, requiring foreign agents and codifiers of material, would be costly: it was to Ireland that Hartlib turned hopefully as a source of money. The scheme offered no particular benefit to Ireland itself.[17]

I have quoted this passage at length because it demonstrates the ambiguous position of Ireland in English thought. Hartlib is sometimes regarded as a significant educational and scientific reformer. Nevertheless, he too regards Ireland as simply a source of income toward the true utopia. Intellectually, Ireland is to be as completely erased as Drogheda and Wexford almost were by that other great seventeenth-century English reformer, Oliver Cromwell. Utopia, for Hartlib, must be created from nothing, and Ireland exists only as obstacle and as raw material toward that creation.

Less dangerously visionary, in *The Complaisant Companion* Head gives as an example of a bull "a Hireling Player [who] being deny'd the augmentation of his Wages, grew angry, and said, *if you want you shall see me in* Ireland *within these two days.*"[18] Ireland functions as the alternate reality where the artist transcends the reality of wage slavery; the manager can be, like a subatomic particle, in two places at once to witness this: here and everywhere. Similarly, Phantastick, one of the English immigrants to Dublin in *Hic et Ubique*, treats the comically impossible as the real. Trying to impress Mrs. Hopewell, he claims,

> I liv'd in *Utopia* three months, where no English Man before durst venture; the Dukes only daughter taking notice of my super-excellent qualifications, as likewise the exact simetrical proportion of my body, fell so deeply in love with me, that I was necessitated to satisfie her desires, to save her life. And to save mine (the *Duke* being informed of what was done) there being no shipping in the harbour, I was fain to put to sea in a Wash-bowl, and the only sayl I had, was the fore part of my shirt. (28–29)

The fantasy operates on a number of levels, but the central illusion is Phantastick's attractiveness. Hic et Ubique (the name of a character) derides Phantastick's sailing gear with typical double entendre: "A yard I grant him. But what did a do for want of a mast[?]" (29). The utopian fantasy is denigrated as impossible because of impotence, which figuratively suggests the inability of utopian dreamers to achieve completion.

Yet in Dublin, at least at first, Phantastick lives in utopia. Asked by Contriver how he does, he responds, "The Duke of *Utopia* lives not merrier than us; we eat, drink, and sleep, without the least care; for our hearts are so continually oil'd by good liquor, that they are antidoted against sorrow" (23). The vintner Thrivewell explains that cash is at a premium in Dublin: "Provision indeed is cheap, because money is scarce; yet good liquor is dear, 'cause there are so many that will pawn their cloaks" (14). Phantastick disembarks from the Holyhead boat well able to take advantage of the situation:

> Here's money lads, and bills of exchange too, which wee'l exchange for Sack: We cannot want, for when we have spent all our English moneys, here's Spanish and French, more than these Ram[-c]rested Citizens know what to do withal. It shall go hard but our wits shall put in for a half share among 'em. (2)

The trouble is that you cannot get from the inebriation that cash buys to success, which, Phantastick assumes, is the point of utopia:

Contriver   Pray on Sir, about your *Utopia*.
Phantastick   I wud keep open house for all roaring Blades, and one part of my pastime shud be to make 'em drunk: the Gentry shud ride home in Coaches, and the servants follow after in wheel barrows. (24)

Ireland is not supposed to require work; in a sense, that turns out to be true for some of the characters, but their methods (marriage and mountebankery) would work equally well in London. Phantastick, however, shows the expectations that the post-Restoration immigrants held regarding Ireland.

Head suggests that Dublin does represent Marin's blank page legally:

Bankrupt	But how wu'd you advise me to secure my self from my debts in *London?* As for protection, by reason of the many abuses occasion'd by 'em, they are cald in, I hear.
Thrivewell	However fear not: Ther's a great Gulf man betwixt you and your creditors.
Bankrupt	I but these letters of Atorney, I fear 'em more, than the lark does the hobby.
Thrivewell	You trouble your self to no purpose.
Bankrupt	But is't not usual for such letters to be sent over, the witnesses being sworn in Chancery.
Thrivewell	Such a thing may be, but then there's a remedy; if e're it comes to that, repair to me, and I'le shew you the hole, that my self crept through upon the like account. (14)

The contrast here is between the specificity of the legal measures Bankrupt fears, and the vague but serene assurance of Thrivewell that London debts have no meaning in Dublin. It may well be that Thrivewell's confidence was justified in the real Dublin, and Head had enormous experience in ducking old debts. Nevertheless, Bankrupt mentions actual legal procedures that place him in danger, and Thrivewell dismisses these fears without ever explaining what the escape "hole" involves.

Elsewhere, Head portrays London itself as dystopia.[19] London is the antithesis of Dublin, depressingly real, and financially strapped:

Phantastick	First then, Houses and Shops are so dear in *London,* that some Shopkeepers are forc'd to sell their wares in the Country.
Hic	I believe so, and their wearing-cloaths too.
Phantastick	The Mercers and Booksellers are deeply in law about the fee-simple of *Ludgate,* O 'tis disputable which shall carry it. As for Newgate that's to be let. (3)

Head, who was himself a bookseller until his gambling debts caught up with him, satirizes the adventurers who think Dublin is likely to be any different. Later in the play, two other (and smarter) travelers compare notes:

Bankrupt	But what way d'ye resolve on for a lively hood.
Trustall	I know not, imployments being so difficult in their obtaining.
Bankrupt	'Tis true, though whole ships of fooles daily arriving vainly imagin the contrary.
Trustall	Had I know so much before, the Indies shu'd sooner have been my refuge. (40)

The utopic impulse is universal, but it is deflated as surely in Dublin as in London. Throughout the play Head repeatedly asserts a real Dublin. The first scene ends with the characters deciding to go to the Feathers tavern rather than to the "London" (5)—both genuine locations in 1663 Dublin. Phantastick confesses to Hic that he is broke and refers to Fletcher's play *Wit without Money*, which was performed in Dublin in 1662 at Smock Alley.[20] Utopic fantasies cannot be achieved in real space, and Dublin is depressingly real.

Despite these references to "present" Dublin, some think utopia, if not discovered, can be created. Contriver represents a projector who regards Ireland as fertile grounds for get-rich-quick schemes. Predictably, Contriver's improvements require the erasure of the landscape:

> The bogs lie near the Mountains, which will afford me earth enough to dam 'em up: but first Ile lay a foundation of hurdles, such as *Dublin* is built on, to support that Masse of Earth. So it shall be; tis as clear as a Mathematical Demonstration. The benefit that will redound hereby, will be triple. First a vast quantity of unprofitable Acres made arable, next a discovery (it may be) of gold and silver Mines, which the barrennesse of the Mountains demonstrate: and lastly metamorphosing a mountainous into a Champian Countrey. Here's the worst on't, I shall loose my name by't. The King will confer on me little lesse than the Title of Duke of *Mountain*, Earl of *Monah*, or Lord *Drein-Bog*. (23).

Mathematical demonstration is an appropriate figure for the plan since abstraction characterizes Contriver's approach. By the time Contriver finishes speaking, a great leveling occurs, creating the new Ireland Ormond supposed necessary. It is, of course, entirely a paper scheme leading to ridiculous titles.

It is not the case that Head is opposed to wealth, deserved or otherwise. *Hic et Ubique* is dedicated to the duke of Monmouth, Charles II's illegitimate son, who in 1663 was around fourteen years old. In singing Monmouth's praises, Head warbles with a charming frankness about what it is he really admires: "Your sublime dignity, quick-springing wit, and large revenues contend for priority, so that you are beheld by all the object of admiration." Unfortunately Ireland is an unlikely place to achieve wealth. Suitably, Contriver claims, "This very day did I find in an old Map, *O Brazeel* with its height" (24). Subsequently Head will satirize English adventurers to Ireland under the same rubric.

In *The Western Wonder: or, O Brazeel*, Head and others set off for the utopic island visible off the west coast of England. Unfortunately, one arrives at "Montecapernia," as O Brazeel invariably disappears into a storm as one gets close to it. The good news is that the native gentry "are generally accomplisht in most respects, and greatly given to that they call Hospitality."[21] The bad news is that the natives are unpromising inhabitants for an earthly paradise:

> It is a thousand pities the People are so sloathful, being given to no manner of Industry, Husbandry, or any useful improvement; which partly occasions the barrenness of the Countery so much to appear, that otherwise by active spirits might easily evince the contrary: for though they have many Hills, Mountains and Boggs, yet they have matchless rich vallies. (32)

The presence of the Irish distinguishes Montecapernia from O Brazeel, the real from the utopic.

In *Hic et Ubique*, a Cromwellian colonel and his surly Irish servant inhabit the historical Ireland that complicates the present. The fire-breathing "Collonel Kil-tory" seeks to perpetuate his hold on Ireland through marriage to the reluctant Cassandra. Misogyny is his characteristic humor:

> No I must smother the ripe sallies of my inflam'd desire and study what it is to be a man again, and how much these admired pieces of imperfection fall short of his merit. Whilst I was scouring the Mountains and skipping the Boggs, not sparing the very spawn of rebellion, I had none of these qualms. I cu'd have then driven a score or two of these white cloven Devils without pity or regard. But since Mrs. *Peace* came acquainted with us, she has perswaded us to change our Head-piece for a soft Pillow, the ground (covered with the spangled Canopy of Heaven) for a down-bed, and that's naught too without a wench. (7)

The advantage of war was its clarity; when doubt is replaced by action, men like Kiltory are in their element. Strikingly, however, Kiltory is lost in post-Restoration Ireland, as indicated by his inability to tell the difference between women and rebellious Irish Tories.[22]

Kiltory represents both the limited impact of the Cromwellian arrivals on post-Restoration Ireland in general and of the army in particular after 1660, "largely unregimented, at times more like a militia than a centralized professional force."[23] A central problem was that there were substantial arrears in pay, and Ormond had insufficient revenues to meet them.[24] By the eighteenth century poor morale and little discipline had made the English army in Ireland "a byword for inefficiency, incompetence and shady practices."[25] The consequence of deeply rooted ambivalence toward the army—necessary to maintain control over the majority Catholic population while at the same time very expensive, and, by law, not Irish—was that few of the Cromwellian soldiers felt inclined to stay. As Karl S. Bottigheimer points out, "Even where land was found for claimants, whether adventurers, soldiers, or creditors of the state, they too often hesitated to plant, and instead sold out to speculators more confident or hopeful of the future of Protestant Ireland."[26]

Kiltory is conned out of land by Mrs. Hopewell, who promises marriage in return for control of his estate, only to reveal that she is already married.

Kiltory	Now Madam, I've done my part, there's nothing wanting but the performance of yours.
Mrs. Hopewell	Which I shall quickly do; according to my promise, I freely bestow on you, all the right and title I have in my self.
Kiltory	That's a guift greater than the riches of the *Indies*.
Mrs. Hopewell	No such matter Sir, 'tis none at all.
Kiltory	How's that?
Mrs. Hopewell	Can you give away another man's interest?
Kiltory	No.
Mrs. Hopewell	Then cannot I give away my self: that man, the Kinsman as I told you, has been my Master this seven years, and shall be all, till I am master'd by death. (57)

Here Mrs. Hopewell's charactonym refers not to herself but to Kiltory. He has, in effect, traded real Irish land for an empty signifier, because Mrs. Hopewell has no capacity to alienate herself. Moreover, the mention of the Indies in connection with Mrs. Hopewell, an echo of the earlier conversation between Bankrupt and Trustall, identifies her with the neutrality of utopic space: for Kiltory, she exists as an object of desire with which he plays on an imaginative level; legally and, consequently, physically, she can have no existence for him.

All is not lost for Kiltory. Thrivewell asks derisively, "Col. is this Debentureland, or are you onely an Adventurer: if so, you may come in among the forty nine men" (57), but there is a kernel of truth in his remark. Since Kiltory is not entitled to land by primogeniture, and the Cromwellian grants provide only an illusory wealth, he must accept the real Dublin and his place in it as a potential merchant and ultimately at best an alderman, for there is no place in post-Restoration Ireland for Cromwellian colonels. In fact he does even better as Mrs. Hopewell's husband becomes an improving landlord: "Your Estate being two hundred pounds per Annum; if you will lend me a years anuity (but conditionally that you shall ne're require it again) till I shall freely confesse, that the improvement thereof hath made me full able" (61). Practical agriculture will eventually enable both Hopewell and Kiltory to live well in Ireland, but this is not a utopic project in the way that Contriver's schemes are. Some of the post-Restoration adventurers and soldiers did in fact become successful.[27]

Thrivewell achieves prosperity the old-fashioned way: he marries it. His wife establishes a rooming house, from which they raise enough money to buy a tavern. A careful marriage has saved Thrivewell from himself:

> When I came over first, I knew not what to have done without her; for, by waiting a great while for a very beneficial employment, which I was promised by this great man and 'tother, all my money was gone, then cu'd I not stoop to be a Drawer, that was so lately a Master. (13)

A combination of unjustifiable pride (associated, as we saw earlier, with the Irish by English commentators) and an erroneous belief in political advancement nearly beggars Thrivewell, but a sensible wife corrects his errors. Peregrine, the most intelligent of the immigrants, continues the pattern of success by marrying Thrivewell's daughter, Cassandra. Even Hic achieves comfort by marrying Sue Pouch, an aging innkeeper. Symbolically, happy endings are contrived by alliance with the pre-existing English in Ireland, rather than through utopic schemes. Incorporated in the material Dublin, some of the new arrivals establish a limited but realizable success. Thus, Dublin ceases to be utopic empty space, where characters such as Contriver seek aristocratic titles, instead becoming an emblem of bourgeois economy populated by an emergent middle class. While the play offers economic realism in contrast to utopic fantasy, the characters are also realistic in a sense absent from most of the English drama of the the early 1660s; as J. Douglas Canfield observes, "The characters of the play remind us of the rest of the world, the 'humane Creatures' exluded from the canon of official discourse—from Stuart ideology to literature as one of the Fine Arts."[28]

Nevertheless, *Hic et Ubique* retains some of the dialogic tension of utopic space through the unresolved presence of Kiltory's servant, Patrick. Patrick is a stage Irishman, for the exaggerated accent and the comical acceptance of his master's right to cuckold him type him as such:

> Fuy by St. *Patrick* agra, he put de fuckation upon my weef. I will tell de tale if thou wil Glunt amee. I came in wid my pishfork upon my back, thou know'st, and I see a greyshy guddy hang upon my weef, and I did creep in like a michear, to the wattle upon de loft abow thou know'st, and there I did see putting the great fuck upon my weef, as if thy own shelf was there Moister. (18)

Despite his denials, Head has some rudimentary knowledge of Irish.[29] And at first in the play, Head presents Patrick as similar to the loyal and stupid comic servant Teg in Robert Howard's *The Committee* (1662).

As the play develops, however, Patrick becomes the practical counterpoint to his master's romantic idiocy. Patrick declines to attack Phantastick and Hic merely because Kiltory is trying to impress Mrs. Hopewell:

Kil-tory	sirrah, did not you tell me you cud fight, upon that account I entertain'd you.
Patrick	Yes, feat at cuff, or skean.
Kil-tory	None serves me but those that durst blow in a charged pistol, and valew a sword no more than a cudgel.
Patrick	See for this, by got a chree he wu'd put some lead in my belly but there was no sharge powder upon the pishtol, he did make intention to cut off my head, feat. (32)

The tumultuous nature of Patrick's speech in his annoyance does not conceal the shrewd analysis of the situation. There is no profit for him or Kiltory in taking pointless risks. Kiltory's indifference to the practical is contrasted with Patrick's pragmatism.

And it becomes clear as Kiltory is duped that Patrick is the more perceptive of the two. When Mrs. Hopewell asks that Kiltory's estate be settled on her, Kiltory tells Patrick to seek a scrivener, and Patrick asks why:

Kiltory	Why thou Bog-trotting, Beetle-head, tell him, I have business for him then.
Patrick	Arrah fuat de Devil must my shelf go make fecth for de Clark, to put sheat upon my moyster, and *Pathrick* himself. (47)

At this point in the play it is clear that Kiltory is an abusive bully and Patrick owes him no particular loyalty. However, Patrick's own future is at stake in the colonel's folly.

Patrick confronts Kiltory directly when the latter is signing over his property:

Patrick	Ub, ub, boo! arrow moyster, wilt tow give away all dine own tings and leave nothing upon me poor *Kilpathrick:* fuate shall my wife *Juane* do for de Cow dat make de buuter-milk, and de bony clabber for dy child and my shelf, and de mullaghane, and de garraane baane, and de garrane dough, thou didst make promise for me.
Kiltory	Sirrah leave thy howling.
Patrick	My shelf no howle, me make speak for you: By St. *Pathrick* and St. *Shone Batty,* my shelf will make no servant for de. (57)

There is a kind of dignity in Patrick's grim rejoinder that he is not howling and he will no longer be Kiltory's servant. As Kiltory denies his obligations, Patrick is released from his. Moreover, the implication is that Kiltory has an illegitimate child by Patrick's wife ("dy child") and that the descendent of Cromwellian soldier and native Irish is involved now in the displacement that Patrick faces without a position in the economy. When the cheat is revealed, Patrick tells Kiltory, "Shoole a crogh, manam a dioule, thou greise micheer, by my soulwation joy a chree, y told dee, de English vid put de sheat pon efry podyes" (57). The tone here is one of contempt, for even with the warning from Patrick, Kiltory cannot save himself. Patrick exits from the stage and the play cursing Mrs. Hopewell.

Patrick's self-interest, cunning, and justifiable wrath give him a real presence that the stage Irishmen of the English Restoration theater lack. His anger at the cheating English, combined with the absence of any explanation of what becomes of him in the play's resolution, emphasizes the central problem of the English in the real Dublin upon which their utopic fantasies were shipwrecked. The Irish were not going to go away, and it was necessary that they be converted, slaughtered, or conciliated. Hugh Reily complains in 1695 about the victor's version of the massacre of the Protestants in the Ulster rising of 1641:

> The Catholicks suffered in much greater Numbers, but dying as it were dumb, like so many Sheep brought to the Slaughter, their Blood made no great Noise, at least in *England;* but the Protestants fell, as I may say, with so many speaking Trumpets in their Mouths, that every individual seemed an hundred.[30]

Head, himself a survivor of the rising, creates in Patrick an embodiment of the silent Catholics. Although Patrick is comic and unable to influence his betters, his presence reminds the audience that although the natives can be silenced, their continued existence means history can be rewritten.

After the restoration of Charles II, a tribunal was established to return land to Catholics found innocent of rebellion. When the claims of too many Catholics were upheld, the tribunal was dissolved, with most cases unheard, leaving a dispossessed and bitter population.[31] Oddly, however, it was planned to preserve the "Writings of Nocents" even if they lost their case, or if their case did not come before the tribunal. The speaker of the Irish Parliament, Sir Audley Mervyn, warned against any such practice:

> Sir, in the North of *Ireland*, the *Irish* have a custom in the Winter, when milk is scarce, to kill the Calf, and reserve the Skin; and stuffing it with straw, they set it upon four wooden feet, which they call a *Puckcan*, and the Cow will be as fond of this, as she was of the living Calf, she will low after it, and lick it, and give her milk down, so it stand but by her: Sir, these Writings will have the operation of the *Puckcan;* for, wanting the lands to which they are relate, they are but Skins stuffed with straw; yet Sir, they will low after them, lick them over and over in their thoughts, and teach their Children to read by them, instead of Horn-books, and if any venom be left, they will give it down upon the sight of these *Puckcan* Writings, and entail a memory of revenge, though the Estate-tail be cut off.[32]

Obviously a gifted and powerful speaker, Mervyn uses a native Irish practice to describe the threat the Irish represent.[33] Mervyn's example describes how the Irish are alien—the practice was apparently unknown in England—and yet at the same time increasingly familiar: only their practice can describe their feelings, and Mervyn has become sufficiently close to Ireland to accept that proposition. And at a time of Protestant authority, Mervyn will not allow Parliament to forget the tenuousness of its position. Describing the ways in which he is not an Irish Catholic, Mervyn at the same time unconsciously affirms that he is not English, as no one in the English Parliament would need at this time to lose sleep over the Irish. Strikingly, however, Mervyn illustrates the dangerous utopic fantasy. If the documents were in some way erased, prior Catholic ownership would cease to be a problem. Dispossession requires a blank page.

Both sides, of course, claimed that they were the truly loyal subjects of the Crown. Gratianus Lucius (John Lynch), dedicating *Cambrensis Refuted* to Charles II in 1662, asserts that

> the natives then, both from their national and inherent disposition, are naturally inclined to loyalty and obedience, while the colonists, from the wrong and perverse bias of their education, as well as from their natural principles of vigorous perseverance, are ever ready and determined to resist and oppose regal government.[34]

But the Protestants have the upper hand, and an attack upon Peter Walsh, an Irish Franciscan and royalist, published anonymously probably sums up the views of those with power:

> His majesty may rationally expect more future *obedience* and *loyalty* from *English* Protestants, than *Irish* Papists; for (I) the *English* Protestants are the *Conquerors*, the *Irish* Papists the *conquered*; and antient as well as modern experience has made it appear, the *conquered* never did (some think morally never will) love the *Conqueror*.[35]

While the dividing lines seem firmly drawn here between English Protestants and Irish Catholics, such divisions could only be unproblematic as long as all were in agreement that the Protestants were, in fact, "English." Peter Walsh makes an astonishingly accurate prediction upon this very point:

> The Country must at length give denomination to all that inhabit it: and the posterity of those that proclaim loudly the English interest, must within an age, admit themselves to be called Irish as well as the Descendants from the first Colony of English planted in *Ireland*.[36]

Despite the Glorious Revolution that placed the Protestants more firmly in control of Ireland than ever, the English of Ireland would ultimately become, at least in English eyes, just a subgroup of the Irish.

TWO

"I've saved your Country, and would gain your Love"

Conquest and Conciliation in the Plays of Charles Shadwell

Charles Shadwell was Ireland's first prolific playwright, producing at least a play a year from 1715 to 1720. Nor was he unsuccessful. A play written and premiered in London, *The Humours of the Army* (1713), was produced as late as 1747; *Irish Hospitality* (1717–18), a Dublin play, was revived as late as 1766; and another London play, *The Fair Quaker of Deal, or, The Humours of the Navy* (1710), had an impressive stage history, being revived up until 1785 in London.[1] Nevertheless, Shadwell has been largely ignored, partly because he did not stay in England, and, like the other playwrights of Ireland in the seventeenth and eighteenth centuries, his identity slides through the categories of national English and Irish literary history. Unlike Richard Head, who was at least born in Ireland, Shadwell was unmistakably English. Indeed, his father was the Whig poet laureate Thomas Shadwell, appointed by William III to replace the Catholic Tory John Dryden; the prologue to Charles Shadwell's first play, *The Fair Quaker of Deal*, says that as Charles was *"born* on Parnassus's *Cliffs he pants for Fame."*[2] Thomas Shadwell was both the inhabitant of Parnassus and anti-Catholic for most of his life, so it is unlikely that his son, Charles, had any sympathy for the religion of the majority of the Irish. Some modern critics see Shadwell as an argument for the non-Irish character of the Dublin theater. J. O. Bartley argues that "the plays are concerned with the English and Anglicized Anglo-Irish of the Dublin area, and they probably reflect that society, for audiences of which they were written, rather well."[3] Christopher Murray describes *Rotherick O'Connor* (1719) as exemplifying the ruling aristocracy's view of the conquest of Ireland as a "victory of enlightenment over barbarism."[4] On the other hand, while La Tourette Stockwell regards Shadwell's comedies of Dublin life as generic ("taken intact [they] apply as well to London as to Dublin"), she regards *Rotherick O'Connor* as "an exceedingly interesting addition to that tiny group of Irish historical plays which were the fore-runners of the Irish Literary Theater."[5] W. S. Clark goes further:

> Thus *Rotherick O'Connor* through its warm characterization of Eva [Dermond MacMurrough's daughter] turns a sympathetic spotlight upon that devoted and honourable Irish patriotism which persistently refused to accept with complacence the English Ascendancy. This play quite evidently was for Shadwell the climax of his endeavour to relate the Dublin drama and theatre to the nationalistic sentiments then gathering force among Protestant as well as Catholic Irish.[6]

Joseph T. Leerssen describes accurately the ambiguity of the play, an ambiguity that accounts for the wide variety of critical responses:

> Although his [Shadwell's] political sympathy lies with the forces that had tried (and were still trying) to subdue Ireland's Gaelic population, he does not view the Gaels as inferior or reprehensible; a sneaking admiration and, if not fascination, at least interest, becomes noticeable. This ambivalence is highlighted by his choice of a controversial topic which in itself contains the germ of all later confrontations.[7]

Leerssen strikes the key note; Shadwell's plays dramatize inherent tensions between conquest and conciliation. The contradictory critical responses accurately reflect the contradictions in the new colonists' life in Ireland.

Shadwell's Whig convictions are clear from internal evidence (a satire on Francis Atterbury, Tory bishop of Rochester, figures prominently) and his source for *Rotherick O'Connor*: Richard Cox's history of Ireland, *Hibernia Anglicana*, which explicitly defends the Norman conquest as beginning the civilization of Ireland.[8] As a consequence of these beliefs, Shadwell regards the English domination of Ireland as a triumph of religion over superstition, and of law over tyranny; Ireland thus participates in progress toward an enlightened and benevolent empire, and Shadwell's plays are an early eighteenth-century example of "The Progress of Poesy." This vision is inclusive. All parts of the empire share in the development (or imposition) of civilization. Yet at the same time, Shadwell is living in Ireland and knows that the English regard the Irish (including the New English) as inferior, and that not merely do the *Irish* not regard the English conquest as a positive event, but that the English of Ireland were becoming increasingly restive about their status as subjects of what they regarded as a sister kingdom, and which England regarded as a colony.

Anthropologist T. O. Beidelman analyzes an analogous situation, that of Christian missionaries in Africa:

> Missionizing is based on a contradictory evaluation of others: Africans and Europeans are equal in God's eye, all with souls worth saving and dear to God, yet Africans clearly have beliefs and customs inferior to Europeans or they would not require conversion. The Kaguru human being merits love and respect, but the culture and society that make that person what he is do not. As Bishop Chambers observed: "To be a friend to the African need not mean giving him your daughter

in marriage, but it does mean understanding and fellow-feeling, anticipating his needs, helping him to rise, and taking trouble to enable him to enjoy the riches of his inheritance in Christ."[9]

As souls prior to salvation, and, presumably, as Christians in the kingdom of God, missionaries and natives are equal, just as subjects of the English empire partake of the benefits of law and true religion equally. But just as the natives are inferior (not, for instance, someone you would let marry into the family), the Irish are nearly as much so in English eyes, and need to be firmly administered for their own benefit. Marriage is less stigmatized between white Irishmen and Englishwomen than it is between missionary and native, but even wealth and title require a significant cash premium for marriage to occur.[10] Yet one cannot be both equal subject and superior administrator without inevitable tensions' arising.

Worse, the missionaries found that to survive and work effectively in Africa, they needed to compromise between idealistic Christian asceticism and (comparatively speaking) the European luxury to which they were used:

> From the African view, the supposedly altruistic missionaries lived incomparably better than their Black brothers and sisters; yet the modesty and frugality of these missionaries' lives appeared seedy and niggardly when compared to other Europeans. To Africans missionary thrift carried none of the meanings which missionaries themselves assigned to it. For Africans, the missionaries were failed Europeans, demonstrably not as successful as those in government or commerce. (Beidelman 68)

Similarly, the lifestyle of the English of Ireland was superior to that of the natives, yet markedly inferior to that of those holding comparable rank in England; lord lieutenants came for parliamentary sessions and decamped for England as rapidly as possible, and the post itself was "commonly used as a means of shelving a discarded colleague who could not be dropped completely, or of giving some impecunious nobleman a chance to repair his fortunes."[11] Disparity of wealth ensured that the distinction (and enmity) between recent conqueror and native would remain. Nevertheless, comparative poverty (or diminished social status) and the consequent absence of the amenities of England rapidly led to English contempt for the English colonists in Ireland. In other words, not just the natives but the colonists' own ethnic group came to regard them as failed Englishmen. This perforce led to the beginnings of a rapprochement with the Gaelic culture that the colonists had displaced.

Whatever the weaknesses of the colonial model when applied to Ireland, Shadwell fits the profile of a colonist. His grandfather was recorder of Galway, attorney general of Connaught and then attorney general of Tangiers—an early example of the roving colonial administrator.[12] His father visited Ireland for four months in 1664 and satirized the country as the home of superstitious and bigoted priests in two plays, *The Lancashire Witches* (1681) and *The Amorous Bigotte* (1690). Charles Shadwell arrived in Dublin as a typical colonial entrepreneur, keeping "the only Office of Assurance for the support of Widdows and Orphans" in Dublin.[13]

Yet easy categorization of Shadwell's views is complicated by his family history. Charles's grandfather, John Shadwell, had as patron James Butler, first duke of Ormond, one of Charles II's most loyal supporters, and a Tory during the exclusion crisis.[14] Shadwell's grandfather also clashed with William O' Brien, governor of Tangiers when he was attorney general, second earl of Inchiquin, and a Williamite. And though the second duke of Ormond welcomed William III, he remained a Tory, was despised by Whigs for his displacement of Marlborough and his cooperation with Bolingbroke,[15] and ultimately became a Jacobite in exile. In the dedication of Shadwell's *The Humours of the Army* (1713) to Major-General Newton (under whom Shadwell served in the army in Portugal), the second Ormond is highly praised: "His Grace the Duke of *Ormond*'s trusting you with the Government of *London-derry* is a certain Sign of Your Faithful Service, Loyal Principles, and Zeal to Monarchy: Such Good Men as you, will always find the Favour of that Great Man."[16] No doubt Shadwell carefully disassociated himself from any sympathy with Ormond after the failed Jacobite plots, but that does not alter the fact that he had once felt sufficiently comfortable with Ormond's politics to view him as a patron. What Shadwell's family life shows is that monolithic assumptions about political loyalty must be carefully qualified. Shadwell is an English Whig supportive of England's imperial ambitions. He is also a playwright who must please as large an audience as possible, and that means tempering his celebration of the Norman conquest and Williamite victory with sympathy for the defeated Irish.

I

Cox claims in his history that the Irish kings were like Indians in Virginia and ruled only by force:

> Nor were there Laws better than their Governours, it was no written Law, no digested or well-compiled Rule of Right; no it was only the Will of the Brehon or the Lord. . . . Every Lord had one of these Arbitrary Brehons who to be sure took Care not to disoblige his patron; the greatest Crimes (as Murder or Rape) were not punished otherwise than by Fine. (xx)

Shadwell's prologue to *Rotherick O'Connor* reiterates the claim that Ireland was ruled by

> *Kings that Govern'd with an Arbitrary Sway,*
> *And slavish Subjects, born but to Obey.*
> *When* Brehon *Laws cou'd reach the Subject's Life,*
> *And none but great Ones, dare support the Strife.*

Irish history for both writers becomes an archetype for modern England. Rotherick and the Stuarts are despots, while Strongbow, William III, and

George I are Whig redeemers. Thus the tragedy exemplifies the establishment of the benign constitutional monarchy that Cox and Shadwell see as the consequence of the Glorious Revolution, which itself was the historical fulfillment of the Norman conquest and the Elizabethan settlement.[17] Cox, who was to become lord chancellor of Ireland in 1703, has no doubt that the English conquest of Ireland has been unreservedly beneficial:

> All the Improvements themselves or their Country received, and their great difference between their Manners and Conditions now and then, is to be ascribed to the English Government, under which they have lived far happier than ever they did under the Tyranny of their own Lords. (xxxix)

Cox, in short, was "an Englishman who happened to live in Ireland."[18]

This was Shadwell's view before he reached Ireland. In *The Humours of the Army,* written after his service in Portugal, Shadwell idealizes British unity by claiming an equality of courage:

> For *Britain's* Sons, by their fore father's led
> To neighboring Realms, in differing Manners bred;
> Some Tincture of the Foreign Soil they have,
> But still retain to be by Nature brave.
> Howe'er in private Contests they cabal,
> Shew 'em a Foe, you'll find 'em *Britain's* all.
>
> (prologue)

The assumption that Scots, Welsh, and Irish are all descendants from a common race obviously solves numerous hierarchical difficulties among the subjects of Britain; cultural differences are epiphenomena. Indeed, a benighted Scotsman is the only soldier who thinks otherwise:

Outside	But my Shoul 'tes a deplorable Story, that we must tay suddenly of a lingering Shackness, when we might march away to the Enemy, and have Time to repent of our Shins.
Hyland	Waunds Mon, won wad thank you study'd to talk mistically on purpose; I have heard more Iricisims [*sic*] fram you, than a whole gang of the Bashon, Sir.
Cadwallader	Come Cornel, praise a Man for her Toings, and not for her Speakings; here is or Frient the Major, has Murtert his share this Compaignt.
Bloodmore	Hang your Words, Truth and Honesty may be express'd by Signs, never find fault with a Man that does not speak as you do.

(12)

This may well echo *Henry V* (3.2), which, David Cairns and Shaun Richards have argued, implies that the "Celts are united in their service to the English Crown. Their use of the English language, however, reveals that 'service' is the operative word, for in rank, in dramatic importance, and in linguistic competence, they are comical second-order citizens."[19] As in Shakespeare, the

English officer represents tolerance and makes peace among squabbling subject peoples. Thus subjugation is preferable to independence for the Celts, in the English view, just as conversion to Christianity by European missionaries is an advantage to native Africans.

Still, even in this play, Shadwell's understanding of the strains of Irish society is more complex than in English drama of the early eighteenth century. There are two Irish men, Outside and the urbane Young Fox, and when Hyland praises the latter as a man of sense, they show racial solidarity:

Outside	Arrah, by my Shoul now I have catch'd you dear joy, for he was Born at *Mac Farty,* in the County of *Tiperary,* as well as my self, he did Suck of the same Nurse, he did eat his Pottatoes out of the same Back-Side, and his Bonny-Clabber came from my moders Bull: den how de Devil shou'd he have more Sence den I. By St. *Patrick* he only speaks his vords one way, and I do speak them an order vay, but we do mean de same ting.
Young Fox	Exactly my dear Country-man.

(40–41)

Outside presumably represents the Irish country gentleman and Young Fox the educated and urbane variety, but despite the humor of the scene, they both close ranks against Scottish critics when Irish character is attacked. In short, Shadwell is aware that there is more than one kind of Irishman, and despite surface differences, they do represent an emergent cultural consciousness. Interestingly, the Irish Protestant (Catholics could not be soldiers in the British army) is as likely a subject for caricature as any native Celt. Like missionaries overseas, he is, if one of the English of Ireland, already a failed Englishman in some eyes.

Regan, Dermond's loyal retainer in *Rotherick O'Connor,* stresses the civilizing character of English rule: "Their Country seems, more civiliz'd than ours;/With Arts and Sciences, they polish all/The rude, the wild, ungovernable Crew" (276). Thus a king functions as a careful steward of liberty and instructor in the arts of advanced society. Rotherick, on the other hand, identifies himself as a tyrant:

> A Monarch's made to Rule each petty Slave,
> To bid him Live, or send him to his Grave.
> Mercy is for a vile Mechanick Soul,
> No humane Passion, should a king controul:
> 'Tis Justice is the Rule that Guides his way;
> And all is Just and Good that Monarchs say.
> (287)

The Hobbesian echo here reinforces an image of Stuart tyranny. Prior to the establishment of a monarchy, in Hobbes's view, "the notions of Right and

Wrong, Justice and Injustice have there no place. Where there is no common Power, there is no Law: where no Law, no injustice."[20] This is, of course, an oversimplification of the Hobbesian position, but Rotherick represents the absolutism that James II (and James III) supposedly threatened and that Hobbes philosophically defended.

For Shadwell, the principles of the Glorious Revolution still need to be defended in 1719 Ireland. Even in his comedy *The Sham Prince, or, News from Nassau* (1718–19) the character Sir William Cheatly (based on a real confidence man who duped the Dublin merchants) is compared with a Tory monarch:

> Despotick Princes will do what they please,
> And ne'er consult the harmless subjects Ease:
> They come, they go, and never tell the Cause;
> Their arbitrary Wills are still their Laws.[21]

Celia, in *The Plotting Lovers* (1719–20), claims that if her father, Tradewell, a domestic tyrant, insists she marry Squire Trelooby, a buffoon from Cornwall, she will play the religious card: "Why I'd threaten to go beyond the Sea, change my Religion, and throw my self into a Nunnery."[22] Not merely political, but commercial and familial structures are imperiled by Toryism.

A prologue to *Rotherick O'Connor* by a Colonel Allen describes the relationship between international support of the Pretender and religion as another target of Shadwell:

> A Popish Priest he ventures to expose,
> Who sticks at nothing to distress his Foes,
> Thank Revolution, we have none of those,
> For such outragious Plagues we're not in Pain,
> They're to be found in *Muscovy* or *Spain*.
> (266, italics reversed)

Ongoing fear of Spain was, after all, perfectly justified: Ormond planned in 1719 to invade England with major Spanish support, including soldiers from the Irish brigades. The reference to Muscovy is also apropos; Peter the Great, who recognized the Stuart claim to England, was actively recruiting Irish soldiers in the early eighteenth century: Peter de Lacy from County Limerick progressed to the rank of field marshal in the Russian army.[23]

Fear of Catholics and the association of them with enmity to the revolutionary settlement remain an integral part of the Anglo-Irish identity in the early eighteenth century. Catholics favor tyranny and arbitrary power, according to Jonathan Smedley: "They own themselves oblig'd to obey an Hereditary Arbitrary Prince, even tho' he shou'd confound all our Establishment, Laws, Liberties, and Religion."[24] Yet the villain Catholicus, a bishop and adviser to Rotherick, represents more than just papal perfidy in *Rotherick O'Connor*—he also represents a not particularly covert attack on High Church Tories. An identification of Catholics with High Church Tories would not make Shadwell unusual. An anonymous pamphlet in 1716 makes the same claim: " . . . the Faction in ENGLAND had not yet thrown off the Mask and discover'd that by High Church, they meant Popery, and by Hereditary Right James III, as they have since proclaim'd him."[25] The reiteration of *faction* denotes the party politics of the time: "The Faction in England corrupted several officers . . . Gordon who serv'd in the Muscovite Army, and others. They listed Men privately, and rais'd Money to carry on their damnable Design, besides what the Impostor had from the Pope, the King of S——, from the Jesuits in France, and elsewhere" (14–15). Strikingly here, the pamphlet links Muscovy, Spain, popery, and faction in a single passage. In an inflammatory summation, the Whig author implies that Tory factions are the real root of England's political instability:

> No doubt of it, it is not Religion that makes a man a High-Churchman, but Faction, a Lust of Power, and a Spirit of Persecution: And every honest Papist who is for Liberty, is a Whig, and will hate Jacobitism. As many Papists as Protestants fought for King William and Queen Anne. . . . I do not believe there's a Nation upon Earth, whether Papist or Turks, not to say Protestants, that would endure such a Faction as our staunch Tories among them. (53)

Thus political difference becomes more dangerous than either religious or national difference, as its root is a desire for power. An anonymous pamphlet published during the Bangor controversy also claims that the Tories are indistinguishable from the worst kind of Catholics: "Shall it ever be said that a Party of scandalous, wicked and profane Clergymen, who glory in being High-Church, but may be said more properly to be *Jesuits* in Masquerade: I say shall these govern us, not only in our Estates, but our Consciences? Amazing Stupidity!"[26] This may be inflated political rhetoric, but that at least indicates that the rhetor thinks somebody will believe it.

In *Rotherick O'Connor* faction is associated with Irish defeat, and, consequently, the losing Irish. Strongbow attributes the disorder of Ireland to partisan politics: "Such is the horrid fate of civil War,/Shame and Destruction, always Fall on those;/Who by their Factions are the Cause of Strife" (289). However, the cunning Catholicus, shifting sides frequently when he sees advantage, seems to imply more than just Irish Catholic deceit, specifically in his search for advantage. To placate Rotherick when he complains about Pope Adrian IV, who first gave Ireland to England, and Alexander's Bull, which confirmed the grant, Catholicus describes the independence of the Irish Church:

> And we of *Ireland,* have never own'd
> The Pope's Supremacy, or Power here;
> For from St. *Patrick,* to this present time,
> Our Church has always, strenuously opposed.
>
> (281)

Here Catholicus echoes a common Church of Ireland argument that the established Church was the true descendant of Saint Patrick's pure, primitive

Church, which had wisely never accepted pontifical authority. When Catholicus sees that Strongbow is likely to win, he becomes a dutiful servant of the pope:

> These *English* are well Disciplin'd to War,
> *Henry* the second is a gallant Prince,
> The Church does flourish much within his Realm,
> And what is our Delight, Church-Men bear some Sway;
> The Pope has sure enough, bestow'd him *Ireland*.
> I begin to think, he had
> A most Religious Right to give away;
> I ought to pay Obediance to the Chair.
>
> (317–18)

Indifferent to religion and national loyalty, Catholicus exemplifies the Tory lust for power. Strongbow is briefly allied with Catholicus, which reveals the danger of subtle churchmen to political order. Shadwell as Whig has little sympathy for the clergy, Catholic or High Church.

More specifically, Catholicus is identified with contemporary politics as he shares Atterbury's views on the question of what to do with Tory traitors. In a pamphlet he published anonymously in 1716, Atterbury argued that "the Question is, whether the Government shall shew Mercy, or take a Reverend Divine's Advice who lately exhorted from his Pulpit, *to slay Man and Woman, Infant and Suckling*, &c." Atterbury was, of course, for lenity: "As there is room for Mercy, so there is Reason for it, and that the less Blood there shall be spilt on this Occasion, the more it will be for the Honour as well as Security of the Government." [27] The Whig view was harsher:

> There is an actual Necessity for taking off the *Leaders* and *Chiefs* of the Rebels, the Laws demand it, the Security of the Government requires it, and no Reasons can be offered to the contrary, but what draws after them the fatal Consequences of weakning the Authority of the Laws in general, of encouraging Crimes of the like Nature, and endangering the safety of our *King* and *Country*. [28]

Indeed, Sir William Thornton, addressing the House of Lords on behalf of the Commons, asserted of execution that "'tis the most effectual Method to prevent any future Insurrection or Disturbances of the publick Repose and Tranquility of the Kingdom, and to render firm and lasting our present happy Establishment." [29] Strongbow similarly fears a renewed attack from Rotherick and thinks the prisoners captured by the Norman and Leinster forces should be executed: "Should proud *Rotherick* Rally,/ and bring his Forces to another Charge;/ We shall repent us we let them live" (324).

But the gag behind Atterbury's plea for mercy for Jacobite prisoners was that it would eventually (in 1722) fit his own case. The potential irony—suspicions about Atterbury's Jacobite connections would have been common—was not lost on Shadwell. Catholicus says, aghast, "I as a Prisoner must suffer Death;/ Heaven forbid! I am not fit to die" (324). Consequently Catholicus argues that the Irish, tired of Rotherick's tyranny, are ready to return to their loyalty to Dermond; the only threat to Strongbow's eventual rule would be want of mercy:

> But should you put to Death their Fathers, Sons,
> Their Brothers and their Kins-Folks, it must not be,
> It will inrage, and bring Destruction on,
> Whilst calmer Means, may bring them all to peace.
>
> (325)

The specious subtlety of Catholicus conceals a traitor whom neither side can trust; his death frees Ireland from a dangerous churchman, and thus the play celebrates Whig victories over Catholics and High Church tories.

Even here, however, Shadwell is aware of the difficulties of simply associating one position with political subversion. Eva, daughter of Dermond, king of Leinster, also criticizes Strongbow's harshness: "(*Aside*) Cruel, barbarous, inhumane Monster!/(*to him*) And would you have them all, to suffer Death?/In cool Blood, must they be butcher'd thus?" (324). Her warm heart, unhardened to what Strongbow calls "The Discipline of War" (324), leads her to the same position as Catholicus, which shows that love of country may also lead to views that threaten political stability.

Like Catholicus, Rotherick himself represents more than Tory despotism. He also reveals the rising threat of pseudo-Irish patriotism to the beneficent Whig government. O'Connor as Irish patriot was an available archetype from the early seventeenth century. Meredith Hanmer allows Rotherick a heroic speech to his troops:

> You right worthy and valiant defenders of your Country and liberty; Consider with what people and for what cause wee are now to fight and wage battell, the enemy of his owne Country, the tyrant over his owne people, the exile fugitive, behold hee is returned backed with strangers, and purposeth to destroy us and the whole Nation.[30]

In Shadwell's play, Rotherick deceives his daughter Avelina and her doomed lover, Cothurnus, Dermond's son, by spouting the rhetoric of love of country: "I am a Tyrant, cruel and revengeful,/Because I love my Country, and oppose/The Man, who gives up all his Land to Strangers" (296). Most important, he uses the language of patriotism when attempting to win Eva by freeing Cothurnus, his hostage, and Regan:

> I love my Country, and scorn that Prince,
> Whom small Revenge for Injuries received,
> Can draw to act a Deed, which all good Men
> Abhor. The selling of his Country
> To the vilest Vagabonds and Strangers,
> Forgive me Charmer, when my zeal displays
> The horrid traiterous Folly of your Father.
>
> (306)

The Tory despot appropriates the language of patriotism for factional purposes and to seduce Strongbow's promised bride. That the tyrant Rotherick can invoke such appeals shows their danger. Nevertheless, his defeat and death show that the Tory danger is contained.

The prologue to *Irish Hospitality* suggests the tone of the Whig celebration of conquest:

> Hibernia *then from Wars, and Tumults free,*
> *Bless'd with a* Bolton, *happy days shall see,*
> *And long Indulge, in Peace and Poetry.*
>
> (202)

The lord lieutenant's presence at the theater is the symbol of an enlightened conquest: the wars over, faction ended, Ireland can enjoy the blessings of civilization. England brings the ruler and the poet, Ireland reaps the fruits. Shadwell's plays, then, explicitly defend a Whig teleology of a fortunate and benevolent empire, justified by its victory over arbitrary despotism.

II

Yet it is important to remember that Shadwell is writing for the theater and needs to reach a larger audience than the duke and duchess of Bolton, especially since Charles Paulet, duke of Bolton, was both personally and politically unpopular.[31] In the same prologue Shadwell, after praising the Roman theater for inculcating virtue and discouraging vice, writes wistfully, "*From which our Scribbling Author wou'd infer,/Each Nation shou'd support a Theatre*" (202). The careful choice of *nation* to describe Ireland indicates Shadwell's awareness of Anglo-Irish resentment at the English view of Ireland as a colony or plantation, and it underlines his need for a larger audience than just Dublin Castle. The same point is made more abjectly in the prologue to *The Hasty Wedding* (1716–17):

> This spacious City, were you not asleep,
> Might one poor *Poet* and a *Play house* keep.
> From this Day forth you're summon'd to appear,
> That each may prop this falling *Theatre.*[32]

Shadwell's party might control the government, but as playwright Shadwell had to please a diverse audience of people unaware that they were supposed to be grateful for his muse.

Economically, Shadwell's audience is diverse. The epilogue to *Irish Hospitality* dissects the audience's tastes:

> Lady's will Smile, if Scenes are modest Writt,
> Whilst your double Entender's please the Pitt.
> There's not a Vizzard sweating in the Gallery,
> But likes a smart Intreague, a Rake, and Raillery.

And were we to Consult our Friends above,
A pert and witty Footman, 'tis they love.
And now and then such Language as their own,
As Damn the Dog, you Lye, and knock him down.

(203)

The stratification of society requires compromise on the part of the play-wright. Since, presumably, among the servants in the upper gallery are native Irish, one of the compromises will be a sympathy for the indigenous inhabitants, by allowing that Irish footmen may have wit and an attractive sauciness.

At the top of the hierarchy was a divided aristocracy and gentry. R. F. Foster says, "The descendants of settler gentry asserted their ascendancy in a polity that had the status of a dependent kingdom, but psychologically and pragmatically partook of attitudes best called colonial."[33] But as the New English became entrenched in Ireland they increasingly recognized that their interests were, if not divergent from English interests, not identical. Before the passage of the Declaratory Act of 1720, which established the authority of the Westminster Parliament over Ireland, one pamphlet author recognized his own quandary:

> And I hope it will be no Offence upon this occasion to add, that altho' I am of *English* Parentage, and entirely attached to the true Interest of *Great Britain*, yet all the Fortune which I have lies in *Ireland:* Nor have I in this World any other View either for my self or mine, but within this Kingdom alone; whose Rights and Privileges I, for this Reason also, the more earnestly desire to transmit down to Posterity.[34]

Of English descent and still British by inclination, the author acknowledges the distance between himself and England to be not merely physical but psychological. Currently independent, he fears subjection because the imperial center regards the colonists as subordinates to be manipulated for imperial advantage.

Anxiety was not limited to the upper class. The strains in Dublin society are explicitly referred to in *The Hasty Wedding*. Squire Daudle, wishing to gain access to the heiress Aurelia, disguises himself as a journeyman shoemaker with a Huguenot master, whom he describes to Sir Ambrose Wealthy:

Squire Daudle   Why and't please your Worship, he was born a Slave, was dragoon'd out of his own Country, upon the account of Religion, and is resolv'd to live miserably, in hopes of getting together as much Money here, as he left behind him in *France.*

Sir Ambrose   A good intelligible Fellow this: I warrant you people of the Country here, grumble at these Foreigners.

Squire Daudle   No, an it please your Worship, not one Morsel; we can't blame the Fellows for being Industrious; but we know and then curse the Gentry, for letting their own Country-men starve, whilst they are employing foreigners.

Sir Ambrose   If our own Countrymen were but as Industrious, they wou'd
not want business; but they never care to work, till they begin
to [g]row hungry.

(38)

French Protestants threaten the artisan class by creating a surplus of labor.
Interestingly, it does not really matter whether Daudle is impersonating a
Catholic or Protestant. One cannot, for instance, tell from the lack of a stage
accent; after reaching Ireland, Shadwell eschews attempting Irish pronunciation—wisely, as an audience of experts would presumably recognize errors. Sir
Ambrose's comment on lack of industry therefore can apply equally well to
either Catholic or Protestant. Whomever Daudle impersonates, the complaint
and response are the same: the Irish are being abused by a gentry that prefers
the work of foreigners to that of the people of Ireland, and the Irish are liable
for their own plight by being shiftless and irresponsible. The dismissal indicates an English perspective, but the complaint reveals that Shadwell has already absorbed something of the "Irish" sense of grievance.

Shadwell, then, could not indulge in an uncomplicated encomium to Whig
triumph for a number of reasons. As a playwright he needed to satisfy a disparate audience. Even as a newcomer to Ireland, he ceased to participate in the
English victory but became instead a member of a colony—like the missionaries in Africa, a failed Englishman. Nevertheless, the Anglo-Irish audience
needed to be humored in the notion that they were a separate kingdom, and *as
a Whig* Shadwell accepted an ideological position that all members of the empire were equal. In Ireland, he could not treat the Anglo-Irish as brutes subdued by enlightenment. S. J. Connolly points out, "Ireland was neither a physically distant nor a racially separate possession. It was a neighbouring island,
whose inhabitants were European in physical appearance, culture, and religion.
And it is this which makes the colonial label less than satisfactory."[35] That
Shadwell soon ceases to treat Ireland as simply a colony to be exploited, but
instead as a fellow member of the empire both worthy of and needing help,
is apparent in the changes he makes from Cox in *Rotherick O'Connor*, and his
treatment of marriage between Irish and English in that play and in *Irish Hospitality*.

Cox, writing in 1689, cannot understand why the Irish would rebel against
the obviously superior English who have brought them civilization, and thinks
it will be impossible for the English to forgive them: "But at this Day the
Provocations are carried so high, and the Irish have abused the English to that
degree of Barbarity and Ingratitude, that it will be hard to perswade the Protestants to trust them again, as to live neighbourly with them any more" [ix].
Perhaps nowhere is the imperial Whig unconscious so apparent: the Irish
should be grateful for being conquered. Even Shadwell's placement of patriot
rhetorical strategies in the mouth of Rotherick shows that he knows that claim

convinces few in Ireland. In fact he goes much further in expressing sympathy for Irish patriotism. Regan, after praising the Norman invaders, apologizes when Eva reproves him for lacking respect for his own countrymen: "I ne're meant,/By praising of these Strangers, to take off/Any Glory from the *Heroes* of my Country" (276).

Characters merely mentioned by Cox are developed at length by Shadwell. Dermond's faithful counselor Regan and the hostage Dermond has given to Rotherick, his own son Cothurnus, face captivity and death with stoic courage:

Cothurnus	I Grant you, our Religion teaches us
	To bear the Ills of Life, without repining.
Regan	To part with Ills we have, we hurry on
	Perhaps to worse; Cowards may wish to die,
	Because they fear to live, but noble Souls
	Can with undaunted Courage, meet the Shocks
	Of Life, and still appear Philosophers.
Cothurnus	There is in Life, no Blessing worth our Care[,]
	But to be free from Slavery and Chains.

(311)

The bravery here is no merely pagan virtue but the consequence of Christian faith. Cox says dismissively of Irish religion, "But whatever the Religion of the Irish was formerly, it is certain that at this Day it is rather a Custom than a *Dogma,* and is no more than Ignorant Superstition" (xxxvii). But Shadwell is clearly closer to the Irish Jacobite Hugh MacCurtin, who attacks modern writers who traduce the "Island of the Saints":

> But alas! their glorious *Fame* in that, and in all other Qualities, as *Valour,* and great promptness to *Learning,* wherein they were undeniably Excellent, is Eclips'd by some modern Writers, branding the Ancient *Milesians* with all the Infamy that Malice and Prejudice cou'd invent.[36]

More importantly, although the play is set in the distant past, the presence of Regan and Cothurnus as living actors on the Dublin stage reinforces Irish Protestant perceptions of themselves as possessors of true Christian simplicity. As Eva says to Regan when he praises the English, "You have forgot you were in *Ireland* born,/Where pure Religion by St. *Patrick* taught:/Is still kept up, with a becoming Zeal" (276). Covert apology for the Church of Ireland or not, Ireland had a "pure religion" prior to the Norman conquest. Indeed in *The Sham Prince,* Sir William Cheatly, professing some scruples at marrying the princess of Passau in a Catholic ceremony, is reassured that in Passau "if your Highness has a mind to be an Atheist, you may have as free Liberty of Conscious there, as if you liv'd in the City of London" (173). Ireland was and remains a center of piety, while London is the home of freethinkers and libertines.

Strongbow exemplifies the change that the conquerors must undergo in Ireland. Cox, for instance, may overlook the issue of whether Ireland was a colony or a sister kingdom—it was not a very pressing issue in 1689, and, in any case, it was much too complicated for simple resolution—but he has no doubts about the authority of the English Crown over Ireland, regardless of the status of the papal gift of Ireland to England:

> But I have spent too much time about these paltry Bulls, and therefore I will leave them, and proceed to the solid and legal Titles, which the Crown of *England* hath to the Kingdom of *Ireland;* and the first is that of Descent from *Eva,* Daughter of *Dermond Mac Morough,* who was actually King of *Leinster,* and whose Ancestors were Monarchs of *Ireland;* the second is by lawful Conquest in a just War; the third is by many solemn Oaths, Compacts and Submissions of the Princes, Nobility, Gentry and People of *Ireland:* The fourth is, by several Statutes, and Acts of Recognition: And the last (which alone were sufficient) is, by above five hundred years Prescription. (8)

Pride of place goes to marriage and possession, but it is clear that possession alone is sufficient. Cox is determined to show that there can be no reason for the Irish to doubt their just subordination to England. Strongbow, unable to claim five hundred years' control in Shadwell's play, nevertheless asserts his rights in a similarly uncompromising fashion:

Catholicus   The Clergy in their Pulpits, shall declare
                       That you have all the Right you would have;
                       We'll found it, on what Principle you please.
Strongbow   The right of Conquest is the Right I own.

(328)

Strongbow will bend Church and people to his control, and even unpromising instruments such as Catholicus serve his purposes.

     Strongbow takes a similar attitude toward his marriage to Eva at first. Eva, in love with Regan, tries to avoid marriage to Strongbow. Wrathfully he tells Dermond,

> Curse on her Female pride, why who am I?
> No doating Fool, that sues and whines for Love:
> I call her to my Arms, as by Agreement made,
> We have sign'd and seal'd and you gave her to me.
> All articles by Generals made, are Sacred;
> And were the petty Girl, a-kin to me,
> She should not dare to put it off one Moment.
> (326–27)

Outraged masculine pride is here equated with military might. Dermond and Strongbow's exchange of Eva, itself a consequence of military aid, is important because it signifies Strongbow's dominance over Ireland: Eva herself is important as a signifier, not as an object of desire. In anthropological terms, she is the gift that seals male agreements.

Strongbow, however, changes his view even as he defeats all possible rivals. Dermond and Cothurnus are killed by Rotherick, Regan is killed by Strongbow's soldiers, and Strongbow kills Rotherick himself. In short, by the end of the play there are no Irishmen of rank available to contest Strongbow's claim to Eva or Ireland. He is apologetic over the death of Regan, and remorse at the cost of his victory transforms him. He says to Eva, "Dry up those watery Eyes, my dearest Princess,/I fight your Father's cause to set you free;/Whilst I remain a Slave, a Woman's slave" (333). When Rotherick attempts to ravish her, she greets Strongbow's arrival with recognition that he has become essential to her: "The Earl of *Chepstow* comes to set me free,/And he is now the only friend I've left" (336). In acknowledgment, Strongbow separates conquest and alliance: "My charming Princess! I'll revenge your Cause,/I've saved your Country, and would gain your Love" (336). The allegory is straightforward: England must rescue Ireland from tyranny, and she must accept this intervention as the boon it is. But conquest and even Dermond's agreement cease to be adequate reasons for Ireland's submission to English rule.

Interestingly, despite the historical fact of Strongbow's marriage to Eva, the play ends with his still courting her.

Strongbow	Comply with my Request, and Crown my Love,
	Be a Parent to your sinking People,
	Obey your Father, own your self my Wife;
	And let us to this Isle, give lasting Peace.
Eva	My heart is swell'd, and so opprest with Grief,
	'Tis pain and Anguish when I utter Words;
	I beg you would command my Fathers Army,
	Rule and govern well his Kingdom, curb his Foes,
	And give his poor, and wretched Subjects ease;
	Whilst I, in one continued life of Prayer,
	Send up my Pious thoughts, to heaven for you.

(337)

Eva's marriage to Strongbow, when it occurs, reflects Shadwell's views of English domination over Ireland. Her subordination in marriage, emblem of the subordination of the kingdom of Ireland to that of England, is the true patriotism, because it will improve the lot of the Irish people. Moreover, Eva does accept his right to rule and protect Ireland from foreign enemies (i.e., Continental supporters of the Pretender). Nevertheless, Strongbow has come to realize that for his conquest to be meaningful, it has to be consensual. Paradoxically, Shadwell's epideictic play about the Norman conquest conciliates its restive Dublin audience by suggesting that their consent is still required. Ireland is worth having and therefore requires wooing, and the tenor of the courtship is that Eva should recognize the benefits of the Whig settlement. There may again be an echo of *Henry V* here in that Strongbow courts Eva just as Henry V courts Kate, despite the fact that she has already been made the central demand of the proposed treaty. The difference is that Shakespeare provides closure (although that is deconstructed in the epilogue) and Shadwell does not, recognizing the New English unhappiness with England and the uneasy movement of the colonists toward the remnants of Gaelic culture.

Even here, the play reflects a careful ambivalence in its incomplete resolution; Shadwell cannot treat the marriage as anything but positive—it was, after all, one of the justifications for English control of Ireland, and descendants of Norman-Irish marriages would have been sitting in the audience—but he cannot celebrate it unreservedly either. A long-held view was that any intermingling with the Irish was a degenerative influence: Raphael Holinshed and John Hooker's *The Second Volumes of Chronicles: Conteining the description, conquest, inhabitation, and troublesome state of Ireland,* published in 1586, reported that "againe, the verie English of birth, conversant with the savage sort of that people become degenerat, and as though they had tasted of Circes poisoned cup, are quite altered" (45). The conventional wisdom was that intermarriage had been a bad thing. Sir John Davies, for example, criticized the "English Lords" who rebelled during King John's reign, for they

> placed *Irish* Tenants upon the Lands relinquished by the *English;* upon them they levied all *Irish* Exactions, with them they married, and fostered, and made Gossips so as within one Age, the *English,* both Lords and Freeholders, became degenerate and meer *Irish* in their Language, in their Arms and manner of Fight, and all other Customs of Life whatsoever.[37]

Davies wrote in 1612, but the work was reprinted in Dublin in 1704, revealing continuing anxiety over the cultural "decline" of the English of Ireland.

Thus when Shadwell dramatizes a happy union between New English and Irish in *Irish Hospitality,* he is creating his most radical statement of sympathy for the Irish and the English of Ireland. First, the colonists have adopted the native tradition of hospitality, which Cox had derided as a mask for political self-interest: "And it was that custom of *Tanistry* which made the *Irish* seek to be popular; and to that end were Hospitable even to Profuseness, and above all things coveted an *outward Appearance,* thereby to attract the Admiration of the Vulgar, and increase the number of their Followers and Abettors" (xxi). Writing closer to Shadwell's time, MacCurtin is again the defender of Irish customs:

> And certainly for what most concerns the antient Times, it appears out of very good, both domestick and foreign, Authors of undoubted Credit, that the *Irish* have always taken extraordinary Care for providing Entertainment for all *Comers;* and that their Hospitality in those primitive Ages, was unparallel'd in all *Europe.*[38]

In Shadwell's play, it is the recent interloper, Sir Wou'd be Generous, who "affects all the Liberality of Sir *Patrick,* but has a mistaken Notion of Generosity, built more upon Pride and Ostentation, than a design of doing good" (204), while Sir Patrick Worthy epitomizes the true spirit of hospitality: "A Genrous temper'd Gentleman, who having a Plentiful Estate, keeps open House to all Comers and Goers, and by his Liberality, makes himself the Country's Darling" (204).

Sir Wou'd be Generous is the second generation of the aristocracy to own an estate to the detriment of Ireland, having bought his from Sir Run-away-Spendthrift, who, according to a neighboring half-mounted squire, "would spend his time in *Dublin*, when he should be runing his Dogs, and before the Hunting Season was half over, he was Fool enough to go to the Bath for his Health, and he no sooner got it, but he whipt to *London*, and there lost that, and his Estate too" (237). Between absentee landlords and hypocrites, Ireland is endangered, dramatized by the fact that Sir Wou'd be Generous plans to murder Sir Patrick out of jealousy.

Shadwell's adoption of hospitality as the mark of an Irish gentleman is striking because as it became more expensive, the upper classes became more cautious, and the custom lasted longest among the archaic and rural gentry.[39] Moreover, hospitality was primarily associated with the Gaelic, Catholic gentry.[40] Sir Patrick therefore represents the interpenetration of Whig ideology and Irish custom. A responsible landlord, he keeps an eye on his own estate; Shela Dermott, the wife of a tenant, frets over difficulties meeting payments:

> O save me! yonder's Landlord coming down the Field; I told your Father he was a stubborn old Fool, that he would not let the Wheat be Thresh'd out, and then we might have pay'd him his Rent; you know Landlord, for all his Generosity, receives the Rents himself. (278)

No middlemen come between Sir Patrick and his property, and his true patriotism is shown by his active participation in the management of his own estate. Even recent immigrants like Shadwell rapidly incorporate the themes of Irish unrest, such as the loss of specie to England.

The accumulation of wealth is a social good when in the hands of worthy men such as Sir Patrick. The Irish custom is translated by him into the Christian injunction to charity:

> I think my self an Earthly Steward, deputed by Heaven, to distribute that Fortune it has entrusted me with, on my Fellow Creatures; what Satisfaction is there, like relieving of the Poor, giving Food and Raiment to the miserable, and stopping the Current of a deplorable Man's Condition. (215)

This is, of course, a traditional justification for the aristocracy. Social hierarchy, created by God, is justified by increased responsibility on the part of the wealthy. The landowner becomes a lovable, paternal figure, such as Addison's and Steele's old-fashioned Tory, Sir Roger De Coverley. And indeed the relationship between Sir Patrick and the Dermotts is a long-standing one: "Thy Family have been Tennants to our Estate above these hundred Years, and always have been Honest" (246). Unlike Shadwell, Sir Patrick is no recent interloper.

Yet the play is informed by Whig perspectives. Even self-control turns into a battle for liberty and limited monarchy. Goodlove, Sir Patrick's friend, life-saver, and, ultimately, son-in-law, makes the analogy while attempting to reclaim Sir Patrick's libertine son, Charles:

> But as our Politick Notions of the World teach us to hate Tyranny and Slavery, and to make noble Stands for the preserving of our Liberty, so we shou'd Subdue the Arbitrary Power of the Flesh—there, self preservation shou'd Exert it self, 'tis then indeed the first Principle of Nature, which we ought to make use of, to depose the Corrupt Monarchy of Sin. (285–86)

There is no reason to think of this as a gratuitous interjection on Shadwell's part. He is writing exemplary drama, and in a pastoral elegy upon his death, he is described as living up to his precepts.[41] Virtue itself belongs to Whigs, and Sir Patrick and his friends are virtuous.

But the central event of Shadwell's conciliatory attitude toward the Ireland for which he was writing is, as in the case of Strongbow and Eva, the emblematic betrothal. Winnifred, daughter of Shela Dermott, is nearly seduced by the libertine Charles; Sir Patrick steps in and marries them by providing Winnifred with a dowry. First the Irish are drawn to England, as the daughter of Gaelic stock is christened with an English name. Second, the potentially absentee landlord son is drawn to virtue and hence Irish patriotism, as he will live on what will one day be his estate. Finally, the Irish and the (relatively) New English are drawn to peace through marriage alliance. Ireland, in Shadwell's view, becomes part of a prosperous and virtuous Whig empire, while preserving the valuable elements of the indigenous culture.

Whereas the Restoration transient Richard Head foresees mostly difficulties for the New English arrivals in Ireland, Shadwell, the English emigré attempting to please a Dublin audience (and apparently succeeding), depicts a happy resolution. Yet Whig apologist for conquest and empire as he is, he nevertheless participates in a movement of conciliation both toward emergent Anglo-Irish dissatisfaction, and toward some aspects of the pre-existing Irish culture. As we shall see, Tories could appropriate that culture even more easily.

THREE

"And mix their Blood with ours; one People grow"

The Ambivalent Nationalism of William Philips's *Hibernia Freed*

William Philips's *Hibernia Freed* premiered in London at the Lincoln's Inn Field Theater on 13 February 1722 and was performed seven times, the last show taking place on Saint Patrick's Day.[1] The play represents several anomalies, starting with its surprisingly lucrative second benefit for the author: £86, 2s. 6d. in cash, and another £52, 10s. in ticket sales; after house charges of £40, Philips took home nearly £100.[2] The composition of the audience on that night attracted attention as well. A commentator in *The Freeholder's Journal* wrote, "I never knew a play so clapped . . . till a Friend put me in Mind that half the Audience were *Wild Irish*."[3] The commentator's categorization of the audience (which would certainly have included numerous Anglo-Irish spectators)—half savage and wholly foreign—suits well with the topic of the play: an Irish victory over the Danes prior to the Norman conquest.[4]

Yet Philips's father, George, was the governor of Derry who encouraged the apprentices to close the gates of the city against Lord Antrim in 1688, and his great-grandfather was a servitor under the Crown during the rebellion of the earls in the late sixteenth and early seventeenth century.[5] In other words, Philips, neither Gaelic nor Catholic, with a Williamite family background, and thus assuredly in Irish terms a member of the "New English," is adopted by the wild Irish in a London audience, and, in the play's dedication to the earl of Thomond, he describes himself as an Irish patriot:

> As Love of my Country induced me to lay the Scene of a Play there; so the particular Honour I bear to, and ought to have for, Your Lordship's Family, oblig'd me to search for a Story, in which one of your Lordship's Ancestors made so noble a Figure; for what is so noble as to free ones Country from Tyranny and Invasion?[6]

But despite the play's celebration of a native victory over foreign overlords, the bard Eugenius ends the play prophesying the subsequent happy conquest of Ireland by the English.

Hibernia Freed has significance in terms of English politics, as Philips was a Tory, a Jacobite, and, at least for a while, a member of Speaker Sir Thomas Hanmer's entourage. Nevertheless, the tensions present in *Hibernia Freed* and probably in its audience are also a function of competing views among early eighteenth-century Anglo-Irish patriots of how Ireland should respond to English assertions of imperial authority. Philips's dedication to the Irish earl of Thomond shows he is no longer English (despite his English name); the closing speech shows he does not desire an independent Ireland either. While appropriating a heroic Irish past, Philips also urges patience with foreign tyranny by incorporating the Irish historical motif of punishment because of guilt and division. Still, although the play indicates an author not unhappy as a subject of Great Britain, the plot implicitly warns the English that the Irish are not to be taken for granted, and the "mix'd blood" of Ireland can be warmed to revolt again.

While the actual effect of English legislation (the Navigation Act of 1663, the Woolen Act of 1699, and the patent granting Wood the right to make half-pence in 1722) on Irish prosperity is debatable, it is clear that "among the Irish gentry at large and in the eyes of Irish public opinion generally, a rather nebulous view was commonly accepted from the 1720s which held English legislation to have been directed against Irish economic interests and to have seriously prejudiced them."[7] Moreover, the *Sherlock v. Annesley* case demonstrated the appellate authority of the English House of Lords over the Irish and led to the Declaratory Act (Sixth of George I) in 1720 which made statutory the British Parliament's right to pass laws over Ireland.[8] The effect of these commercial and legal persecutions was that, as Foster says, "those who in the 1690s called themselves 'the Protestants of Ireland' or even 'the English of this Kingdom' could see themselves as 'Irish Gentlemen' by the 1720s."[9]

Jonathan Swift exemplifies the wrath of the Protestant Irish gentry over these developments, and their growing self-identification with Ireland. In a standard modern edition of *A Proposal for the Universal Use of Irish Manufacture*, for which the editors use the 1735 Dublin edition of Swift's works, Swift quotes a member of the hierarchy of the Church of Ireland:

> I heard the late Archbishop of *Tuam* mention a pleasant Observation of some Body's; *that* Ireland *would never be happy 'till a Law were made for* burning *every Thing that came from* England, *except their* People *and their* Coals: I must confess, that as to the former, I should not be sorry if they would stay at home; and for the latter, I hope, in a little Time we shall have no occasion for them.[10]

The anonymous 1720 edition published in Dublin is much more indicative of Swift's mood at the time.[11] Following the colon after "Coals," Swift originally wrote, "Nor am I *even yet* for lessening the Number of those Exceptions" (6). Disturbing as it must have been to some to have a dean of the Church of Ireland emphasizing his disagreements with the English—there was little doubt that Swift was the author[12]—the violence of Swift's original version must have been very shocking—and probably accounts for his revisions—because a united front of protestants, as well as the protection of England, against the bitterly oppressed Catholic majority, was perceived by many as essential to the maintenance of the Protestant interest.

John Toland, the Irish religious controversialist, underlined the dangers of the Sixth of George I in a pamphlet published in London: "Nothing should be attempted, that might bring about the Possibility of a *Union of Civil Interests* between the Protestants and Papists of Ireland, whose antipathies and Animosities all sound Politicians will ever labour to keep alive."[13] Swift's *Proposal* was dangerous because in his use of the word *Irish* he suggested a potential alliance where the definition of nationality would be geographical (rather than religious). The anonymous *An Answer to the Proposal for the Universal Use of Irish Manufacture* (Dublin: 1720) redraws the boundaries:

> If he means by *Ireland,* the native *Irish* his Country-men, as I believe he does, I must confess that he has once spoken truth; They have been chastiz'd by *England* with great Severity, and I am in great hopes that they will take warning for the future. . . . But; if he means the *English* settled in *Ireland,* who are best known by the name of *Protestants;* what Reason have they to Complain, [and] if they have they do not. (12–13)

The native Irish deserve what they received, and the gentry are not Irish. Religion defines identity, and Swift is dangerously mistaken.

However, there were at least some friendly relations between native Irish and New English immigrants, the Protestants of Ireland increasingly did not identify with the English, and Swift consequently represents the temper of the time. Philips writes in his dedication to Thomond,

> Tho' the Histories of *Ireland* are not writ in such a manner as to intice many Readers, (a Misfortune however, not particular to that Nation) yet none are ignorant that Your Lordship is lineally descended from the Monarchs of it. (2)

Despite the claim that there are not many readers of Irish history, Philips was participating in a resurgence of interest in a Gaelic past. Interestingly, one of the centers of this resurgence was London. Sarah Butler's *Irish Tales: or, Instructive Histories for the Conduct of Life,* also about Irish victories over the Danes, was published in London by Edmund Curll in 1716.[14] Dermo'd O'Connor published his translation of Geoffrey Keating's *Foras Feasa ar Éirinn* in London and Dublin in 1723; O'Connor's career is evidence both that a Gaelic scribe could make a living in London, and that, at least in Ireland, Irish and English language cultures and Catholics and Protestants interacted more widely than has been assumed.[15] Indeed, O'Connor presented a copy of his work to the prince of Wales, who, according to the *Dublin Intelligence,* received it with "esteem and favour."[16] In any case, it is clear that the Anglo-Irish in London on some occasions regarded themselves and were regarded as "Irish." Or rather, as D. W. Hayton remarks,

Still conscious that they represented the "English Interest" in Ireland, and capable of thinking of themselves as both "English" and "Irish" in different contexts, they were fond of exuberant statements of Irish patriotism, and denounced what they saw as English economic exploitation while realizing that the possibilities of action and remedy were restricted.[17]

Trickwell, in Philips's *St. Stephen's Green,* probably indicates Philips's contempt for those who went to London and denigrated their heritage:

> For I have observ'd that none Despise *Ireland* so much as those who thrive best in it. And none so severe in their Reflections upon it, as those who owe their Birth and Fortune to it; I have known many of 'em, when they come first to *London,* think there is no way so ready to purchase the Title of a Wit, as to Ridicule their own Country.[18]

Stage Irishmen are replaced by English wannabes like the shifty Lady Volant in Philips's comedy, and Irish Protestants are proud of Ireland—while at the same time seeking fortunes in England. Love of country competes with dependence on the English economy.

O'Connor's translation of Keating was dedicated to William "O Bryen," earl of Inchiquin and cousin of Thomond, and among the subscribers was Thomond. O'Connor's dedication to Inchiquin refers to his royal Irish ancestry and praises the O'Briens for

> having filled the Throne of *Ireland* for twenty nine Successions, (as appears from the subsequent Genealogy of your Lordship's most Illustrious House) and with signal Bravery have repelled the Invasions of foreign Enemies, and gave a fresh supply of Life and Vigour to the Cause of their expiring Country.[19]

Despite O'Connor's glowing reference to the expulsion of foreign invaders, Jacqueline R. Hill has shown that "patriot" sentiments, particularly in the first half of the eighteenth century, should not be regarded as evidence of dissatisfaction with the link with Britain.[20] Thomond, for instance, was a member of the Irish Privy Council, which, according to Lord Chancellor Wyndham, was "a post really of consequence here."[21] On the whole, the privy council was opposed to patriot sentiments.[22] Moreover, his father-in-law, the duke of Somerset, was an important Whig, although not always reliable on party grounds.[23] Still, one could be, as Thomond was, a loyal Whig Protestant and nevertheless proud of an Irish heritage.[24]

Furthermore, Thomond represents the close ties between some members of the Irish power structure and the Gaelic, Jacobite aristocracy of Ireland that had been expelled after 1691. Knowing he was dying without an heir, Thomond asked his cousin, the sixth Viscount Clare, an officer in the French army in an Irish brigade and the son of one of the Wild Geese, if he would convert to inherit the earldom (the offer was cleared with George I). Clare declined, but Thomond left him 12,000 pounds to show there were no hard feelings.[25] At least one member of the Catholic hierarchy was closely related to members of the Protestant aristocracy. Christopher Butler, Catholic archbishop of Cashel from 1712 to 1757, was closely related to the duke of Ormond.[26] Philips would almost certainly have been aware of ties between the Protestant Old English and their Catholic cousins; the dedication to his 1698 tragedy *The Revengeful Queen* claims the protection of the duke of Ormond "because your Family have vouchsafed to be the Patrons of mine for several Generations."[27]

Thomas Bartlett suggests that Catholic families tolerated a token conversion by a family member to maintain control of the land, which would indicate further close ties between some Catholics and Protestants.[28] The mere fact that the Normans (and Elizabeth and Cromwell and William III) had conquered Ireland did not eliminate pride in a royal past or sympathy for relatives who retained allegiance to a defeated religion. Many Catholic landowners retained possession of their land because Protestant relatives or neighbors held the legal title of the land for them, while perjuring themselves by claiming they were doing nothing of the sort; the earl of Fingall is perhaps the most prominent example.[29] The ties of blood, class, and proximity were strained by religious differences but not destroyed.

Philips himself was a Tory with Jacobite friends. He represented Doneraile in the Irish Parliament as a member of the Tory interest from 1703 to 1713.[30] Fascinatingly, he visits Paris with Sir Thomas Hanmer in 1713 and cautiously intimates that Hanmer was an enemy to the Hanoverian succession. As for Philips himself, Lord Newcastle quotes him as saying, "For his own particular, he wod dey to serve the King." This does not make Philips any less the anti-Catholic Anglo-Irish politico. He also tells Father Inese that the Pretender "should shew kindness to protestants, and have as many of them about him as his present condition could allow."[31] Philips's sympathies were with the country party and those still loyal to the Stuarts. As a member of the imperiled Protestant interest in Ireland, he remains sensitive to the fears that a Stuart restoration would threaten the status quo.

Still, in his attitude toward the Irish Philips is clearly more in agreement with Swift than with his anonymous enemy of *An Answer*. That vituperative Protestant says of the Irish,

> Tho' their Crime was as great [as Arachne], their Punishment does not seem quite so bad: they have been metamorphos'd, but into what? not Spiders, but Men, they have been tra[n]sform'd from Savages into reasonable Creatures, and delivered from a state of Nature and Barbarism, and endow'd with Civility and Humanity. (12)

This, of course, is similar to Sir Richard Cox's view of England's enlightened colonial administration, discussed in chapter 2.

On the contrary, in Philips's view, Ireland was the land of learning prior to conquest:

O'Brien   Hibernia! Seat of Learning! School of Science!
             How waste! How wild dost thou already seem!
             Thy Houses, Schools, thy Cities ransack'd, burnt!

(3)

Rapacious foreigners have made Ireland what it is, and they are far from being pillars of enlightenment. The Irish were far too kind and charitable to the needy invaders:

Agnes   Hibernia, ever kind to the Distress'd,
                  Ever for Hospitality renown'd,
                  Receiv'd ye famish'd, and reliev'd your Wants;
                  Gave Towns to build, and fruitful Plains to till.

The virtues of Ireland, hospitality, generosity, and piety, are responsible for its plight. Nor do the Irish lack worthy heroes. O'Neill, in love with O'Brien's daughter, Sabina, is a Celtic Achilles:

> Thus *Thetis'* Son forsook the sanguine Plain,
> And War and Glory courted him in vain.
> At *Deidama's* Feet supine he lay,
> Resign'd himself to Love's more gently Sway.
>
> (23)

The Irish, however, are brave warriors only by necessity, preferring the arcadian paths of Irish romance; the invaders are irredeemably bloodthirsty savages.

According to Swift, the Irish are in the position of Arachne:

> The Goddess [Athena] had heard of one *Arachne* a young Virgin, very famous for *Spinning* and *Weaving:* They both met upon a Tryal of Skill; and *Pallas* finding herself almost equalled in her own Art, stung with Rage and Envy, knockt her *Rival* down, turned her into a *Spyder,* enjoining her to *spin* and *weave* for ever, *out of her own Bowels,* and *in a very narrow Compass.*[32]

Punished for their abilities, the Irish are restricted from exporting their goods. But more importantly, the English are to blame for Irish poverty. Athena has fallen from her position as goddess of wisdom, just as the English are acting unwisely in their treatment of Ireland. The choice of Arachne is especially important as the English trade restrictions fell hardest on Protestants, who controlled the weaving industry.[33]

In Philips's play, the Irish nobility have been forced to collaborate in the torment of the Irish:

> O'Brien lives to see his People Slaves,
> Himself a Slave, a poor precarious King,
> Compell'd to rob and strip the lab'ring Hinds,
> To feed the *Dane* and support his Riot.
>
> (2)

This indignity is emphasized when Turgesius ignores O'Brien while lusting after O'Brien's daughter, Sabina: "I feel, I see to what I am reduc'd;/To pay Obedience to the Victor's Will/and stand neglected like a common Slave" (16). Philips's identification with the Irish places him in the position of questioning

English methods of rule (particularly under the Whigs), if not English rule itself. In short, Philips, as Irish Protestant, makes sense out of contemporary events through identification with a Gaelic past. The play is not directed to the "English of Ireland."

The anonymous *Answer* again provides the hardline view on Irish subordination:

> The Protestants of *Ireland* are sensible that Nature and Circumstances, as well as Constitution and original Right, have plac'd them under a Dependence upon their Mother Country, whose Protection and Justice they have the utmost confidence in, and think it their great happiness, that they have her to depend upon; because they cannot depend upon themselves, much less upon them whose Properties they enjoy, and whose enmities can never be extinguish'd as long as the Motives of Interest, Religion, and national Aversion endure. (14)

Many Irish Protestants, however, did not see the Catholic natives as a threat; God had protected them in 1641 and again in 1690. Nor did they see England as the "Mother country" but rather as a sort of an elder sister.[34] This is not to deny the deeply rooted anxieties that exploded into active oppression in the 1760s and 1790s, but some Irish Protestants were prepared to blame Irish unrest on English mistreatment.

Like Strongbow in the first half of Shadwell's *Rotherick O'Connor*, Turgesius uses as his justification for demanding gratification of all of his demands (including Sabina) the right of conquest:

> And what like Conquest gives a Right to Empire?
> He, who possesses greatest Fortitude
> Should rule the World and Trample on Mankind.
> The Lyon hence subjects the savage Herd,
> The Eagle hence insults the feather'd kind.
>
> (27)

It is not much of a stretch to see the British lion represented, particularly in the context of "savage" herds, the standard epithet for the Irish. The difficulty of this argument that "might makes right" is immediately pointed out by Sabina:

> How well such precepts suit a Prince's Mouth
> Which instigates his Subjects to rebel!
> Ye lab'ring Hinds! who sweat and drudge for Life,
> Away with all your Implements of Toil,
> Be bold, and dare, and bravely seize a Crown!
>
> (27)

The argument of the *Answer* is that the English conquest has improved the lot of the Irish. The emphasis here on the lower classes reminds an audience of the poverty of the native Irish peasantry, poorer than the French and much more destitute than the English.[35] That fact makes nonsense of claims that English imperialism has improved the lot of the Irish. Sabina says that when "Human-

ity and Temperance are scorn'd,/Justice and Virtue are of no Regard"; consequently, a virtuous acceptance of natural subordination is discredited by the
very rulers who need that attitude to maintain control.

Of course to a Jacobite, whether in England or Ireland, the usurping invader
could never be entitled to "natural subordination" on anyone's part. God had
set the bounds of society and determined natural rulers. Thus O'Brien states
that empire itself is pernicious to the conquerors:

> Faith, Justice, Laws, Obedience, Gratitude,
> Are Cob-Web Bonds when Empire is in View.
> Man breaks thro'all, and when the Toy is gain'd,
> Care mounts the Throne and Suspition broods.
>
> (32)

When a crown unjustly destroys an existing government, the moral ligatures
that hold society together are broken. Ireland here is no longer a spider spin-
ning out her entrails. Virtue becomes as weak as a spiderweb among the foreigners who enjoy their prey without restraint; eventually, their lack of self-
control will lead to their undoing. To a Jacobite, this is a promise of Stuart
restoration. But to an Irish patriot this is a warning that English avarice under-
mines the postrevolutionary settlement in Ireland. In other words, it would be
to the advantage of the English to treat Ireland as a sister kingdom, rather than
as a colony.

Swift writes in the *Proposal,*

> The Scripture tells us, that *Oppression makes a wise Man mad;* therefore, conse-
> quently speaking, the Reason why some Men are not *mad,* is because they are not
> *wise:* However, it were to be wished that *Oppression* would, in Time, teach a little
> *Wisdom* to *Fools.*[36]

It is here that Philips associates himself with the *Answer* rather than with Swift.
The anonymous Protestant responds, "He [Swift] stimulates them with an
Aggravation of their Wrongs, and instead of Oyl pours Vinegar into their
Wounds. . . . Wise-men more frequently make Oppression light by bearing it"
(6–7). The recurring remedy to which O'Brien resorts is stoic endurance.

Eugenius begins the play by stating that private persons can be happier than
rulers:

> On Thrones, in Triumphs, crown'd with all we wish,
> The Mind is on a Rack, conscious of Ill.
> But virtuous Actions can secure her Rest,
> Spite of Calamities or Fortune's Frowns.
>
> (2)

O'Brien, when not ranting about his state, comes to agree with this. Indeed,
were it not for obligations to his people, and a father's responsibility to protect
his daughter, he would prefer private life:

> The Loss of Empire and the Loss of Pow'r
> We may support, while Reason is our guide.
> Better be subject to the *Danes,* than as
> This *Dane,* to ev'ry Passion be a Slave.
> Reason directs us to the Choice of Good,
> And while obey'd, the Mind enjoys sweet Peace
> In lowest state, conscious of no Reproach.
>
> (30)

The traditional stoic glorification of reason is balanced against Turgesius's appetitive nature. Passivity in the face of imperial vice becomes the moral opposite of Turgesius's restless action. The virtuous man is greater than the mere ruler and rises superior to fate. As O'Brien says firmly,

> When Fortune smil'd, and left no room to wish,
> This Land, then blest, and I the Sovereign Lord,
> Virtue and Honour I had still in view,
> And so instructed her.
> Now of my Crown, of Empire dispossess'd,
> In virtue still I find a blest support,
> And borrow strength from thence to bear my griefs.
>
> (41)

The virtuous Irish nobleman makes light of his burdens by bearing them.

The soothing oil Philips pours on Irish wounds comes with a wry acknowledgment of necessity. Agnes pleads with O'Connor when he seeks to challenge Erric, who has attempted to violate her honor:

> Oh whither would'st thou go! with Passion blind,
> By Love, by Honour, I conjure thee stay.
> Would'st thou expose thee to his Rage, and draw
> Inevitable Ruin on us all.
>
> (17)

Outnumbered and defeated, the Irish must tolerate some affronts because worse will follow if they do not; after all, the Irish gentleman can tolerate the attempted rape of Ireland (Agnes) when it does not succeed. Swiftian rage can only make the situation worse. Thus reason, virtue, and practical considerations all argue for a placid acceptance of imperial wrongs.

Again, this attitude has implications for the English political scene. The Country party insisted that private life was superior to the feverish and sycophantic atmosphere of the court; Philips's patron, Hanmer, alone turned down four offers to join the Oxford ministry.[37] Necessity could make a virtue out of the quiet life as well. Tories accused of Jacobitism had little choice other than stoic endurance in the period after the Hanoverian succession. Philips dedicates his 1724 tragedy *Belisarius* to General John Richmond Webb, who, despite a distinguished career and the admiration of George I for his bravery, was deprived of his posts and forced to sell his commission by the Whigs in 1715. He was linked with a Jacobite association known as "Burford's" in 1722, and the last two years of his life were spent in extreme retirement (DNB).

Belisarius reiterates many of the themes of *Hibernia Freed*. The court is by its nature vicious, and the jealous courtier Hermogenes plots to bring down the virtuous Belisarius. Vitiges, king of the Goths, betrays Belisarius, despite the latter's kind treatment, in order to regain his kingdom: "Resistless Bait! tho' infamous the Means,/We blindly follow or are weakly led,/So strong the appetite to rule."[38] Valeria, who also turns on Belisarius because he prefers Almira, nevertheless is grateful for divine justice after Hermogenes blinds Belisarius and is destroyed for it:

> Oh Providence how Just!
> The Wicked of their Prudence to divest,
> And Folly give for Guide, when impiously
> They deviate from thy Laws.
>
> (47)

Ultimately, God will take a hand and punish those who desire power unjustly. The individual, however, can do nothing except wait for divine intervention. Like O'Brien, Belisarius, deprived of power and wealth, stands on his virtue rather than rebel: "My Honesty, my Virtue is my own,/Thank Heav'n! innate, by practice too confirm'd,/Beyond the Reach of wild despotick Pow'r" (30).

No doubt stoic passivity was reassuring to any stray Englishmen who wandered into the Lincoln's Inn Field Theater to see *Hibernia Freed,* but it does not explain why a "wild Irish" audience would not only tolerate supine acquiescence but applaud it. Ultimately, of course, the Irish are victorious in the play. But also Philips is relying on a traditional Irish view that their defeats at the hands of various invaders were a well-earned punishment for their own sins and divisions; the Irish brought their troubles upon themselves. There is a kind of gloomy satisfaction among Irish historians that the Irish have so greatly provoked divine wrath. Possibly, there is also an excuse involved; i.e., the Irish would not have lost if they had not broken training.

Catholic historian Peter Walsh in 1682 writes grimly that as a general habit, "never have we read of any other People in the World so implacably, so furiously, so eternally set upon the destruction of one another." In fact, Saint "Columb-Cille" warned them of "Turgheise" (Turgesius) in particular:

> So that Almighty God, the great Justiciar, the great Striker of them from above, might justly say to them at this time, what he had formerly said to the *Jews* by the mouth of his Prophet *Jeremy. In vain have I stricken your children they received no correction.*[39]

Implicit in Hugh MacCurtin's *A Brief Discourse in Vindication of the Antiquity of Ireland* is the argument that the Irish, like the Jews, are a disobedient chosen people and must suffer accordingly. Turgesius reduced the Irish "at last to such Bondage and Slavery, as far surpassed the *Egyptian,* or any other that has been known any where on Earth."[40] O'Connor's 1723 translation of Keating summed up the view that the Danish conquest was punishment for Irish sins:

> For the Inhabitants were become very profligate and corrupt in their Manners, and a Torrent of Vice and Prophaneness had overspread the Nation, but prevail'd chiefly among the Nobility and Gentry, whose Pride, Injustice and Ambition, deserv'd the severest Inflictions from the Hand of Providence; so that the cruel *Danes* were used as Instruments by divine Vengeance, to scourge and correct a wicked and debauch'd Nobility, and an immoral and licentious Populace.[41]

Patient endurance of foreign conquest may be ignoble, but endurance of the rod of the Lord is quite another matter.

Eugenius tells O'Brien, "Fatal Disunion and intestine Strife/Have render'd us a Prey to foreign Pow'r" (2). Immediately we are told of a new disaster: Rannald, Prince of Kerry, has refused to aid O'Brien's son, Lucius, unless he is given Sabina; when told she is engaged to O'Neill, "*Rannald,* incens'd, withdrew. Too few the rest/To vanquish, scorning Flight—they fought—they dy'd" (6). One of the Irish lords, Herimon, says no hope remains, and Eugenius reads the moral:

> Rash Man! Are we still harden'd in our Sin?
> Nor yet taught Wisdom, unsubdu'd our Pride?
> Groveling our Senses, ignorant and blind,
> Dare we brave Pow'r, eternal, infinite,
> And dare we Worms expostulate with Heav'n?
> (6)

Whom the Lord loveth, he chastizeth, and the Irish Jobs ought neither to despair nor question providence.

It is important to stress that Philips is not making an allegorical pitch for Protestant unity (disunity being one of the traditional faults of the Irish). The heroic past Philips invokes is specifically that of a preconquest Ireland:

> Our Griefs swell higher, when recording Bards
> Sing to their Harps the mighty Deeds of *Ir,*
> The hundred Battles by *Milesius* gain'd,
> And paint *Gadelus* Fame, and shew us sprung from them.
> (10)

The discord that Philips dramatizes as deadly cannot be reduced to sectarian differences. The O'Briens were noble as Catholics and remain noble as Protestants. The "Irish" unity that Philips suggests as admirable is a curious inversion of an Anglo-Irish argument for equal rights with England based on the fiction that there are few Irish left.

As early as 1612, John Davies stated that after Henry II,

there have been since that time so many *English* Colonies planted in *Ireland,* as that if the People were numbred at this Day by the Poll, such as are descended of *English* Race would be found more in number than the ancient Natives.[42]

Richard Cox agrees "that four parts in five of the Inhabitants in *Ireland* are of *English* Extraction."[43] Cox's point is that any talk of Irish independence is idle because few of the Irish are left. And William Molyneux, in *The Case of Ireland's being bound by acts of parliament in England* (1698), goes even further and says there are a "mere handful" of the native Gaelic population left; Molyneux uses this argument to reverse Cox and to legitimate "the ascendancy's claim to power in Ireland by reducing the original inhabitants of the country to the status of non-people."[44] But all of these writers are claiming that the mixed race left in Ireland is predominantly an English race. The Irish are insignificant and few.

Philips, however, writing for Thomond, cannot make any such claim; the O'Briens did not dwindle to insignificance. Eugenius, at the end of the play, lavishes praise on the eventual English conquerors:

> Another Nation, famous through the World,
> For martial Deeds, for Strength and Skill in Arms,
> Belov'd and blest for their Humanity.
> Where Wealth abounds, and Liberty resides,
> And Arts and Sciences shall flourish ever.
> . . . .
> They shall succeed, invited to our Aid,
> And mix their Blood with ours; one People grow,
> Polish our Manners, and improve our Minds.
>
> (57)

One is tempted, granted the political strains between England and Anglo-Irish patriots, to see this as tongue in cheek. Even if the speech is serious, however, Philips is stressing that the English were invited in—the Irish were not conquered. Moreover, the resultant race is genuinely mixed, not English. Also, the master narrative to which Philips attaches his version of nationalism is Irish, not English; the validation of the English arrival comes from a Gaelic bard, just as much as the validation of Irish history comes from an Anglo-Irish playwright. And what the play *shows* is an Irish victory over a foreign invader. Despite the important dramatic position of this speech—the last lengthy speech in the play—the play as a whole is a celebration of indomitable Irish resistance. Ultimately, stoic endurance is replaced by an overthrow of the invader, and there lies Philips's warning to the English.

Erric says to the aghast Agnes, "Let me enjoy the Sweets of Wealth and Pow'r,/Let Slaves and Beggars preach against the Means./I stand possess'd of those, and they are thine" (14). Stoic as the Irish are, the rapacity of the foreigner drives them to their limits.[45] Significantly, the invader has none of his own. Erric is willing to destroy the peace by bringing Turgesius and Sabina together. Indicative of the invaders' moral standing is Turgesius's first reponse when told of the women:

> I will have them both.
> When my Desires shall droop, when cloy'd with them,
> Or when new Beauties give new Appetite
> I'll cast them off to thee; to other Slaves.
>
> (24)

The resultant events are recounted in almost every seventeenth- and eighteenth-century history of Ireland. Turgesius calls for women to be presented to him and his lords. Instead, noble youths dressed as women arrive and, when alone, stab the Danes to death.

The imperial appetite, here manifested as sexual appetite, cannot wait for gratification. Warned by Erric that O'Neill has defeated the Danes in Ulster and has reached O'Brien's camp, Turgesius cannot wait so much as a night:

> Shall it be said, I left my Love through Fear,
> Because O Neill has stolen a victory?
> No, at my leisure I will punish him.
> This Night shall be devoted to my Love;
> To morrow to Revenge, my second Joy;
> Perhaps to Morrow it may be my first.
>
> (50)

The flippancy of the last line puts in stark relief the instability of Turgesius's power. Hubris and will combine to work God's retribution upon him after he has served God's purpose in punishing the Irish. O'Neill tells Turgesius, "From my Dominions I have driven thy Troops,/And now am sent by Heaven to punish Thee" (51). The savage nature of Turgesius, the same that drives him to conquer, leads him inevitably to create the circumstances of his own doom. The Irish, when driven too far, do not miss the chance.

Earlier in the play, Sabina pleads with Turgesius,

> Oh be not deaf when the Afflicted sue!
> Oh let thy Virtue master thy Desires!
> Give way to Pity, let thy Mercy rule,
> Mercy, the brightest Ornament of Crowns!
>
> (39)

The application to England (at least to the Irish in the audience) would have been clear: as conquerors, the English will have their way, but virtue requires that the English limit their assault on Irish trade and rights. This plea, however, shows the conflicted nature of Philips's play. On balance, his anti-imperialist theme suggests that it is in the nature of conquerors not to circumscribe will and, thus, to create the seeds of their own destruction.

Presented in London, the imperial capital, the play cannot be understood as a subversive manifesto urging Irish rebellion. Throughout, Philips counsels patience to the Irish and restraint to the overlords. But if the Irish are being punished by God for their sins, it is probable that there will be a limit to their bondage, and the presentation of the Danes forbodes that the principle of empire creates its own destructive antithesis. Whatever the English response to Irish complaints in the early 1720s, *Hibernia Freed* dramatizes (overoptimistically) a win-win situation. Either the English will retreat in their assaults on Irish dignity and prosperity, or they will destroy themselves. As O'Brien declaims,

> Fortune not permanent to bless or curse,
> With rapid Force has bore'n us down the Hill;
> Thro' craggy Cliffs and over rugged Vales.
> Now she ascends and smooths the Path before us,
> And opens fairer Prospects to our View.
>
> (20)

No wonder the wild Irish applauded enthusiastically.

Philips's celebration of the mixed blood of Ireland—a Protestant participation in a heroic Celtic past—is an important precursor to the Anglo-Irish patriot fervor of the 1770s. Still, it also shows a recognition of the problem of English imperialism and Irish Protestant patriotism. For if the English and Irish could not grow into one people, the play's dialectic of imperialism argued that the English empire would disintegrate as surely as had the empire of the rapacious Danes. Under such circumstances, without divine intervention, the position of protestant patriots such as Philips would prove difficult. But if Philips foresaw a problem (perhaps facilitated by Stuart invasion?), the attendant difficulties of allegiance to "Protestantism" and "Ireland" simultaneously were still minor in his lifetime. *Hibernia Freed*, however, remains interesting as an example of a Tory appropriation of Irish history. After Shadwell and Philips, Irish history could be borrowed by any Anglo-Irishman with a political agenda.

FOUR

Robert Ashton's Heroic Palimpsest,
The Battle of Aughrim

The story I have to tell
Was told me by a teacher
Who read it in a poem
Written in a language that has died.
—Richard Murphy, *The Battle of Aughrim*[1]

From the perspective of the late twentieth century, the slaughter of Irish foot soldiers (as many as seven thousand) at Aughrim in 1691 seems like an extraordinarily pointless episode, worth mentioning only because it was the bloodiest battle ever fought on Irish soil. Brendan Fitzpatrick writes,

> Who these men were and what they thought they were being killed for will never be known. They were not dying for Louis XIV or James II, both of whom had now lost interest. Nor were they dying as property-owning Old English, for these had fled with the cavalry. They were not dying as Catholics, because the Papacy had not supported the war. They were not "dying for Ireland," because there was as yet no romantic myth to die for. It is hard to avoid the conclusion that they died for nothing at all.[2]

Nevertheless, the battle became the occasion for the creation of a heroic Irish past, one in which both Protestants and Catholics shared, and the subject of one of the most popular plays written in Ireland prior to the twentieth century, particularly among the lower classes, who suffered most grievously from the consequences of the battle. Aughrim's symbolic construction illustrates the complexity of cultural relations in eighteenth- and early nineteenth-century Ireland.

Robert Ashton's *The Battle of Aughrim* (1728) has attracted little recent attention or serious consideration. J. R. R. Adams calls it "the Ulster Folk play *par excellence*" and dates its first publication to 1756.[3] More sympathetically but without elaboration, Norman Vance points out that the play is a "Drydenesque heroic tragedy" and "a polished piece"; this defense of Ashton would be more compelling were it not for the fact that Vance accepts Adams's date of 1756 and renames Ashton "John."[4] Anne M. Brady and Brian Cleeve also accept the erroneous dating of the play, and oversimplify by claiming the work is written from the Orange viewpoint. They do, however, point out the work's extraordinary popularity among Catholics: "The reason is its portrayal of Sarsfield and his lieutenants as epic figures. Ashton's intention was to make the Orange victory the greater. The result, as in *Paradise Lost,* was for the villains to steal the story."[5]

Sarsfield and his lieutenants do not steal the story, but, for the first time in penal-era Ireland, they are glorified as participating in it, and this generates a complex response to the play over the next century and a half. *The Battle of Aughrim* functions on two levels. First, it is a celebration of the Williamite victory, modeled after heroic drama, and reflecting the continuing anxieties of the "Protestant interest." Second, it is a lament for Catholic patriotism, influenced by Addison's *Cato,* and suggesting the increasing awareness of the Protestants that they were now, if not Irish, no longer English. Thus, the play appeals to two strands of Irish culture and dramatizes a meaning for the battle that resonated for well over a hundred years. Third, the presence of both strands makes the play a tragedy about the New English who are caught between a desire to be Irish and loyalty to England. I am suggesting three readings of the play that might, in a different work, create a central and irresolvable contradiction. In *Aughrim,* however, the two seemingly incompatible sympathies are in equipoise, so that both Catholics and Protestants were attracted to the play for generations.

The duality of the play is emblematized by a reference to earlier drama. When General Dorrington leaves the English with a threat, Colonel Herbert responds, "There spoke a *Tamerlane*" (24). From the spelling, the reference would seem to be to Rowe's play (1701), perhaps the most frequently produced play in Ireland in the eighteenth century, and one religiously revived on important political holidays with the lord lieutenant in the audience, such as 4 November, when the play would be performed in honor of the anniversary of the birth of William III, or 5 November, in memory of the Gunpowder plot.[6] In *Tamerlane,* the title character is clearly an analog for William III, while Bajazet represents either James II or Louis XIV; Tamerlane is "the Scourge of lawless pride, and dire Ambition/The great Avenger of the groaning World," who overthrows Bajazet "but to redress an injur'd People's Wrongs,/To save the weak One from the strong Oppressor."[7] Herbert may be speaking ironically, but he nonetheless establishes the possibility of viewing Dorrington and the army of James II as patriots fighting for liberty.

And this idea is strengthened by the subsequent identification of St. Ruth not with Rowe's Tamerlane but with Marlowe's Tamburlaine. St. Ruth promises that when he has defeated De Gincle at Aughrim, "then as a Terror to the following Age,/I'll bind him like *Bajazet* in a Cage" (38). Rowe's character cages Bajazet for the sake of justice. Marlowe's character, like St. Ruth, is a bloodthirsty conqueror who shows his hubris by his mistreatment of Bajazet. Cruelty is associated with the French by reference to the earlier play, while the Irish officers are patriots. The Protestant fear of the Catholics is reinforced through the portrayal of St. Ruth as Marlowe's dangerous conqueror, while Catholics are complimented by Dorrington's representation as a defender of Irish liberty against foreign oppression.

I

The Battle of Aughrim's reception over time is the best evidence for its complexity. The play initially comes out in 1728—and disappears. Virtually nothing is known about Ashton. J. T. Gilbert, writing in 1861, claims "Robert Ashton composed a large quantity of fugitive verses on various local topics" and quotes a broadside:

> A Poem in honour of the Loyal Society of Journeyman Shoemakers, who are to dine at the Bull's Head in Fishamble-Street, on Tuesday, October the 28th, 1726, being the anniversary of St. Crispin, written by R. Ashton, S. M., a member of the Society. John Blackwood, Master; Thomas Ashton and William Richardson, Stewards.[8]

The "S. M." is problematic. If it represents a degree, it was not received at Oxford, Cambridge, or Trinity, nor does it correspond to any Masonic title of which I am aware. Yet "shoemaker" is not very appealing either (aside from the fact that it is printed as one word in the broadside and "S. M." would seem to imply two), since Ashton apparently did move in good circles.

The 1728 edition includes an encomium by "Charles Usher, T. C. D." Ussher (1694–1770) was from a branch of one of the most important Anglo-Irish families. Grandson of Sir William Ussher and son of Adam Ussher, archdeacon of Clonfert, he received a B.A. from Trinity in 1715 and an LL.D. *honoris causa* in 1747.[9] He was also an M.P. for Blessington, 1765–70.[10] Ussher was thirty-four in 1728, which makes his friendship with Ashton scarcely that of college chums. Ashton writes in the prologue,

> But should the play fall short, upon my Truth
> You may impute it to our Author's Youth:
> Scarce tender Twenty, faith a childish Age,
> To bring so great a Subject to the Stage.[11]

And his age is basically the end of information about Ashton. Strikingly, subsequent commentators will suggest a life for him, but what exists from the above evidence is a young man with friends among Trinity barristers and artisans, a flexibility that is evident in his work.

Moreover, while there are at least twenty-five editions of the play between

1770 and 1840, there is a gap of twenty-eight years between the first and second edition (1756).[12] Part of the explanation may be that Ashton's printer, Sylvester Powell, went bankrupt in 1729. Richard Norris, for whom the book was printed, was interested in Irish subjects, having been one of the publishers of Dermod O'Connor's translation of Keating, *The History of Ireland* (1723), but there was, apparently, insufficient demand for a second printing of *Aughrim*.[13] Nevertheless, it is significant that the play explodes in popularity in the 1770s with the rise of Irish Protestant nationalism, while *Aughrim's* popularity is by no means limited to the Protestants.

In 1804 "C.J." writes in the periodical *Ireland's Mirror: or, a Chronicle of the Times* that

> Perhaps a more popular Production never appeared in Ireland; it is in the hands of every Peasant who can read English; and like the Songs or Poems of the Bards, in Scotland, is committed to memory, and occasionally recited. Of the Author, some account would be very acceptable: such an account as might disprove the assertion as to his suicide.[14]

Although recitation from memory is characteristic of epic, the reference to bards indicates the incorporation of Ashton's drama into popular culture. At the same time, the suggestion that Ashton committed suicide turns him into a Romantic poet/hero, an Irish young Werther.

Yet when C.J. finally gets around to reading the work he is appalled at the play's success and creates a fictional history for Ashton:

> He was the son of JOHN ASHTON, who distinguished himself by engaging in a conspiracy with Lord Preston and others, against our GREAT DELIVERER, king WILLIAM III.—ASHTON'S FATHER, like HAMILCAR, has sworn *his* young HANNIBAL at the altar, *not* to be a *mortal foe* to ROME, but a *devoted fanatic* to its Interests, through, and in, every mode of BLOOD, BIGOTRY, and SUPERSTITION.
>
> The "Battle of Aughrim" was, much to the dishonor of the Author, AVOWEDLY written for the Vulgar, and never was a publication so well adapted to catch not only the FLATS, but the FANATICS; and fig up the PADREEN Mare.[15]

The stunning array of capitalizations and italics, by no means characteristic of the publication, shows an almost hysterical response, and the difficulty of evaluating a play that treats the Catholics evenhandedly in the aftermath of 1798. John Ashton was assuredly not the father of Robert Ashton as he was executed in 1690, approximately eighteen years before the best estimate of Robert's birth.[16] Still, C.J. identifies Ashton with a notorious traitor, devotion to Rome, and vulgar approval because he senses the subtext of the play's sympathetic treatment of Catholics. The misreading is obvious; as we shall see, St. Ruth's statements in favor of instituting the Inquisition in Ireland clearly mark him as the villain. But what is frightening is that the remnants of Carthage remain in the West and threaten the empire.

In an edition of 1841 in which *Aughrim* was printed with John Michelburne's *Ireland Preserved; or, the Siege of Londonderry* (1705)—the plays were frequently printed together—the Reverend John Graham, M.A., remarks that the play is by "William Ashton, of whom all that we know is, that he was but eighteen years old when it was written; and, that when it first appeared, a complimentary letter, in verse, from Charles Usher, Esq., of Trinity College Dublin, was prefixed to it."[17] Graham inadvertently marks the play as Protestant: the renaming of Ashton as "William" and the emphasis on Usher's letter from a center of the Protestant establishment (Trinity) emphasize the Williamite character of the play. Graham, a Church of Ireland minister, had not gone back to look at the initial edition, or he would have discovered both the correct name and the fact that the prologue only claims Ashton is "not twenty." Nevertheless he is apparently sure that Ashton is on the side of the ascendancy.

But an awareness of Ashton's polymorphous politics gradually develops. In 1842 in Ennis, Thackeray buys "six volumes of works strictly Irish" for eighteen pence; he reads the play on a rainy night in Galway. Thackeray comes within two decades of the play's date: "It must have been written in the reign of Queen Anne, judging from some loyal compliments which are paid to that sovereign in the play, which is also modelled upon Cato." Thackeray is a sophisticated reader; his recognition that Addison's tragedy about doomed Roman patriotism is an influence on *Aughrim* helps to account for his characterization of Ashton: "The author, however, though a Protestant, is an Irishman, (there are peculiarities in his pronunciation which belong only to that nation,) and as far as courage goes, he allows the two parties to be pretty equal."[18] Despite the gibe at accent, Thackeray can see retrospectively what must have been difficult to see in 1728: Ashton, through his choice of literary models, creates a dramatic Irish Protestant nationalism.

Two important figures in the creation of Irish nationalism, literary and political, William Carleton and Charles Gavan Duffy, recalled *The Battle of Aughrim* from their youth in Ulster. Duffy recalls both the book and its seller:

> There were no regular bookseller's shops in Monaghan, but a couple of printers sold school-books; and at a weekly market there was always a peddlar who supplied, at a few pence, cheap books printed at Belfast, of which the most popular were the "Battle of Aughrim" and "Billy Bluff." The drama of the battle was in the hands of every intelligent schoolboy in Ulster, who strode an imaginary stage as Sarsfield or Ginkel, according to his sympathies.[19]

The peddler, Duffy goes on to say, sometimes pretended to sell books proscribed by the government. The populist nature of *Aughrim* is apparent both from its seller and its audience; it is both illicit (a kind of rogue literature like "Billy Bluff") and patriotic. The patriotism can be applied in either direction, since "Billy Bluff" was a United Irishmen satire on religious intolerance and government espionage, the author of which, James Porter, was executed for his role in the rising of 1798.[20] The duality of *Aughrim*'s appeal ("Sarsfield or Ginkel") mirrors the paradox of its embodiment: heroic drama sold as a chapbook for a few pennies.

Carleton indicates the play was still being produced in the Ulster of his youth. Since Carleton knew the play by heart, at ten he became "stage director

and prompter both to the Catholic and Protestant amateurs." The popularity
of the production was enormous: "The crowds that flocked to it, both Catholic
and Protestants, would, if admitted, have overcrowded the largest theater in
Europe." Indeed, the weight of the crowd was enough to collapse the loft of
the barn from which Carleton watches his production.[21]

But Carleton also goes on to stress the real danger of the play:

> In the town of Augher, this stupid play was acted by Catholics and Protestants,
> each party of course sustaining their own principles. The consequence was, that
> when they came to the conflict with which the play is made to close, armed as they
> were on both sides with real swords, political and religious resentment could not
> be restrained, and they would have hacked each other's souls out had not the audi-
> ence interfered and prevented them. As it was, some of them were severely if not
> dangerously wounded. (1, 28)

The identification by both factions with Ashton's play is striking. Whereas
tragedy is supposed to allow the purging of communal guilt through the identification of a scapegoat, *The Battle of Aughrim* dramatizes both parties as sufficiently virtuous as to rekindle the unresolved conflicts nearly a century after it
was written. Carleton calls the play stupid, not because its author is inept, but
because Ashton presents too well an apparently irresolvable conflict between
religions and governments. The actors and audience are made stupid participants in a civil war where all of the wounded are Irish.

II

The Battle of Aughrim is a celebration of a heroic victory that preserved English liberties from papist tyranny, and is an expression of Irish Protestant
anxiety caused by the war with Spain and Austria.[22] The epilogue is delivered "by one representing a Press-master, attended by sailors," who delivers an
unusual threat to unruly critics: "Away on board the Fleet, I'll take 'em
all,/The *Spaniards* face, and give 'em t'other Fall" (48). Although by 1728 the
French and English were allies, any European conflict reminded the Irish Protestants of the Pretender's presence on the Continent and of the Irish brigades
of France and Spain, the descendants of Sarsfield's Wild Geese. Sir Robert
Sutherland claimed that Austria and Spain had agreed by secret treaty to place
James III on the throne, and writes, "I know very well how easy and common
it is to laugh at the Name of the *Pretender* . . . as a Political *Bugbear* or *Scare
Crow*. . . . [But] there is not a Day, nor an Hour, in which the necessity of Attention to this great Point, does not appear."[23] In a pamphlet attributed by the
Eighteenth-Century Short Title Catalogue to Benjamin Good, the author supports the alliance of England, France, Denmark, and Sweden as necessary to
protect Great Britain from "an evident and concerted Design to invade his
Majesty's Dominions in favour of the *Pretender*, and to raise *War* and *Rebellion*
in the Heart of his Kingdoms, in the Name of a *Popish* Impostor."[24]

In another pamphlet, Charles Forman emphasizes the consequences of the Austrian-Spanish war to Ireland:

> while the *Irish* Regiments are suffer'd to continue in the Service of France and Spain, they will always [provide] those Nations with Instruments to carry on their Designs against us, and prove a Nursery of inveterate Enemies to *Britain* as long as she continues under the government of the August House of Hanover.[25]

As he makes clear elsewhere in the pamphlet, Forman admires the descendants of the Wild Geese as fighting men; the trouble is that their Catholicism threatens Protestantism and, consequently, reason and liberty.

In a collection of anti-Catholic pamphlets going back to 1686 and collected in 1728, "a Presbyter of the Diocese of Derry" accuses the Catholics of cruelty and murder when attempting to make converts, while asserting that clerics are sent by the Church of England armed "with Reason, and not with the Power of the Sword."[26] Fear of the Pretender and popery is thus capable of uniting Dissenters and Anglicans: whatever their disagreements, the Protestants of Ireland stood together against the Catholics. The anonymous author of *The Tallies of War and Peace,* also printed by Sylvester Powell, warns potential enemies that the Protestants are united: "For they may depend upon the unanimous Vigour of a brave and wealthy People, who are always ready to sacrifice their Lives and Fortunes for the Honour of his Majesty."[27]

Ashton's St. Ruth embodies Protestant fears. After the French-Irish victory, he promises,

> *James* shall return and with great pomp restore
> Our *Romish* Worship to the Land once more,
> And drown the *Hereticks* in crimson gore.
>
> (3)

Charles Chalmont, the historical marquis de St. Ruth, was a figure of terror for European Protestants because of his actions in suppressing the Huguenots after the revocation of the Edict of Nantes in 1685.[28] Ashton is careful to remind his audience of this past:

> You know, my Heroes, I have oft embru'd
> These hands in Blood, and Heresy subdu'd,
> So on this Day, *Rome's* Banners shall be spread,
> To send those Locusts, reeling to the Dead.
>
> (17)

Although St. Ruth is French, in the play he also stands as a symbol for Catholic Spain. After the restoration of James, "then to protect our Faith, we will maintain/An *Inquisition* here, like that in *Spain*" (14). *Inquisition* functions here as the code word for the international Catholic conspiracy against liberty.

Nowhere is St. Ruth's ruthlessness and perfidy more clear than in his slaying of the captured Colonel Herbert. This historical event was capable of multiple interpretations. The anonymous author of *An Exact Journal of the Victorious*

Progress of their Majesties Forces under the Command of Gen. Ginckle, This Summer in Ireland (London: 1691), discussing the casualties, refers to "Coll. *Charles Herbert*, first taken Prisoner at the beginning of the Fight, and afterwards inhumanly murther'd by the Rebels when they saw the Battel lost" (22). But George Story, Ashton's probable source, is rather more understanding:

> The *Irish*, upon their advantage in the Centre of the Battle, had taken some Prisoners (as has been said) but not being able to carry them off, they killed Col. *Herbert* and one or two more; which several have lookt upon as a piece of cruelty: and yet it's no more than what has often been practised in such Cases, and that to a greater degree.[29]

In fact, Story compares the incident to Henry V's action at Agincourt. Thus Story, normally anything but impartial, allows room for a sympathetic view of combat necessity that Ashton declines to take.

Instead Ashton focuses on Herbert's death to show noble English bravery and the importance of it in the face of sneaking Continental villains like St. Ruth. When the battle is in doubt, Herbert rallies his troops by pointing out the devilishness of popery:

> Relieve your Brethren, and with Fame subdue
> *Rome's* wooden Idols, and their monkish Crew,
> Those vile Oppressors of our sacred Laws,
> Then side with me, and Heaven will join our Cause.
>
> (22)

The emphasis here is on the blasphemous despots of Catholicism rather than on the Irish or Jacobitism. After the capture, St. Ruth, fearing Herbert's escape, decides, "I'll hinder that, by heaven he surely dies,/And to my Fury falls a sacrifice" (34). Herbert's murder is not a military necessity but the act of a bloodthirsty villain. The dying Herbert drags himself onstage, offers a speech in praise of William, Anne, and "th'illustrious Hanoverian Line," and shows himself a true martyr with a saintly soul:

> Hear this, O Lord of Mercy, I beseech,
> Fain would I more—But Death just stops my Speech,
> Forgive my Murderers, as I freely do,
> Even from my Soul; so wretched World adieu.
>
> (34)

In Ashton's treatment, the Irish are innocent of Herbert's murder. Sir Charles Godfrey, the English youth who fights on the Irish side because of his love for an Irish maiden, changes sides when he sees the corpse of Herbert, his murdered brother-in-law, and accuses the Irish generals of the crime:

Sir Charles   Long let them [British forces] prosper, nor retire
                  hence,
            Till you atone for murdered innocence.

Sarsfield	As Heaven is Witness—or the conscious Sun,
	I knew not of it, 'till the fact was done,
	I never could with such an Act comply,
	As wilful Murder.
Dorrington	By the Gods, nor I.

(37)

The murder of Herbert justifies victory over the Catholic forces, but the guilt is all French.

Herbert's death is dramatically glorious. His wife, Lucinda, Sir Charles's sister, asks him not to go to the battle because of a dream, but the dream reveals his apotheosis rather than a tragic death:

> Last night methought I seen you wrap'd in Fire,
> All clad in Flames, while Angels did surround
> Your lovely Form, and bore thee off the Ground:
> Then I beheld thee as a Cherub rise,
> And so aloft to the celestial Skies.

(25)

The enjambment (extremely unusual in the play) from lines two to three "surrounds" the form of Herbert as the play surrounds his heroism; his apotheosis is the heroic structure of *The Battle of Aughrim*. The play turns the brave English victim into a blessed martyr.

The British officers are as noble as foreign Catholic tyrants are satanic, which explains Ashton's choice of verse. When, in the prologue to *Aureng-Zebe*, Dryden bids farewell to his "long-loved mistress rhyme," and subsequently writes his serious drama in blank verse, he helps to end the short-lived experiment (1662–c. 1680) of rhymed heroic drama. Still, the form gets its start in Ireland with Katherine Philips's translation of Corneille's *Pompey* and the earl of Orrery's early heroic dramas,[30] and the mere fact that apparently no one except Ashton writes one for a period of over fifty years does not mean that heroic drama was theatrically dead. For instance, *Aureng-Zebe* was revived in London in February 1727, and Lee's *Sophonisba* was revived in July 1728.[31] *Aureng-Zebe* was also revived at Smock Alley in Dublin in April 1730, and the editors of *The Dublin Stage* point out that their calendar is almost certainly incomplete.[32]

Thus Ashton, while clearly not au courant, nevertheless had heroic drama available as a viable theatrical option. Dryden's defense of rhymed serious drama distinguishes between the imitation of common nature in comedy, and a serious play's dramatization of

> Nature wrought up to an higher pitch. The Plot, the Characters, the Wit, the Passions, the Descriptions, are all exalted above the level of common converse, as high as the imagination of the Poet can carry them, with proportion to verisimility. Tragedy we know is wont to image to us the minds and fortunes of noble

persons, and to portray these exactly, Heroic Rhime is nearest Nature, as being the noblest kind of modern verse.[33]

By choosing Aughrim as his subject and heroic drama as his genre, Ashton asserts that the battle possessed an epic quality, comparable to great English victories of the past.

When St. Ruth arrogantly claims that the English will flee from Athlone at the mention of his name, Sarsfield praises English valor:

> I know the *English* Fortitude is such,
> To boast of nothing, though they hazard much.
> No force on Earth their Fury can repel,
> Nor would they fly from all the Devils in Hell.
>
> (4)

Praise of an enemy shows, of course, not merely the estimation in which the enemy is held, but indicates the knightly worth of Sarsfield; he is also, however, underscoring the superiority of the British to the French:

> See what their *Edward* did on *Cressey Plain,*
> Or where at *Poicters* [*sic*] he the Field did gain;
> Then tell me would those *Britains* fear your Name.
>
> (5)

Herbert makes the same point exhorting the British officers: "Think how our *Henry* taught proud *France* to yield/At *Agincourt,* and bravely won the Field" (24).

Ashton's dedication of *Aughrim* to Carteret, lord lieutenant, states, "The Effects of [the battle] was the entire Subversion of Popery and Arbitrary Power, and surely an Action which acquir'd so much glory to the *English* Nation ought not to be forgot, when matters of far less moment are daily adapted to the Stage" (A 2). Written at a time of Protestant anxiety, when the Declaratory Act of 1720 and the controversy over Wood's patent made it seem as if England had forgotten Irish sacrifices, Ashton glorifies a Protestant victory over foreign and domestic Catholics, one that ranks with England's past triumphs. De Gincle and Herbert save Ireland, and only heroic drama can adequately represent the glorious 12th of July.

III

The Battle of Aughrim is a lament for the defeat of Irish patriots modeled after Addison's tragedy *Cato.* With increased awareness that James III represented no threat to Ireland, growing outrage over English treatment of Ireland as a conquered province, and, most importantly, a developing sense that even the members of the Protestant gentry were no longer English, a willingness on the part of the Protestant gentry to incorporate the non-English history of Ireland into their own ethos becomes apparent.

Despite the common worries about the Pretender, many Irish Protestants, and even, perhaps, Dublin Castle, had ceased to lose sleep over the matter. Jonathan Swift writes about dinner parties at Carteret's where neither are Tories barred "nor, at such Times, do the natural or *affected* Fears of *Popery* and the *Pretender*, make any part of the conversation."[34] In *The Intelligencer* no. 8, Swift has Mad Mullinix ask Trim,

> Why ever in these raging Fits,
> Damning to Hell the *Jacobits?*
> When if you search the Kingdom round,
> There's hardly twenty to be found;
> No, not among the *Priests and Fryars.*[35]

These are not entirely reliable sources; Swift was frequently accused of being a Jacobite, and Mad Mullinix may be Swift's caricature of one as well. Yet the caricature itself is significant and shows how the Irish are transformed from dangerous savages to comic butts as the Protestants feel increasingly secure.[36] There is even increasing tolerance for Irish soldiers, apparent from the fact that the French were allowed to recruit for their Irish brigades while the English authorities looked the other way.[37] Although it was illegal for Catholics to serve in the British army at all, and Irish Protestants were allowed only in the cavalry, there is evidence that Catholics were covertly being recruited.[38] Nor were the Irish soldiers of the Continent permanently banned from Ireland; many returned and lived in obscurity.[39] Indeed, some achieved a tenuous place in society. Peter Drake, whose family left Ireland after the surrender of Limerick and who fought at Ramillies, was related to the earl of Fingall and spent most of his last years with the earl and other relatives.[40]

Soldiering was, after all, one of the few career outlets available to the gentry anywhere in Europe; thus, Irish officers in foreign armies were comparable to Scottish Jacobites in the Russian navy and French Huguenots in many of the armies of Protestant Europe.[41] In Ireland, where Catholics were barred from the established Church, the bar, and politics, the only available option other than trade, medicine, and the priesthood was foreign service, but the penal laws were only one reason for Irish Catholics to join foreign armies.[42] As gentlemen, Catholics were not so much a threat to Ireland's security as they were potential competitors for limited assets in a poor country, and no doubt many Protestant gentry were simply glad they were pursuing opportunities elsewhere.

Along with this, there is a rising sense of admiration for the expatriates, even a sense of solidarity with them. Charles Forman's fears about the Irish brigades are combined with his admiration for them, and his belief that Great Britain is entitled to ask France and Spain to dissolve them is based on a stunningly naive premise: "Are they not *British* Subjects, and has not *Britain* a right to demand it?" (37). The problem, of course, is that Forman's fellow subjects were barred from service in Britain's armies. As Henry Grattan said later in the century, "We met our own laws at Fontenoy. The victorious troops of England were stopped, in their career of triumph, by the Irish Brigade which the Penal Laws had shut out from the ranks of British history."[43] Nevertheless, Forman in 1727 has made a statement unthinkable in 1691: the Irish are *fellow* subjects of the British empire, not cowardly rebels richly deserving punishment.

Swift exemplifies the shifting attitudes toward Irish soldiers abroad in a letter to Charles Wogan (2 July 1732), an officer in Dillon's regiment in the French army:

> In these Kingdoms you would be a most unfashionable military Man, among Troops where the least Pretension to Learning, or Piety, or common Morals, would endanger the Owner to be cashiered. . . . I cannot but highly esteem those Gentlemen of *Ireland*, who, with all the disadvantages of being Exiles and Strangers, have been able to distinguish themselves by their Valour and Conduct in so many parts of *Europe*, I think above all other Nations, which ought to make the *English* ashamed of the Reproaches they cast on the Ignorance, the Dulness, and the Want of Courage, in the *Irish Natives;* those defects, wherever they happen, arising only from the Poverty and Slavery they suffer from their inhuman Neighbors, and the base corrupt Spirits of too many of the chief Gentry &c.[44]

English troops quartered in Ireland are contemptible while Irish troops abroad are learned and brave. Equally important, any failings on the part of the indigenous population are a function of English oppression. It seems clear that Swift identifies with the Irish soldiers abroad, despite his status as a minister of the Anglican community.

By 1728, the New English in Ireland increasingly regarded themselves as Irish suffering oppression by the English. D. George Boyce sums up the chief difficulty with treating eighteenth-century Ireland as a colony in the sense that, for instance, Rhodesia was a colony: "The New English, like the Old English before them found it impossible to resist Irish influences and Irish ways, and they were quick to resent the assumptions of outsiders."[45] The Wood's halfpence controversy was, as Edmund Curtis says, "a small triumph for justice compared with the greater wrongs of the time, but it was important as the first note of Anglo-Irish opposition to the selfish domination of Ireland by England."[46] Nor did the defeat of the halfpence measure render the Anglo-Irish parliament quiescent.[47]

John Browne made his opinion known that Ireland needed Wood's halfpence, was forced to testify to the council of England, and found his name mud in Ireland, and doubted his safety if he returned:

> I have fallen into Circumstances which render me suspected as a *Patriot;* I hope my Reader will, however, have Good-Nature enough to *compare* the latter by the former Part of my Life; to *consider* the *Circumstances* of my respective *Misfortunes;* and to believe, that *no Prospect of Gain, no Hopes of Reward or Preferment,* much less

a *poor Resentment* without any Interest of Temptation whatsoever, could engage me in any Thing hurtful to my Country.[48]

Browne, although New English, feels he must defend himself as an Irish patriot and distance himself from any suggestion that he has simply been paid to defend the English interest. He signs his defense "A Sincere, *tho'* Unfortunate, Lover of *my* Country" (16). By the 1720s, agreement with English policies renders an Irishman's patriotism suspect.

The Anglo-Irish identification with Ireland takes many forms, from amusement to outrage. In a comic poem, undergraduates escaping Trinity College must deceive the porter, Paddy, by having two friends speak to him in Irish and claim to be from the same place:

> Paddy will boast on this occasion,
> His *Name* and *Family* and *Nation*
> Call ev'ry ancient Hero forth
> Describe his Merit, shining Worth,
> Sum all his Ancestors, brave Fellows,
> That suffer'd on, or 'scap'd the Gallows.[49]

Paddy is comical, and wiseguy undergraduates have not changed much in a little over two and a half centuries, but it is a given that some of the undergraduates will speak Irish and that Paddy will accept that they are interested in Irish family histories. The verse may be condescending, but it is also affectionate.

Trinity was also the scene of the new Anglo-Irish assertiveness over the matter of choosing a senior fellow. When Provost Richard Baldwin appointed John Palliser to the fellowship over Arthur Forde, he was greeted with a "Protest of all the Senior Fellows in Trinity College Dublin, (except one) against the *Provost*":

> And however the Exercise of that Power might be allowed in the Reign of King *Charles* the First, and be fitted for this Kingdom in a State of Rebellion and Ignorance, when a *Provost* from *England* might fairly be presumed to have more Learning than all his assessors of *Irish* Education, and at the same time to be much better affected to the Government; certainly the Power must be exerted with a very ill Grace in the Reign of *King George,* in an Age of Liberty and Learning, when a *Senior-Fellow* may fairly be presumed as knowing and the Society as well affected to his Majesty as their Governor.[50]

The fellows clearly regard themselves as Irish and the provost as an alien and presumptuous Englishman; they resent that their learning and loyalty should be questioned by an interloper. Trinity belongs to (or ought to be under the control of) the Anglo-Irish scholars.

At its extreme, this evolving sense of Irish identity included outrage over the condition of the indigenous population. Thomas Sheridan (Swift's friend), in number 6 of *The Intelligencer* concludes that travels in Ireland arouse two feelings:

An indignation against those vile betrayers and Insulters of it, who Insinuate themselves into Favour, by saying, It is a Rich Nation; and a *sincere Compassion* for the Natives, who are sunk to the lowest Degree of Misery and Poverty, whose Houses are Dunghills, whose Victuals are the Blood of their Cattle, or the Herbs in the Field; and whose Cloathing to the Dishonour of God and Man is Nakedness.[51]

The position of Sheridan is ambiguous. He presents himself as distinct from the natives (although the Sheridans were, in fact, Irish), but he is also Ireland's defender against those who would insult it. Neither oppressor nor victim, neither English nor Gael, he seems to occupy a space between the two for which in 1728 there was no term, and this is the position in which Ashton finds himself.

Sarah Butler's *Irish Tales* (1716) and William Philips's *Hibernia Freed* (1722) are examples of the tentative movement toward an appropriation of ancient Irish history by the Anglo-Irish, but *The Battle of Aughrim* is the first sympathetic treatment of recent Catholic Irish history by the Anglo-Irish, and it rehabilitates the Irish by comparing them to defeated patriots of the Roman republic. Within two minutes of the beginning of the play, after Sarsfield laments the fallen state of the Irish, Colonel O'Neal responds,

> Fear not, my Lord, but scorn the Revolution,
> And like great *Cato* smile at persecution.
> . . . .
> Then let us, Sirs, like him disdain to fly,
> But dig our graves in Honour e're we die,
> Or like true honest Souls, retrieve our Liberty.
>
> (2)

The reference to Cato and the assertion that they are fighting for liberty constitutes a radical shift from standard Anglo-Irish propaganda about the Irish, and, moreover, it differentiates them from St. Ruth.

Addison's stuffy and static tragedy *Cato* was widely admired and frequently staged in the eighteenth century; Voltaire thought it sublime, and the last words of American spy Nathan Hale before his execution were paraphrased from it. *Cato* was staged in Dublin on 25 November 1723, 9 March 1730, and probably numerous other times.[52] Addison's title character is a Whig hero: "Greatly unfortunate, he fights the cause/Of honour, virtue, liberty, and Rome."[53] Caesar, on the other hand, is not a great conqueror but a great criminal, as Cato tells Decius:

> Alas, thy dazzled eye
> Beholds this man in a false glaring light,
> Which conquest and success have thrown upon him;
> Didst thou but view him right, thou'dst see him black
> With murder, treason, sacrilege, and crimes
> That strike my soul with horror but to name 'em.
>
> (23)

Even in defeat Cato is superior to Caesar.

This comparison is relevant to *Aughrim* because the prologue explicitly relates Caesar to William:

> Never did *Cæsar* do an Action bolder,
> And was our Author but a little Older,
> Not *Pompey's* triumphs nor great *Scipio's* Fame
> Could once compare with glorious *William's* Name.

Caesar, at least, is no greater than William; Pompey and Scipio, heroes of the Roman republic, are beneath him. The prologue emphasizes Ireland's status as a part of a now secure empire, as George II is called "Great *Augustus*" in the epilogue.

While these associations support the triumphal theme of Williamite victory, they also make the Irish into noble, though doomed, patriots. After St. Ruth's death, O'Neal declaims to Sarsfield,

> Hope now is vain, no Succour can be found,
> And Death displays his sable Flag around.
> But yet forbear, too soon to yield to Fate,
> Nor sell our Lives at an ignoble Rate;
> Here let us stand, and here attend our Falls,
> As once *Rome's* Senate waited for the *Gauls.*
>
> (39)

The irony here is that the Irish are depicted as servants of Rome, but of the Roman republic, while the English are, at various times, either brutal, savage Goths, or the tyrants of imperial Rome. O'Neal and Sarsfield represent republican virtue, not popery.

Once this perspective is taken of the play, the English become simply another noxious invader. St. Ruth hails O'Neal as the descendant of other brave Gaels who defeated murderous foreigners:

> Thy Predecessors with Heroick Fame
> Once quelled *Erthugises* the haughty *Dane,*
> When he in Triumph lay encamp'd between
> The Hill of *Tarah* and the lofty *Screen:*
> They cross'd the *Boyn* and in the dead of Night
> Slew all his Guards and put his Troops to flight.
>
> (3)

Not merely is St. Ruth equating the Danes and English as rapacious Vikings, but Ashton is accepting as legitimate a heroic Gaelic past that English historians, such as Sir Richard Cox, derided as fictitious.

Ireland itself becomes a lost Eden. Colonel Talbot's daughter, Jemima (Sir Charles Godfrey's beloved), laments her paradise lost:

> Hail sweet *Hibernia*, hospitable Isle,
> More rich than *Egypt* with her flowing Nile;

> Fair Garden of the Earth, thy fragrant Plains
> Are seats of War; and thy sweet purling Streams
> All run with Blood, and Vengeance seems to trace
> The shining remnants of *Hibernia's* Race.
>
> (12)

The shock of war is mirrored in the sudden transitions at the ends of lines three and four to the violence described at the beginnings of lines four and five. War has destroyed all except the "shining remnants" of the land that the descendants of Egypt have made superior to its predecessor. Sarsfield continues the metaphor after the defeat:

> So *Adam* when he was from *Eden* driven,
> He yet look'd back, to view his promis'd Heaven,
> Then with a Soul all cover'd with despair,
> He grudg'd that Paradise he could not share.
>
> (42)

Thus Ashton laments the exiles forced to live in a fallen world. Adam's fall may well have been fortunate, as was the Williamite victory, but Sarsfield has no prophetic vision of a redeemer.

If from one perspective *Aughrim* is heroic drama, with Herbert as martyred victim, from another it is an elegy for a lost Ireland, with Colonel Talbot as sinless sacrifice. The Talbot of the play is not the earl of Tyrconnell; although a colonel at the accession of James II, Talbot was promoted rapidly to general of the army.[54] But the name alone might lead one to expect an unsympathetic treatment. After all, Tyrconnell was not the only Talbot to achieve notoriety as a Jacobite.[55] Yet Ashton parallels his death with Herbert's. St. Ruth calls Talbot "thou *Irish Scipio*," and Sarsfield, told of his death, mourns "as brave a Soul, with honour fir'd,/As ever yet by force of War expir'd" (16). When the Irish receive a setback, Talbot inspirits them with his oratory (15), and his death is that of a Roman hero, according to his daughter:

Jemima   Oh!—is he Dead?—my Soul is all on Fire,
          Witness ye Gods! he did with Fame expire;
          For Liberty—a Sacrifice was made,
          And fell, like *Pompey*, by some Villains blade.

(17)

Perhaps the best evidence for the parallel functions of Herbert and Talbot is the fact that Ashton has gone to the trouble of inventing two women to grieve for them.

Jemima too sees an apotheosis for Talbot, as Lucinda saw one for Herbert:

> The Clouds fly open and he mounts the Skies!
> O see his Blood! it shines refulgent bright,
> I see him yet—I cannot lose him quite
> But still pursue him on—and lose my sight.
>
> (18)

Jemima's earlier vision of Ireland's shining blood turns out to foreshadow her father's tragic death, but Williamite or Jacobite, all good colonels go to heaven. Both sides have their heroes and victims. Moreover, while apotheosis is a convention of elegy, Jemima's and Lucinda's vision may evoke the *aisling* poetry of eighteenth-century Ireland, thus again connecting Ashton sympathetically with the defeated indigenous population.

Not surprisingly, Sarsfield is the most important of the Irish patriots. After the defeat, he hopes to die in single combat rather than

> Like *Hannibal* the *Carthaginian* Chief,
> Who when by *Scipio* he was overthrown,
> He fled to *Africk*, like a Vagabond,
> Cloath'd as a Slave, dejected and obscure,
> He wander'd all alone from Door to Door:
> Then shall an *Irish* Soul, submit like him,
> To forfeit Honour, and renounce a King[?]
> (40)

Sarsfield's great fear of course is historically fulfilled; he becomes, briefly, the wandering soldier of fortune, before his death fighting for the French. But Ashton presents him as rejecting the role. Sarsfield's characteristics are courage and loyalty, not merely military skill, and in denying that he will be Hannibal, he denies that the English are Scipios. Confronted by the English generals, Sarsfield, O'Neal, and Dorrington "*retreat fighting*" (43), presenting both an emblem of the continuing existence of the Irish brigades, and a refusal, on Ashton's part, to treat the defeat of the Irish as poetic justice.

The play ends with Dorrington, who had earlier demanded the surrender of Gincle in arrogant language, captured and taunted:

Gincle	Hail mighty *Dorrington*, thus low we bow (*Bowing*).
	Shall we disown the Prince of ORANGE now?
	Must we disband our Legions and restore
	Your abdicated King to rule once more?
	It could not be, I did the Act disown,
	For mighty WILLIAM yet enjoys the Throne.
Dorrington	Forbear, my Lord, nor thus insult me so,
	Is this right Usage for your captive Foe?
	Had but *St. Ruth* surviv'd the Tragick fight,
	To *Dublin* Gates you would have taken flight,
	For know, proud Conqueror, by your Lordships leave,
	Our soldiers were superior and as brave.

(46)

Gincle may have a right to celebrate, but that does not make his mockery chivalrous. In the prologue we are told that the Irish "fought that Battle bravely which they lost,/even like *Hectors* as for a time they stood," and there may be an echo of *Troilus and Cressida* in Dorrington's response. Told that the soldiers are cheering for Achilles' victory over Hector, Ajax says somberly, "If it be so, yet bragless let it be,/Great Hector was as good a man as he" (5.9.5–6).

IV

Ashton's enterprise is inherently fragile. Sympathy for the Irish could be interpreted as treason, but diminishing the Irish serves only to diminish the victory. In this his play reflects the battle it describes, as at times the Irish appeared to be about to rout the English. The play's recurring epic simile of impending shipwreck describes the delicate balance of forces.

Gincle   Or as two Friends, who with Remorse survey
                    Their Vessels sever'd on the raging Sea,
                    Each gets a Plank, and his Companion leaves
                    To the wild mercy of the Wind and Waves.
                    As long as possible his Friend he views,
                    Each forc'd at last, a different Fate pursues;
                    One sinks, while t'other gains the Shoar at last,
                    There mourns his Fellows loss, and grieves for what is
                        past.

                                               (27–28).

Gincle makes this speech to his fellow British officers—that some of them may not return is the immediate application—but he also doubts the outcome of the battle as a whole. Catholic victory is a distinct possibility, with the resultant shipwreck of the Protestant settlement.

Lucinda warns Herbert in a similar metaphor of the impending death she has foreseen for him:

                 The Mariner he ploughs the foaming Seas,
                 And from his Bark the pleasant Land surveys:
                 He leaps with Joy, and to his Comfort sees
                 The pregnant Banks, all overspread with Trees,
                 Then as he strives to enter with the Tide,
                 A Rock unseen, his vessel does divide:
                 So e're he can the happy Port attain,
                 He's swallow'd with his Cargo in the Main.
                           (26)

Thus personal disaster comes unexpectedly, in the same way that the peaceful and apparently quiet Ireland of the Protestant interest is always in jeopardy from the possible return of the Pretender. The position of trade and agriculture, under threat from English legislation, is rendered even more tenuous by the underlying threat of a Jacobite invasion and a Gaelic rising.

The central character of the play, Sir Charles Godfrey, also uses the mariner metaphor, in this case mistakenly:

> Now like the Mariner I leave the Shoar,
> And put to sea in search of Golden Oar,
> Through boisterous Surges plough the troubled Main,
> 'Midst Rocks and Tempests, and at last attain
> A Bay of Love and Pleasure for my Pain.
>
> (10)

Godfrey, however, like the Irish soldiers, is a victim of the shipwreck of Ireland. Ashton's tragic hero represents the impossibility of reconciling New English Protestant interests with Catholic Ireland. A daring fiction on Ashton's part, Godfrey sees Jemima, Talbot's daughter, and he immediately asks for her hand, introducing himself rather brusquely:

> I am a *Britain* of a *Saxon* Race;
> Sir *Charles Godfrey* is my lawful Name,
> My Father in our late great Monarch's Reign
> Was by a band of villains basely slain.
>
> (9)

Not merely is he the son of the murdered judge of the popish plot, but his sister, Lucinda, he confesses to Talbot, is married to the Colonel Herbert who is with the troops who have just captured Athlone. All of this is irrelevant. In love with Jemima, he vows to fight for the Irish, and he does so bravely for a while.

To some extent this is the traditional *topos* of *Hibernis ipsis Hiberniores*, a subject to which even Story turns his attention after the slaughter of the Irish by British forces:

> But as the Nature of Man is apter to degenerate than improve; so do the *English* oftner fall in love with the Barbarous Customs of the Irish, than on the contrary. . . . for put a drop of Wine into a pint of Water, and it presently so far incorporates, as you can by no means discern it: so is it often with an *English* Family that has the Misfortune to be planted amongst the meer *Irish;* for it soon becomes of the same stamp with themselves.[56]

This is an extremely odd observation from Story, considering his agenda; mentioning English assimilation into Ireland in the context of a complete subjugation of the Irish, suggests a profound pessimism that inevitably it will all have to be done over again: the English settlers will soon regard themselves as Irish.

Sir Charles simply makes the transition faster than most. Ashton's emphasis on Sir Charles's Protestant, Saxon heritage, and the traditional representation of Ireland as a woman (in this case Jemima), may show that ideally the relationship between the New English victors and the Irish would be wedlock rather than rape. But even though Talbot accepts Sir Charles's suit conditionally after Sir Charles's praise of Jemima and his promise to fight for Ireland, his initial response shows his skepticism: "Eloquence well tun'd, young *Marcus* what remains?" (9). Cicero may be indicated by "Marcus," although Tully would have been the more common name in the period, but for an audience watching the play, Cato's unstable and passionate son, Marcus, would first come to mind.

Addison's Marcus, while brave, has difficulty with his priorities. Although his noble brother, Portius, and the Numidian prince, Juba, are equally in love, they know that the war against Caesar comes first. Marcus, on the other hand, must be continually reminded of his duty. He recognizes his own fault: "Pardon a weak, distempered soul, that swells,/With sudden gusts, and sinks as soon in calms,/The sport of passions" (9). Marcus dies nobly—"what pity is it/That we can die but once to serve our country"—but Juba and Portius are rewarded dramatically by getting the women they deserve.

The conflict between love and duty also informs *Aughrim*. Sir Charles has fallen in love with Jemima and Ireland, but old loyalties die hard. Indeed, his father comes back as a ghost to remind him of them: "The whistling Winds did sing,/How promp'd by Love, you fought against your King,/And how you would your Country extirpate" (35). Sir Charles ultimately stands for all the Protestant settlers of England despite the specificity of his grievance: "Joyn not those vile licentious Rebels Cause,/Who slew thy Father in Contempt of Laws" (36). Whether an audience thinks of the popish plot or 1641, the ghost of Sir Edmondbury Godfrey walks the stage as a demand for vengeance and allegiance to old loyalties, as surely as do the ghosts at the beginning of Frank McGuinness's *Observe the Sons of Ulster Marching to the Somme*.

There is no solution to Sir Charles's divided loyalties. He immediately fights for the British and is killed for his pains. He too acknowledges his guilt, as he dies in Jemima's arms:

> For know thou fair angelick heavenly Maid,
> I'm perjur'd, damn'd and have my Love betray'd.
> The Scorn of Mankind let me ever be,
> Nor let bright Heaven shine on a wretch like me.
>
> (43)

Whether he fights against Jemima or his father, Ireland or England, he is disloyal. Jemima, bereft of Irish father and New English lover, commits suicide. The tentative union of Irish and New English is tragically doomed at Aughrim.

Ashton imagines Sir Charles Godfrey at Aughrim as a way of dramatizing the problem of the Protestant Irish in the 1720s. Increasingly drawn to see Ireland as a kingdom of which they were subjects, rather than as a colony of which they were alien settlers, increasingly sympathetic—or at least wishing they could be sympathetic—to the native, Catholic population, they were on the horns of a dilemma. Without English armies they could not hold on to their lands. With English control came the humiliating experience of being regarded as inferior subjects whose rights must always come second to the needs of England's merchants and manufacturers.

Ashton has no solution to this divided consciousness, but *The Battle of Aughrim* remains an extraordinarily fascinating play nonetheless. The verse is frequently wretched, not surprising in an author not yet twenty, and a charge that can be made of Keats's early verse as well. Ashton, however, is a brilliant theatrical architect: epideictic heroic drama for the British, a moving lament for the Wild Geese, a complex tragedy for the New English, the play's theatrical effectiveness is demonstrated by a production life of over a century.

FIVE

"Our own good, plain, old Irish English"

Charles Macklin (Cathal McLaughlin) and
Protestant Convert Accommodations

Sir, you took Lodgings in the name of "Macklin," and here, yesterday, a person came, and called you by some strange name—"*Maclotlin!*" or "*Maclottin!*" Indeed, it is impossible to pronounce it.
—Spoken by an English landlady attempting to evict Macklin because of his apparent use of an alias.[1]

When Shadwell and Philips incorporate a Gaelic heritage into their plays it is partly a response to patronage and, consequently, the aristocracy; Butlers and O'Briens either were descendants of or were related to the pre-Norman aristocracy that had converted prior to the eighteenth century and whose place in the postrevolutionary settlement was therefore assured. Another, more recent, group of Protestants came from the lower reaches of the gentry and consisted of converted Catholics, pressured by the penal laws into changing religion either to preserve family lands, or to achieve access to the professions. These converts' attitudes toward the revolutionary settlement remained ambivalent. No doubt the conversion of some was purely pragmatic and had little effect on their identity (that is, they continued to be "culturally" Irish and even attended Mass covertly). But for some, conversion meant a genuine belief in Protestantism (or, at least, a rejection of Catholicism) and an adoption of the ascendancy's attitudes toward the native Catholics.

Still, this group of converts perforce could not accept racist stereotyping of the Irish, while at the same time it was difficult for them to support Irish nationalism as they could not afford to be suspected of disloyalty. The embarrassments of accommodation are thus a part of the Protestant identity in Ireland. Converts could with complete honesty embrace historical arguments about Irish political independence from England; after all, they were the descendants of the original Irish. They also, however, needed political cover to save them from accusations of covert sympathy with the disaffected elements of the Catholic community, and the "patriot" movement provided that shelter precisely because many of its leading figures remained anti-Catholic. In short, converts of the mid-eighteenth century are transitional figures who pave the way for the complete identification (political, historical, and dramatic) of the patriots with Irish culture which occurs in the 1770s.

Charles Macklin as a convert embodies the diverse allegiances of this group, complicated by a few internal conflicts that were a consequence of his personality: proud, hot-tempered, physically powerful (he killed one man and beat the actor James Quin savagely during the interlude of a performance), yet insecure because of his Irish, lower-class background. His plays portray warm-hearted and loyal Irishmen and satirize English attitudes toward the Irish, while at the same time espousing "patriot" political attitudes. However, he substitutes for the Irish a Scottish scapegoat. Immediately after his death, an obituary described why he changed his name: "The real name of the family, however, was M'Laughlin, which to render more pleasing to an English ear, was familiarized to Macklin."[2] Macklin's plays, like his name, retain Irish roots but are "familiarized" to English and Irish Protestant ears. His life represents the uneasy consolidation of the Irish and the English of Ireland into a shared identity as "Irishmen."

In the eighty-six years after 1703, 5,500 of the Irish Catholics conformed to the Established Church.[3] This relatively small number is at least partially a consequence of the elites' recognition that widespread conversion was not desirable.[4] Reasons for conformity included a desire to enter professions closed to Catholics (such as the bar or armed services) or to retain family land. The former reason led to competition for scarce positions, and the latter limited the availability of land to upwardly mobile members of the Protestant interest, thus intensifying social conflict.[5]

Those who converted were also divided among themselves. L. M. Cullen argues that "rising families not only conformed outwardly to the Established Church, but identified themselves wholly with its aims." The most prominent example of this identification is John Fitzgibbon, earl of Clare.[6] On the other hand, Kevin Whelan proposes that "it can no longer be safely assumed that 'converts' were a loss to the catholic interest."[7] Some converts were exploiting legal loopholes, and others even represented a parliamentary interest sympathetic to Catholics.

Thomas Russell's family represents the divided loyalties of the converts. His great-grandfather had had to choose between his wife's Protestant relatives and his own Catholic, Gaelic relatives for guardians for his children:

> When Mr. O'Clear was considering of making his will he sayd: "if I leave my brother O'Clear guardian to my children, as he is a dissapated man he will spend their fortunes but he will educate them in my religion (he being a Catholick and

wife of the reform'd religion); but if I make my brother Bradshaw (his wife's brother) their guardian, he indeed will preserve their fortunes but they will lose their religion." This divided him for a long time, but at last he dicided in favor of property and made Bradshaw guardian, leaving to each of his children 500£, esteem'd not an inconsiderable fortune in these days.[8]

The cultural product of this decision, Russell himself, was a pious Protestant (as evidenced by his self-recriminations when he indulged his propensity for wine, women, and song), yet sympathetic toward the Catholics. His divided psyche is also indicated by his progression from serving officer in the British army to leader of a revolution striking for Irish independence.

All converts remained unmistakably Irish. Even a distinguished parliamentarian such as Edmund Burke, whose father converted in order to practice law,[9] could be slighted by a patriot rabble-rouser like John Wilkes for his Irishness alone; Wilkes dismissed Burke's oratory, saying it "stank of whiskey and potatoes."[10] Contempt for the Irish cannot be accounted for solely on the basis of religion, although dislike of Catholics was part of the English psyche. Novelist Henry Fielding, fervidly anti-Catholic and a good friend of Macklin (who had acted in his plays), is sympathetic to the plight of the poor Irish in London. In *Amelia* (1751), the Irish victim of a bully is charged by the assailant with battery:

> The Justice asked the defendant, What he meant by breaking the king's peace—
> To which he answered,—"Upon my shoul I do love the king very well, and I have not been after breaking any thing of his that I do know; but upon my shoul this man hath brake my head, and my head did break his stick; that is all, gra." He then offered to produce several witnesses against this improbable accusation; but the Justice presently interrupted him, saying, "Sirrah, your tongue betrays your guilt. You are an Irishman, and that is always sufficient evidence with me."[11]

Fielding, himself a magistrate, clearly regards the Irishman as the victim of prejudice and ignorance.

Nevertheless, Fielding also accepts stereotypes about the Irish as duelists and fortune hunters, and the Protestant landed gentry are special objects of his satire. In *Tom Jones* (1749) Mrs. Fitzpatrick describes to Sophia her life as the captive wife of a jealous and ignorant Irish squire. Sophia offers condolence: "Indeed, Harriet, I pity you from my soul!—But what could you expect? Why, why, would you marry an Irishman?" Fielding allows Mrs. Fitzpatrick a rebuttal:

> "Upon my word," replied her cousin, "your censure is unjust. There are, among the Irish, men of as much worth and honour, as any among the English: Nay, to speak the truth, generosity of spirit is rather more common among them. I have known some examples there too of good husbands; and, I believe, these are not very plenty in England."[12]

Unfortunately, this statement of tolerance is radically undercut by the novel. Several chapters describe Fitzpatrick as a vile and self-interested brute (both a duelist and a fortune hunter). Nor is Mrs. Fitzpatrick a good character witness for the Irish. Aside from the fact that she is an adulteress, her defense of the Irish seems primarily motivated by her desire not to appear a complete fool for marrying an Irishman.

And Fielding is one of the most tolerant and urbane voices in eighteenth-century English literature. The ordinary bigoted Englishman must have indicated his contempt for the Irish more overtly. R. B. MacDowell has argued that working-class Irish immigrants to England did not feel themselves to be aliens.[13] Macklin's experiences make this claim dubious, as he experienced significant social problems, despite enormous talent and the legitimate fear that his ability as a pugilist inspired. When Macklin attempted to make money independently of the stage through a combination of lecturing and sales of refreshment, a part of what limited success the venture had came from the comic Samuel Foote's mockery of him. Macklin's lecture on the causes of dueling in Ireland was interrupted by a question about the time. Told half past ten, Foote said,

> "About this time of night, every gentleman in Ireland, that can afford it, is in his third bottle of claret, consequently is in a fair way of getting drunk: from drunkenness proceeds quarrelling, and from quarrelling, dueling, and so there's an end of the chapter." The company seemed fully satisfied with this abridgement; and Macklin shut up his lecture for the evening in great dudgeon.[14]

Macklin's annoyance might have been an act. The anonymous *M——ckl——n's Answer to Tully* (not by Macklin) indicates how indebted Macklin was to Foote's comic relief.[15] But other critiques of Macklin's lectures were straightforwardly antagonistic: "How inimitable are your Criticisms on the Works of that Sublime Spirit, the doubly immortal *Shakespeare!* . . . How does he receive that Honour which you, tho' born in *Ireland*, condescend to bestow [on] him, by calling him your Country-man?"[16] Appreciation of Shakespeare is exclusive, and even the second-best Shakespearian actor of his age, if an Irishman, should not pretend to understand what he portrays.

Some of this embarrassment shows up in Macklin's early play *The New Play Criticiz'd, or the Plague of Envy* (1747). Sir Patrick Bashfull, traveling in London, denies his heritage: "I am originally descended from the Fitz-Bashfulls of France—tho' indeed our Family was of Irish Distraction first of all." On the one hand, Sir Patrick is proud of being Irish, while on the other he wishes to conceal his heritage to avoid slights:

Harriet	Then you have several good Poets in Ireland.
Sir Patrick	Yes, to be sure, Sir, there is hardly a gentleman there but knows every one of the Ninety Nine Muses, and can speak all the Mechanical Sciences by Heart, and most of the liberal Languages except Irish and Welch.
Harriet	And how happens it that they don't speak their own Language.

| Sir Patrick | Because, Madam, they are ashamed of it; it has such a rumbling Sound with it. Now when I was upon my Travels I liked the Language so well that I learned it.[17] |

The comic errors make Sir Patrick likable rather than an object of scorn (he is so nervous that he also calls Heartly, the male lead, "Madam"), but his defense of the Irish language and Irish learning invoke pathos because the erroneous boasts are a function of insecurity. He immediately sings an Irish song, which draws praise, but he must claim that Irish is not his native language. Macklin, who was a native Irish speaker, is, perhaps, drawing on his experience in England for this scene.

In England, then, the problem for immigrants was Irishness irrespective of religious belief. Meanwhile in Ireland, Catholic converts remained objects of suspicion, and patriot agitators insisted on drawing a line between Protestants and Catholics which the English were increasingly inclined to ignore in connection with the Irish. This left converts in a gray area. Charles Lucas attacks unspecified converts, comparing them disadvantageously with the professed Catholics: "There are none so dangerous, as those, who, in Publick, are *Protestants* by Profession, in Private, *Papists*, in Policy and Practice. Those, who from Conscience, profess the *Popish* Religion, openly and honestly, deserve tenderness and Pity, and are much less dangerous to the establishment."[18]

Thomas Sheridan represents the insecurities of the Protestants of Irish descent. The Kelly riot in 1747 illustrates not just class tension—part of Sheridan's problems came from his claim to gentlemanly status, to some an insufferable assertion from an actor, whatever his descent—but insecurity and religious tension.[19] An anonymous pamphlet suggests that Charles Lucas advised Sheridan to defend himself by playing off sectarian anxiety:

And he came unto L——s and said, what shall I do, for the men of *Conaught* are upon me.
And L——s said unto S——n, fear not neither be thou dismayed: Are there not Papists in the Land of *Conaught?* and are not the Papists Rebels?[20]

Paul Hiffernan, political controversialist and enemy of both Sheridan and Lucas, mocks Sheridan because of his hysterical assertion of Protestant purity:

But the cream of the jest is, his declaration, that if he thought himself indebted to the MECHEL'S dancing for any part of the extraordinary receipts of this winter, as they are *Papists*, and subjects to the *French* king, he would instantly refund, or rather apply it to some *public* charity, to shew his *love* to the *present establishment*, and have the exquisite pleasure of inserting a *dear* paragraph in the journal.[21]

The barb is directed at contradictory attitudes. Sheridan booked a Catholic act and then worried over the possibility that it might be responsible for his profits. It does not really matter whether the charge is fair; Hiffernan's satire makes sense only if Hiffernan thinks Sheridan or the public will believe Sheridan is nervous about being suspected of Catholic sympathies.

Sheridan is a convenient target for antipatriot polemicists, because the patriot politicians actually were conflicted over incorporating a heroic Irish past into political arguments and the apparent necessity of sympathy for the Catholics who represented the legacy of that past.[22] Lucas found it necessary to apologize for his public suspicion that the Kelly riots might represent the tip of a Catholic plot.[23] He also recycles the argument (dramatized in *Rotherick O'Connor*) that the Norman invasion was an attempt to help the oppressed Irish:

> Lastly, consider to what End have our *Ancestors*, brave free-born *Britons*, left their native Climate, to settle in this *remote*, and then *uncultivated Isle?* Was it not at the request of an oppressed King, and injured People, to restore their *Rights* and *Liberties*, and to impart a *free* and generous Spirit to the *Whole?*[24]

The whole of Ireland of course was not participating in the rights and liberties of the British constitution. But the argument for those constitutional rights, that the Normans had come to preserve the Irish from tyranny, implied that they should.

Lucas was even prepared to accept the possibility that Irish Catholics had some justification for their outbreaks of rebellion. Certainly the Irish were justified in overthrowing the Danish conquest: "The *Irish*, in general, were, absolutely treated worse, than the *Victims* of the most *Savage Barbarians;* as bad, as the *Spaniards* used the Mexicans; or, as inhumanely, as the *English*, now, treat their Slaves, in *America*." The political code is in the equation between the Danish domination of Ireland and the English domination of America. England and Denmark are related through metonymy, with *oppression* as the shared term, and, with Ireland as the modern victim of foreign domination, the English become universally as oppressive as the ancient Vikings.[25] But it is hard to see how Lucas could have avoided the application of this same metonymy to the Protestant oppression of Catholic Ireland, with the same potential threat that the Irish represented to the Danes: "No wonder they [the native Irish] should have become *implacable Enemies* to their *lawless, inhuman, perfidious,* their *worse,* than *Savage Oppressors:* when we find the *deluded Wretches,* always treated, worse, than *a good man* could treat *Brutes!*"[26]

I am not accusing Lucas of inconsistency; the confusion in his attitudes is closer to multiple personality disorder. On the one hand he claims the Irish victory over the Danes as a noble example of patriotism, while on the other hand he remains unwilling to allow their descendants, the Catholic Irish, any share in Irish political power. The religion of the Catholic Irish is the problem, not their culture, in contrast to the English, who regarded Catholic and Protestant Irish as nearly equally culturally deficient.

Playwright, essayist, and novelist Henry Brooke shares the same dual consciousness. Brooke whips up Protestant hysteria against Catholics during the Jacobite rising in Scotland in 1745 by invoking 1641:

> They say to us, *had we lived in the Days of our Fathers, we would not have been Partakers with them, in their Oppressions and Massacres: But herein they confess themselves to be the Children of those Men,* by whom our Maidens were polluted, by

whom our Matrons were left childless; by whom our Grandsires were butchered, and their Infants dashed against the Stones.[27]

By the 1760s, Brooke is writing in defense of Catholics at the instigation of Charles O'Conor, although Brooke's need for money assuredly played a role in his authorship of *The Tryal of the Cause of the Roman Catholics.* Subsequently, Brooke would go on to edit the anti-Catholic *Freeman's Journal.*[28]

Yet Brooke too professes enthusiasm for Irish antiquities, publishing *Prospectus of a Work to Be Entitled Ogygian Fables* (1743) and *A History of Ireland from the Earliest Time Proposed* (1744).[29] An anecdote, published after Brooke's death, suggests that he could be as flattered by Irish praise as English:

> A young man, of the name of Dary, or Mac Dary, who lived on the banks of that river, addressed some verse to him in the Irish language. He was so highly pleased with this little nosegay of native flowers, that he resolved to learn the Irish language, a resolve, with many others, which he never put into execution.[30]

Like the unwritten fables and history, good intentions toward the Irish did not result in any real rapprochement—at least in his own life. But it should not be forgotten that his daughter, Charlotte Brooke, published the important early collection of translations of Irish poetry, *Reliques of Irish Poetry* (1789), and Brooke was responsible for her early education.

Anti-Catholicism was not a function of class. For example, Archbishop Stone argued in 1751 that Anthony Malone, prime sergeant and close ally of Henry Boyle (the powerful speaker of the house), could not be trusted with important office because his mother was a Catholic.[31] Malone is an example of how those with Catholic relatives could rise in Irish society; nevertheless, he is also an example of the suspicion that went with a Catholic heritage.

In this atmosphere of ambivalence toward things Irish, both in those of Irish descent and Anglo-Irish "patriots" espousing reformation of the Irish political structure as well as legislative and juridical independence, Macklin's own experience becomes politically charged, especially because his sympathies were with the patriots, both in England and Ireland; he was, for instance, a friend of John Wilkes.[32] At the same time, Macklin becomes with success almost ostentatiously unashamed of his Irish past. Sir Callaghan, the Irish lover of *Love à la Mode* (1759), while comical, is the most admirable character in the play, and his Irish descent informs his courtship of Charlotte (of Norman stock):

> Sir Theodore is my uncle only by moder's side, which is a little upstart family that came in vid one Strongbow but t'other day—lord, not above six or seven hundred years ago: whereas my family, by my fader's side, are all the true old Milesians, and related to the O'Flaherty's, and O'Shocknesses, and the McLaughlins, the O'Donnegans, O'Callaghans, O'Geogaghans, all the tick blood of the nation—and I myself, you know, am an O'Brallaghan, which is the ouldest of them all.[33]

The mild brogue and inclusion of Macklin's own family, the M'Laughlins, plus the ultimate success of O'Brallaghan's wooing, reveal an unwillingness to compromise with Irish heritage; the hero is Irish and proud of it. O'Dogherty, the wise patriot of *The True-Born Irishman* (1762), refuses to allow his wife to anglicize him: "And pray, above all things, never call me Mr. Diggerty—my name is Murrogh O'Dogherty, and I am not ashamed of it" (111). Nor was this affectation on Macklin's part. The sale catalogue of his library shows a substantial Irish collection, along with a manuscript play, presumably by Macklin, called *Love Is the Conqueror, or the Irish Hero.*[34]

In the latter part of his life Macklin also ceased to apologize for being a native Irish speaker. In 1765, Samuel Johnson and Macklin engaged in a round of linguistic one-upmanship, as Johnson tried various languages on Macklin to humble him, while Macklin managed to keep up his end of the conversation in each:

> Johnson, growing more determined from the failure of his attempts, at last addressed him with a string of sounds perfectly unintelligible. "What's that, Sir?" inquired Macklin. "Hebrew!" answered Johnson.—"And what do I know of Hebrew?"—"But a man of your understanding, Mr. Macklin, ought to be acquainted with every language!" The doctor's face glowed with a smile of triumph. "*Och neil en deigen vonshet hom boge vaureen!*" exclaimed Macklin. Johnson was now dumfounded, and inquired the name of the lingua. "Irish, Sir!" "Irish!" exclaimed the Doctor. "Do you think I ever studied that?" "But a man of your understanding, Doctor Johnson, ought to be acquainted with every language!"[35]

Even if the story is apocryphal, something like it is true, or should be. Johnson and Macklin had too much in common not to have argued: proud, strong, self-made men, they were unlikely to have deferred to one another. Importantly, however, Macklin is asserting that Irish is a language with which the learned should be familiar, a position a long way from Sir Patrick Bashfull's unwillingness to acknowledge that he is a native speaker.

Yet in an uneasy pairing with Irish pride, Macklin's plays consistently endorse the calls for political reform common to sporadically anti-Catholic writers such as Lucas and Brooke. In *The School for Husbands* (1761), Townly is chastised by Angelica for wooing when he should be seeking a way to reform the philandering Lord Belville: "Sir, you were called into our cabinet to assist us in punishing my lord, and in redressing this lady for the general weal—and like a selfish minister you would neglect the business of the nation to gratify your own private passion" (155). Private morality and public morality are thus closely related, an important patriot creed. In *The Man of the World* (1781), Sidney castigates Sir Pertinax for his self-interested approach to politics:

> Indeed, sir, I believe the doctrine of pimping for patrons, as well as that of prostituting eloquence and public trust for private lucre, may be learned in your party schools—for where faction and public venality are taught as measures necessary to good government and general prosperity—there every vice is to be expected. (259)

In *The True-Born Irishman* Macklin attacks the Castle through Count Mushroom, a fop who abuses O'Dogherty's hospitality by trying to have an affair with his wife, and who, according to Cooke, was meant to ridicule *"Single Speech Hamilton,"* who was then Secretary to the Earl of Halifax, Lord Lieutenant of Ireland" (235). The English as a whole are abusing the Irish, and some of the Irish are aiding them. Referring to the practice of buying parliamentary votes, O'Dogherty says sourly, "We have a great many among us that call themselves patriots and champions, who, at the same time, would not care if poor old Ireland was squeezed as you squeeze an orange—provided they had but their share of the juice" (101).

Macklin's patriot politics made him popular in Dublin, but it also connects him with the virulent anti-Catholicism of some of the patriots, a position that may well have made him uncomfortable. He was not alone in this awkward area of supporting patriots while probably regarding their sectarian views as lamentable; Charles O'Conor of Belanagare, defender of Catholic rights, was moved to support Lucas as well.[36] Macklin, to his credit, never gives in to the anti–Irish Catholic virus. In his first play, *King Henry the VII, or The Popish Impostor,* he calls attention to Irish inactivity in the 1745 Stuart rebellion. Sevez, the papal legate, asks Frion, a rebellious Scotsman, about Ireland's support for Perkin Warbeck (an analog for Charles Stuart):

Frion   Th'Apostate Slaves are fallen off from *Rome,*
           And firmly fixt in the Usurper's Cause;
           Kildare, Clanrikard, with many others
           On whom we built absolute Assurance,
           Have, at their own Charge, arm'd their Friends
               and Followers
           And join'd the *English* General, *Poinings.*[37]

The mention of existing loyal Irish noblemen in connection with the name Poinings reminds an English audience of loyal Irish subordination to the law that gave the English Privy Council the right to amend Irish bills. The Kildare and Clanrikard families were, of course, Protestant in Macklin's time, but he depicts the Irish (and by extension Catholic converts) as more loyal than the Scots, who are willing to turn traitor for any plausible pretender. Macklin's politics show the uneasy compromise being worked out between Irish nationalism and some limited relief from paranoia about Catholic insurrection.

In the same vein, he tweaks British hypocrisy about the presence of Irish soldiers in the military. Lord Belville is humbled in *The School for Husbands* (1761) by a press gang. When they lay hands on him, he protests that he is a lord, and the corporal responds, "O be quiet—be aisy, my dear soul, for if you was the lord leeftenant of Ireland you must go when you are commanded" (168). While Irish Protestants were allowed to serve in the cavalry, neither Catholics nor Protestants were allowed in the infantry, since they supposedly were a threat to discipline. The manpower demands of the Seven Years' War, however, forced regiments to find manpower wherever they could, and violations of the restrictions assuredly occurred—an eighteenth-century version of

"Don't ask, don't tell."[38] Irish and English audiences are not being challenged here, but they are being reminded of the gap between the law and practical necessity.

Tolerance toward Irish Catholics was in some ways more possible in England than in Ireland. Hugh Reily's defense of Catholics, originally published in 1695, was reprinted in London in 1762. In it, Protestant schemes for the conversion of Ireland, emphasizing conversion, exile, or death, are attacked as unchristian:

> Here we have a hopeful Scheme of a Protestant *Thorou' Reformation*, where knocking Arguments are urged, not to convince People's Judgments, but in effect to beat out their Brains, a Practice never thought of, much less used by the most renowned of our Primitive Christians towards the very Heathens.[39]

Apparently unfamiliar with the conversion of Norway, Reily wrote a Catholic apologia that praises Catholic fidelity to the church of Saint Patrick and accuses Luther and Calvin of "new Revelations" (20). The late reprint of this work implies increasing confidence in England that Catholics were not a danger to public security. Irish Protestants were not so sanguine.

Macklin's background is crucial to understanding his Irish patriot politics. Modern commentators point out that the early biographies of Macklin are unreliable, but what is striking about them is the ubiquity of his Irish identity. Whether or not the stories are true, memorialists were unable to separate Macklin from them. The anecdotes reveal an Irishman abroad, facing slights and likely to respond dangerously when treated with disrespect. Macklin was somewhat unusual, no doubt: his achievements as actor, director, and playwright, as well as his temper and ambitions, exposed him more to ridicule. Moreover, because of his success, we have more information about him than about most Irish actor-playwrights. Still, the tone of the commentaries, their awareness of the effect of history and geography on events, implies a wider applicability than just to Macklin's experience abroad. Family, class, and nation figure repeatedly in the biographies of Macklin published shortly after his death.

Macklin died in 1797, yet immediately a mythology developed about his connections with the Irish aristocracy and their displacement. A restrained obituary merely describes loyalty to the prerevolutionary order: "The M'Laughlin's, originally respectable, suffered greatly from an unfortunate attachment to the Stuarts; and the fortunes of the family were at the lowest ebb before our hero saw the light."[40] There is no heat in this identification—Jacobite fears had been extinguished generations before, at least in England—but there is an inference that Stuart loyalty is crucial to understanding Macklin. On one level, this account explains why he became an actor, as poverty forced the landed gentry into trade, crafts, or entertainment. But there is more to it than that, as Kirkman's biography makes clear:

> The circumstance of CHARLES MACKLIN's having been carried away, in a turf-kish, from the scene of action, near the Boyne, on that memorable day which gave freedom to Ireland, and transferred the property of the old possessors to new masters, is still spoken of by those, whose grandfathers, if living, could scarcely remember the event, but who have had it from father to son by oral tradition. (Kirkman, 13)

This story, to which Kirkman wholly subscribes, despite the fact that it would make Macklin 107 at his death, makes Macklin a transitional figure. His family's loss is Ireland's and, ultimately, the stage's gain, but the echo of the Moses story suggests that Macklin will be forced to serve a country other than his own.

Macklin's divided loyalties receive further elaboration in another early biography. William Cooke claims that Macklin told him that

> at the celebrated siege of that city [Derry] in King William's time, he had three uncles within the walls, and three without, who distinguished themselves, though on opposite sides, with a bravery (to use the old man's phrase) "that kept up the honour of the blood of the M'Laughlins." (2)

Again, there is no shred of evidence supporting this story; it reads like a novel by Sir Walter Scott wherein kin are forced to fight against kin because of political upheaval. But it reveals both kinship divisions and acceptance that bravery and honor existed on both sides of the divide, a sort of pseudo-biographical *Battle of Aughrim*. Kirkman also describes Irish pride in a preconquest past when discussing Macklin's antecedents:

> At that time family pride ran as high in Ireland, as it ever did in any part of the world; and the families of M'LAUGHLIN, or O'KELLY, would not have thought themselves very much honored by an union with those of LLEWELLIN, DOUGLAS, or HOWARD. (9)

Diminishment has occurred in that Macklin the actor is incomparably inferior socially to his ancestors; recollection of that aristocratic past remains.

Sliding social status has a specific cause, and Cooke reminds his readers of the penal laws and their consequences:

> His mother, by the restraining laws of Ireland at that time, which gave to the next Protestant heir the inheritance of every landed property from the Popish possessor, provided the latter did not conform to the Protestant religion, lost her little farm by the operation of this cruel law. (9)

In this account the disinherited are objects of sympathy because they are victims of intolerance. Kirkman draws the connection between religious belief and social degradation. Macklin's destitute mother married Luke O'Meally, a Williamite who owned the Eagle Tavern on Werburgh Street (Kirkman, 17). This accommodation merely increased her worries as her growing son turned into a rogue and vagabond, "*Charles a Mollucth;* or, in English, *Wicked Charlie*" (Kirkman, 24): Macklin's mother "began to be indifferent what line of life her son moved in; no matter how low or how contracted, provided she could persuade him to preserve his morals untainted and his religion unchanged" (Kirkman, 53). Ambition and Catholicism conflicted; to choose fidelity to religion meant accepting poverty and social contempt. Thus when Macklin converts, around the age of forty, despite his claim that his Protestantism was "as staunch as the Archbishop of Canterbury, and on as pure principles" (76)—a claim that should be treated with serious skepticism, as Macklin may never have married the mother of his children[41]—the emotional baggage of conversion is psychologically linked to betrayal of family for financial and social acceptance.

Further, Macklin was both from the lower class and afflicted, at first, with an Irish accent. Aspry Congreve's biography of Macklin mentions another incident that serves to type the actor:

> A late Irish Judge, however, has been frequently heard to declare, that he remembered him a very inferior servant in Trinity College, Dublin; where he used to stand in the menial capacity of errand boy on the students and fellows of the seminary.[42]

Despite the patronizing overtones echoing in the judge's declaration, Macklin came to be able to joke about his early employment. Cooke argues that part of the success of Macklin's plays in Dublin was a consequence of this service, "what he used jocularly to call himself—a *College man* (being a badge-man to the College,) and from this situation could remember the ancestors of most of the people of distinction in and about Dublin" (Cooke, 304). This, of course, cuts two ways. If Macklin could remember their grandfathers as students, the Protestant gentry presumably could not forget that he was originally a menial. Macklin's success and Protestantism, while making him less threatening, could also not erase the historical legacy of Irish Catholic dispossession. Insofar as Macklin's plays support the patriot agenda this past made that agenda inclusive, but his social, ethnic, and (formerly) religious compatriots still outnumbered the Protestants, and Macklin's joke about being a "college man" reiterates the exclusivity of Protestant rule.

Macklin's allegiance to his own Irishness, apparent in his plays, is in contrast with the practical necessity of losing his accent. Kirkman writes, "With the judicious, his Irish accent was an objection which they allowed his acting in a great degree, counterbalanced;—with the lower order, his being an Irishman was an objection, however admirably he might act" (64). Macklin succeeded in shedding this identifying and, for an actor, disabling Irish characteristic. Actors need multiple accents, and Macklin developed them. In a revival of Charles Shadwell's *Humours of the Army* for Macklin's benefit night in 1746, Macklin played the Welsh officer Cadwallader, rather than either of the Irish officers.[43] Two of his best roles were as the Scotsmen Sir Archy Macsarcasm and Sir Pertinax Macsycophant in *Love à la Mode* and *The Man of the World*, respectively.

Indeed, Macklin could play an Englishman well enough for Cooke to claim that the genesis of Sir Callaghan O'Brallaghan was a meeting with an Irish officer in the Prussian service:

> He was so extremely simple and unsuspicious, that when Macklin (who passed himself off for an Englishman all the while) attributed his successes with the ladies from having a *tail behind*, as common to all Irishmen, he instantly pulled off his coat and waistcoat, to convince him of his mistake, assuring him, "that no Irishman, in *that respect*, was better than another man. (224–25)

Again, there is no reason to believe this story is true. Kirkman offers an entirely different version; a brother of Macklin's mother, Captain O'Flanagan, recruiting in Ireland for the "German service," almost persuaded Macklin into joining him (Kirkman, 46). But Cooke's version implies that Macklin was not above denying a common heritage to make his countryman the butt of a joke. Cooke goes on to suggest that the model for O'Brallaghan was "educated in the simple manners of the interior part of Ireland, where an unsuspicious temper, courage, generosity, and fidelity, are qualities that seem particularly congenial to that soil" (Cooke, 232). These are, of course, particularly valuable qualities in a servant, or a subject people, and the marked condescension of Cooke's praise reinforces denigration of the Irish, rather than working against it.

Fortunately, O'Brallaghan transcends these stereotypes. His bulls usually show either wit or virtue:

Sir Callaghan	Ho! to be sure, madam, who would be a soldier without danger? Danger, madam, is a soldier's greatest glory, and death his best reward.
Mordecai	Ha, ha, ha! That is an excellent bull! death a reward! Pray, Sir Callaghan, no offence, I hope—how do you make out death being a reward?
Sir Callaghan	How? Why, don't you know that?
Mordecai	Not I, upon honour.
Sir Callaghan	Why, a soldier's death in the field of battle, is a monument of fame, that makes him alive as Caesar, or Alexander, or any dead hero of them all.

(56)

The Jewish suitor, lacking honor, assumes a contradiction where none exists. The Irish suitor, possessing both courage and honor, parries smoothly. O'Brallaghan is also not a fortune hunter. The other suitors are gulled into believing Charlotte is poor; O'Brallaghan shows his decency by standing by his offer: "Madam, my fortune is not much, but it is enough to maintain a couple of honest hearts, and have something to spare for the necessities of a friend; which is all we want, and all that fortune is good for" (75).

O'Brallaghan has been made carefully nonthreatening to both an Irish and an English audience. As an officer in the Prussian army, he is rather more likely to be Protestant than Catholic. One Scotsman, annoyed at the satire on his nation, pointed out the nationality of O'Brallaghan's regiment:

> An *Irish* officer in the *French, Spanish,* or *Austrian* service, would have been more agreeable to the general received notions of mankind. But such an incoherent medley of heroics and stupidity as *O Brallaghan* is dished out here by his country-man, never has been exhibited before, nor ought to be borne by any audience that would lay a claim to rationality.[44]

In fact, that O'Brallaghan is not the typical stage Irishman draws attention and criticism. The Scottish critic is relying on religious antipathy. France, Spain, and Austria were Catholic countries with numerous Irish soldiers; but, in any case, whichever anecdote about the genesis of the play one prefers, Macklin is calling attention to Irish soldiers' serving in Protestant foreign armies because they could not serve in the English. Where the critic wants to remind his readers of the threat that the Irish represent, Macklin portrays them as loyal exiles who deserve better.

Macklin was fighting an uphill battle. After his death, another anonymous biographer charged him with reverse discrimination in *Love à la Mode:*

> Though this piece does not want character and satire, yet it must be observed, his partiality for his country has transported him a little from the strictness of drama; for, out of four lovers, he makes an Irish officer the only one that is disinterested.—A character so widely different from what experience has, in general, fixed on the gentlemen of that kingdom, that, although there are undoubtedly many amongst them possessed of minds capable of great honour and generosity, yet this *exclusive* compliment to them, in opposition to received opinion, seems to convey a degree of prejudice, which as a dramatic writer, and a countryman, he should be studious to avoid.[45]

In short, Macklin's violation of stereotypes is an aesthetic offense because the stereotypes, based on general experience, are more or less true, despite occasional exceptions. Since drama is concerned with the probable, in the opinion of this neo-Aristotelian critic, O'Brallaghan's generous and altruistic love is an example of reprehensible bias in favor of the Irish.

Yet this critic's comment is more subtle than just knee-jerk bigotry against positive Irish characters. Macklin's problem is exclusivity. If Macklin wishes to dramatize the exceptional Irishman, contrary to normal expectations of character development, he also should not have limited the exception to the Irishman. That is, if cultural stereotyping is objectionable, then it should always be objectionable, and Macklin should not have relied on it in connection with the oafish English country squire, the ignoble Jew, and the grasping Scotsman. Macklin has merely substituted a different scapegoat to get the Irish off the hook.

This charge is largely true. Sir Archibald Macsarcasm is a pale object of contempt compared with Macklin's attack on Scottish politicians in Lord Bute's administration in the character of Sir Pertinax Macsycophant in *The Man of the World*.[46] The hero, Egerton (Macsycophant's son, but raised by an English uncle), represents patriot politics:

Egerton	(*With a most patriotic warmth*) I own I do wish—most ardently wish for a total extinction of all party—particularly that those of English, Irish, and Scotch might never more be brought into contest or competition; unless, like loving brothers, in generous emulation for one common cause.
Sir Pertinax	Hoo, Sir! do ye persist? what! would ye banish aw party, and aw distinction between English, Irish, and yer ain countrymen?
Egerton	(*With great dignity of spirit*) I would, sir.
Sir Pertinax	The damn ye, sir—ye are nai true Scot. Aye, sir, ye may leuk as angry as ye wull; but again I say—ye are nai true Scot.

(218)

O'Brallaghan is a virtuous Irishman. Egerton can only be virtuous because raised by the English. In the former case, altruism and benevolence are natural, in the latter acquired, since Egerton could not have inherited them from the wholly vicious Macsycophant. Egerton's desire for equality in the empire recalls Shadwell's allied soldiers in *The Humours of the Army*, and, as in Shadwell's play, the discordant note is struck by the Scotsman. But Hyland is at least silent under correction; Macsycophant, foiled in his plans for greater political power through the marriage of his son, storms off unreconciled, saying, "My vengeance leeght upon ye aw together" (269). Disinterested justice is not possible for "a true Scot." Macklin, the victim of racism, succeeds in English and Protestant Irish society but, having done so, substitutes another object for victimization.

Kirkman attributes Macklin's anti-Caledonian tendency to a desire for profit. In connection with *Love à la Mode* he writes,

> Some gentlemen of North Britain were, during the first run of the Farce, highly exasperated at the character of *Sir Archy*, which they imprudently declared was a satire upon the whole kingdom of Scotland. This circumstance turned out exactly as the author imagined it would; the resentment of the Caledonians provoked the mirth of others, and spread the fame of *Love-a-la-Mode* all over town. (402)

Macklin appears here to have appealed to English prejudice by allowing the victims to draw attention to themselves. But this explanation requires that Macklin be aware not only of English prejudice, but also that complaints about it will draw only laughter from complacent English audiences. In short, Macklin uses prejudice to succeed.

But if Macklin is not a good candidate for sainthood, he is a major influence on increasingly positive portrayals of Irishman on the English stage.[47] In Dublin, he introduces characters whom the Anglo-Irish recognize as their own:

> At the first performance when Messink staggered on as Fitzmongrel, a drunken Irish beau, a gentleman in a box impulsively cried out, "Why that's me! But what sort of a rascally coat have they dressed me in?" Divesting himself of his own gold-laced one, he called out to Messink, "Here—I'll dress you!" and flung it to the startled actor amid loud applause.[48]

Comical as this instance is, it indicates that the cultural idiom of Dublin is no longer West British, for the play worked only with Irish audiences. The English did not identify with these characters while the Dublin audience did.

Moreover, even the English language ceases to identify the English of Ireland. Mrs. O'Dogherty has adopted "Diggerty" as her name in London and comes back affecting an English accent—unsuccessfully, as she sounds more like a cockney than a member of the aristocracy. To effect reconciliation with Mr. O'Dogherty, she must resume her Irish pronunciation:

> And as to yourself, my dear Nancy, I hope I shall never have any more of your London English; none of your this here's, your that there's, your winegars, your weals, your vindors, your toastesses, and your stone postesses; but let me have our own good, plain, old Irish English, which I insist is better than all the English English that ever coquets and coxcombs brought into the land. (111)

The introduction of "stage English" as a source of amusement for the Anglo-Irish reveals that London English is by now merely a variant in the empire, and Dublin English equally defining. Something is lost here, as the Irish language becomes largely irrelevant to an Irish identity in the eyes of an economically comfortable theater audience. But when an O'Dogherty (who from his social position must be either a convert or the descendant of a convert) praises Irish English, the Catholic converts symbolically both claim a place in the existing Irish power structure, and force the Protestants of English descent to admit that they are sundered from their English coreligionists because they no longer speak identical languages. In short, the English of Ireland are now Irish—or at least think they are—and subsequent playwrights are able to take the Irish heritage as their own unapologetically.

SIX

"Beneath Iërne's banners here I stand"

Francis Dobbs, Gorges Edmond Howard, and Irish Drama of the 1770s

John Almon, a radical journalist and friend of John Wilkes,[1] published, in 1770, an edition of Molyneux's *The Case of Ireland*, with a new preface in which he praises ancient Irish valor and warns that England can no longer afford to disregard Irish patriot grievances:

> For let fancy present us but for a moment, this island we speak of, not inhabited by the descendants of *Britain*, nor those who are blended with these descendants, by every natural and civil intercourse, not by men—who have or wish to have the same interest, at worst no opposite interest to that of Britain . . . but let that Island be filled with a race of ancient Irish, fierce, active, robust, patient of hunger and toil, proud in being the posterity of these heroes who chased the prowling Danes from their country, plumed as they were at that time with repeated victories over the prostrate Saxons . . . Instead of being so rich a jewel in our crown, what a thorn would *Ireland* be in our side?[2]

In 1772 the Catholic historian Sylvester O'Halloran also recalls Irish victories over the Danes in the context of Irish patriot sentiments:

> Do we look for incentives to the brightest actions for national liberty? Let us behold *Ceallach in Caishel:* a prince gallant, brave, and young, insidiously imprisoned by the Dane; and threatened with perpetual confinement in a foreign land, if he will not consent to deliver up his country a prey to these strangers. Instead of acquiescing to demands so injurious to his people, he *privately* directs his successor . . . to make no kind of concession to the Barbarians, and to take advantage of this negociation to arm his country to their destruction, without any regard to his particular fate. How noble a subject for the Muse![3]

In 1773 Gorges Edmond Howard published *The Siege of Tamor* (not, apparently, performed until 1774),[4] a tragedy about Malsechlin's victory over the Danish king Turgesius (the same subject as Philips's *Hibernia Freed*, although Howard gets the name of the victorious Irish king right); and Francis Dobbs has produced in 1773 and published in 1774 *The Patriot King; or Irish Chief*, a tragedy about Ceallachan's defeat of another Danish invader, Sitric (subsequently produced in Belfast in 1777).[5]

In each case, the plays commemorate Irish victories over foreign invaders, as well as the patriotism and courage, against overwhelming odds, of the native population. Moreover, the plays represent two important patriot themes during the rising tide of Irish nationalism in the 1770s: national unity and political reform. Gorges Edmond Howard, a Dublin alderman, adds to the story of Malsechlin a youthful Niall from Ulster, the heir of Malsechlin's enemy, who aids in defeating the Danes and marries Malsechlin's daughter. Francis Dobbs, one of the founders of the Volunteers, dramatizes an ideal hero who conjoins private and public virtue. In Dobbs's play, even the Danes are integrated into the Irish state, because Ceallachan marries Sitric's sister. Howard and Dobbs are not identical in their political sentiments: Howard, for most of his life, supported the government, while Dobbs was a radical reformer (at least in his early years). Howard translates "patriotism" into "faction," while Dobbs regards "patriotism" as the identifying characteristic of the virtuous political party in Ireland. It may well be that both playwrights incorporate Irish subjects since many in Ireland were annoyed at James Macpherson's piracy of Irish mythology for Scottish purposes. But most importantly, these Irish Protestant playwrights, although politically opposed, use Irish history to express their political views, and contribute to the nationalistic sentiment for Irish rights, at least in the limited form that would be embodied in Grattan's Parliament. Some of the English of Ireland had become wholly Irish, just as in the same period, North American colonists ceased to regard themselves as English, coming instead to see themselves as American.

I

As an alderman, Howard was a member of the urban middle class that would most strenuously insist upon maintaining the "Protestant ascendancy" in the 1790s.[6] Moreover, from at least 1753 he finds himself on the wrong side of the patriot movement. In his introduction to his own works, published in 1782, Howard looks back ruefully on a legal treatise, *His Majesty's Hereditary Revenues,* and the pamphlet attacks on him:

> Thus did I suffer for as much political scribbling as would fill a tolerable volume; (nine parts in ten of which, I wish not a trace to remain on the face of the earth) although I could with safety say, were I this instant expiring, that I never intentionally published a line against the real interest of my country, or the character of any individual. I ever had a soul above such things; nor does there live a man, who loves his country, its constitution and legal liberty more: I had no other intentions or views, than to explain and conciliate; but faction knows no greater offense.[7]

Howard presents himself here as seeking a common ground. Crucially, however, he disassociates himself from "faction" and refers to his love of country without using the term *patriot*.

Joep Leerssen has argued that patriotism was simply a virtue in the eighteenth century, and therefore should not be seen as having political and nationalist overtones: "It is true, yet again, that Patriot thought made more of *virtue* (and, by implication, of the virtue of *amor patriae*) as a political quality; but it is no less true that non-Patriot and even anti-Patriot writers could lay equal claims to those virtuous ideals."[8] While it is certainly true that both sides claimed to love their country, Leersen is mistaking rhetoric for content, as the word *patriot* quite clearly had a partisan signification in the English language. It first received wide usage in the English language during the fiercely partisan exclusion crisis of 1681, and was appropriated by the Whigs under a cover of public-interest politics.[9] Dryden clearly regarded patriotism as a gilding of opposition (read: treason) when, in *Absalom and Achitophel* (1681), he had David comment on his enemies, "Good heavens, how faction can a patriot paint."

The anonymous *The History of the Rise, Progress, and Tendency of Patriotism by a Freeholder* makes the distinction between *theoria* and *praxis* explicit. Leerssen's definition of *patriotism* certainly was operative in the eighteenth century:

> Some define it thus: *Patriotism* is a certain Turn of Mind and Spirit drawn from Reason and Observation, which determines a good Man at all Events, to prefer the publick Happiness to his own private Welfare, and to sacrifice for it, when necessary, both his life and fortune.

Clearly this version of patriot thought could belong to anyone, as the relevant characteristic of a patriot is his desire to serve the public. In practice, however, patriotism is a mask for greed and a radical agenda:

> The second Definition, to the Sense of which most of the greatest Men have strictly adhered, is this: *Patriotism* is a bloated Sound delightful to the Ears of the great Vulgar and the Small, ever in the Mouths of those who would, at the Expence of the Multitude, enrich and elevate themselves, Children, Brothers, Sisters and Confederates. To this Species of Patriotism we may ascribe the Destruction of States and Communities, the subversion of Kingdoms, Dethroning of Kings, the Loss of publick Credit, futilous Debates and Negotiations, Rebellions and Murders, Places and Pensions, Stars and Garters, Axes and Halters, Carts and Coaches, with a long *Et cætera* of several other very useful and ornamental Matters, which I shall hereafter treat of.[10]

Despite the gibe at great men, which typically in midcentury would have indicated an attack on Walpole and the government, the commentator clearly associates patriotism with a radical agenda dangerous to established order, and assumes that the rhetoric of patriotism masks a venal self-interest.

Further, Leerssen rejects the idea that patriotism can be associated with nationalism, because "the concept of the 'nation' in eighteenth-century usage does not refer to a cultural or historical, let alone a racial-genealogical entity, invented by the nineteenth century" (14). On the contrary, as Howard Weinbrot has shown exhaustively, both England and Scotland understood the concept of "nation" in racial and cultural terms, were careful to trace the mixed cultures that made up the British synthesis, and ultimately created a well-developed literary nationalism long before the nineteenth century.[11]

The Irish too developed a conception of nation in racial and cultural terms. In *The Antiquities and History of Ireland* (first edition 1654, revised 1658) James Ware is merely making an anthropological observation when he states that the Irish were originally descended from the British, but their blood was mingled with that of many others.[12] By 1689, Richard Cox has a distinct animus behind the same claim: "And 'tis certain they are at this Day a *mixt* People, if it were for no other Reason, but that there is hardly a Gentleman among them, but has English Blood in his veins."[13] Cox asserts this position to deride claims of Milesian purity; the Irish ought to accept English authority since they are a mongrel race, partially related to the English, and therefore not a separate nation.

Sylvester O'Halloran accepts the mixed-race hypothesis but makes a wholly different use of it in the 1770s:

> For, though unhappily for the antient kingdom, *unnatural* distinctions have but too long been kept up by artful and designing enemies, to the almost entire ruin of the whole; yet are we in fact, but *one* people, and as unmixt a race as any in Europe. There is not at this day a Milesian, or descendant of Strongbow, whose bloods are not so intimately blended, that it would be impossible to determine which should preponderate.[14]

Over time, the mixing of races creates a new race. At least the Old English and Celtic Irish are one race and, by implication, a nation. O'Halloran is even more inclusive in a later work, and defends his practice with reference to English scholarly habits: "What British historian, attempts to draw a line of separation, between the old Britons, and those of Saxon, Danish, Norman, Flemish, Dutch and German origin? He combines them all under the general title of Britons or Englishmen, and they all equally glory in these epithets."[15] Notably, O'Halloran is drawing a line between the Irish and the Britons. But the expansiveness of the definition of "English" also allows the English of Ireland to claim themselves as Irish as geography creates a shared national consciousness; over time, proximity and intermarriage create a new race.

To sum up, the racial and cultural consciousness that allows nationalism, and an identification of nationalism with particular patriot positions, was already in place by the 1770s. In Ireland in the 1770s the term *patriot* meant the radical reformers in favor of free trade, parliamentary independence, and parliamentary reform, not generalized lovers of the public welfare (although they assuredly thought that these reforms would benefit the public). Literary nationalism, however, could be appropriated both by the patriots and the Castle and its supporters, such as Howard.

Howard's allegiance to the the government is apparent even from attacks on him when he was apparently on the outs with George Townshend, lord lieutenant. In 1770 George Faulkner published an advertisement mocking Howard; Howard responded with an angry letter that Faulkner printed. Robert Jephson, Townshend's master of horse and a playwright, wrote anonymous poems about the controversy and published them under Faulkner's and Howard's names.[16] In both, Howard is pilloried as a timeserver. In Howard's own supposed epistle, the viceroy, Lord Townshend is disguised as Lord Sanch:

> But now, when too late, I perceive, to my cost,
> My friendship misplac'd, and my confidence lost;
> And find, that contempt is the only reward,
> I'm likely to gain from this pitiful Lord;
> Why, so it diverts him accounts it no matter,
> What characters he and his colleagues bespatter.[17]

The ungrateful Castle has failed to defend Howard, and he has lost all allies in the City and government. In the supposed commentary on his pseudo epistle, Howard's situation is not so desperate:

> For my own part, however unwilling I may be to encrease the number of absentees, as long as I keep my places, I am resolved to leave the kingdom for ever, as soon as I can obtain leave to sell these employments, which I have dearly purchased by thirty years' slavish attendance.[18]

This was, of course, the standard (and fully justified) charge of the patriots against those who supported the government: the administration bought support with lucrative offices and pensions. Government supporters, on the other hand, identified their opponents with faction.

When, in response to a rejected money bill in 1769, the viceroy prorogued Parliament, an anonymous pamphleteer blamed the patriots and, in particular, Lucius O'Brien:

> If you ask me to whom I attribute this Calamity;—I say, To You, Sir, and to other Members in Opposition to Government (who, by a strange Abuse of Words, are usually distinguished by the Name of Patriots) together with those powerful Leaders of Factions, who lent you a Majority on that Occasion.[19]

The rhetorical strategy of government supporters was to substitute the term *faction* for *patriot;* the self-interest of particular groups underlies the apparent benevolence of lovers of country. In Howard's *Apothegms and Maxims on Various Subjects, for the Good Conduct of Life,* under "Patriot and Patriotism" occurs the following remark identifying personal ambition as the source of conflict: "There is, and ever will be, a natural strife between court and country. The one will get as much, and the other give as little as it can" (*Works,* 2, 193). Howard, publishing anonymously in support of the Castle, carefully disassociates himself from the patriots: "It is incumbent on every Man who understands the Matter in any Degree, and has a real love for his Country, to do all in his Power to prevent his Fellow Members in Society from being imposed upon and led astray in so momentous a Business."[20] Both parties claim to possess "love of country," but *patriotism* identifies the party seeking a dangerous level of independence for Ireland out of self-interest, reversing the charge of the patriots.

The political crisis caused by rejection of the money bill led to a series of attacks on the patriots. In an anonymous pamphlet entitled *A Stricture upon Observations on a Speech by an Impartial Observer,* which marginal notes on the copy in the Royal Irish Academy suggest is by either the Reverend William Dennis or the Right Honorable Arthur Malone, the substitution of *faction* for *patriot* is made explicit:

> You an honourable patriot, have devoted one pamphlet to the wants and necessities of the people. Without a requisition from the throne you have increased the abuse against government. You have pompously arrayed an army of words, which may be martially employed in the suburbs of London or forests of America. You have given the peaceful treasure of your mind to disturb ministry, and solicit popular affections that this ministry as well as the colonies may feel the phrenzy of faction.[21]

Patriots, it turns out, really are all the same. Whether they raise popular unrest in England, America, or Ireland, their virtue is merely "the phrenzy of faction." Without the support of the king or the ministry, patriots can only appeal to the mob.

The defeat of the money bill called forth defenses of Poynings's Law and vilifications of the self-interest of the patriots, who were endangering the checks and balances of the constitution by encroaching on the prerogatives of the Crown and the Crown's viceroy:

> It is easy to perceive everything was hazarded to shew party strength, and that the mighty struggles to get into that House, as well as those within, are all exerted for personal ends and to support an unconstitutional aristocratical power: Let not government be abused for stemming this torrent, the head of which arises from our general corruption; let us not sell our birth-right for a mess of pottage.[22]

The viceroy, Lord Townshend, was also convinced that he was fighting "the dominion of aristocracy in Ireland."[23] In this view, the patriots are being used by the managers of aristocratic factions in Parliament. Far from being lovers of country, the patriots are tools of privilege.

Howard does not deny the existence of patriotism. For instance, Henry Flood, after his conversion to the government's side in 1774,[24] is called a patriot, in Howard's "Extempore of the Speech Made by the Right Honourable Henry Flood in the House of Commons of Ireland, on the Twentieth of December, MDCCLXXIX, on the Resolutions Respecting the Extension of the Trade of Ireland":

> That what Philosophers relate,
> Is true, that Spirits transmigrate,
> Lo! how FLOOD's language flows!
> With fire of GRECIAN patriot rage,
> And sweetness of the ROMAN sage,
> No bounds his fancy knows.
>
> (*Works*, 1, 63)

Despite the prosaic title, the verse form indicates a Pindaric ode, a serious poem on a serious subject. In connection with the trade bill, a government officeholder, like Flood, could achieve a unity of purpose with the patriots. True patriotism involves service of country under wise direction.

Benign neglect is Howard's policy suggestion toward the patriots. In the *Apothegms*, under "Faction," Howard suggests that if simply ignored the opposition will go away: "Schismatics both in religion and the state are like a top; if you scourge them, you keep them up; but if you neglect them, they will go down of themselves" (*Works*, 2, 79). The danger of faction is that it leads to mob rule: "Popular tumults have worse effects upon common safety, than the rankest tyranny, as it is easier to please the humour, and either appease or resist the fury of one single person, than a multitude. A licentious mob is an assembly of tyrants" (*Works*, 2, 107). Clearly, Howard is a conservative with no interest in greater public representation in Parliament, and equally clearly no ally of patriot reformers.

Both Castle supporters and patriot opposition in the dispute regarded themselves as Irishmen and emphasized it. A pamphlet pleading for calm in the money bill dispute stresses national identity:

> As an Irish man, I feel, what it would be unmanly not to feel; a distress for the consequences which must necessarily follow from such a measure; such as contrariety of opinions between men of the same nation; an over-heated party zeal in those who were for or against the measure; a jealousy in Great Britain for the rights of the crown, seemingly invaded by the warm assertion of constitutional privilege in an I——h H——e of C——s; in short, I feel for all those unsocial errors and fatal feuds, which are concomitant to hastily-adopted opinions, and inattentive surveys of the most materially constitutional principles.[25]

A recurring theme in the pro-Castle side of the pamphlet controversy was the danger Ireland incurred in contesting the English ministry's right to impose imperial costs on Ireland.[26] Yet both sides present themselves as acting in the interests of Ireland. In the passage above, "an Irish man" worries over the "jealousy" of "Great Britain"; subordinate to Great Britain, the Irish are nevertheless distinct from them. Strikingly, virtually no appeals are made to imperial obligations; that, it appears, was a matter for English pride, and had little or nothing to do with how the Irish contest was perceived by pamphlet commentators.

No new intellectual schema was required to explain patriot factionalism. In

1766 Charles O'Conor recurs to the common theme of Irish historiography discussed in connection with Philips in chapter 3: internal division. The Irish were "in their Infancy, a martial and free, in their Progress, an industrious and legislating, People: In their Prosperity, learned, religious, hospitable; in every Period, factious and turbulent." In fact Malsechlin's chief difficulty with Turgesius was this Irish tendency to put local interests ahead of national:

> The Oligarchs of the Time, were rather unanimous in rejecting their King, than the common Enemy: They loved their Country only in the second Place: Domestic Animosities, personal Revenge, were uppermost; and to the Gratification of these Passions, they sacrificed every Consideration favourable to their native Country, or useful to their own common Safety.[27]

The application of this lesson is apparent in Howard's choice of subject.

The dangers of faction and division are dramatized in *The Siege of Tamor*. The play begins with Moran, bishop of Meath, and Reli, prince of Bressney, discussing the Danish siege of Tamor, and Moran talks Reli into treason:

> Nor are you stranger to my many sufferings,
> The slights and all th' unmerited indignities
> With which our monarch hath of late oppress'd me;
> But above all, when he bestow'd the primacy
> Against my right, against his royal promise,
> (Which should be sacred as holy writ)
> On a mere stranger, that mean, servile, flatterer,
> The proud SIORNA, his new-chosen fav'rite.
>
> (*Works*, I, 174)

Siorna, of course, turns out to be brave, wise, and nobly opposed to surrender to the pagan Vikings. Moran represents the self-interest that underlies human behavior, particularly of those who seek public position. Siorna tells Malsechlin that loyalty cannot be bought, as those who seek favors from the king "build new demands on ev'ry free compliance,/And one rejected cancels thousands granted" (*Works*, I, 233).

It is tempting to regard this as a patriot jab at the Castle's traditional habit of buying support—Howard may still have been smarting from Jephson's satire—but the play as a whole suggests that people who betray Ireland are a symptom of Irish factionalism. Turgesius knows and takes advantage of the Irish tendency to division. Told by Zingar that Niall's Irish troops will be slow arriving at Tamor, Turgesius corrects him:

> Much you mistake; these hardy islanders
> Are fleet as stags, of ev'ry suffering patient;
> Nor lack they aught but union with themselves,
> To send the world their gauntlet of defiance.
>
> (*Works*, I, 203)

Against such formidable opposition, taking advantage of Irish treachery is prudent. Turgesius accepts Moran's help, while telling his officers to make sure the traitors are killed as soon as the Danes control the walls of Tamor because "he who betrays one master will another,/Whene'er the lure of self-advantage prompts him" (*Works*, 1, 184). Rebellion replaces lawfully constituted authority with tyranny.

Even the virtuous Niall's father was a traitor, and Malsechlin doubts Niall as a consequence:

> How! shall the offspring of his faithless sire
> By whose unnatural aid, the savage Dane
> Hath pour'd upon this heav'n-forsaken isle
> The flood of war in boundless desolation,
> Be friend to us, his country, or to freedom?
>
> (*Works*, 1, 204)

The problem of Ireland is encapsulated in fear of potential allies because of the behavior of "faithless" sires. The burden of history limits the capacity of Ireland to unite in the face of destruction. In disguise, Niall has saved both Malsechlin and his daughter, Eernestha, from the rapacious Danes. He cannot, however, avow his own name, for as Malsechlin's adviser, Donnal, informs him, "The king as yet regards you as his foe" (*Works*, 1, 205).

Malsechlin is the wise ruler who can separate personal animosities and, indeed, private obligations from kingly duty. O'Conor describes him as the epitome of administrative virtue:

> Malachy, as Prince of *Meath*, rescued his Country from Thraldom: as King of *Ireland*, he distinguished himself by the Equity of his Administration, by his Skill in War, and by his Moderation after Victory. He distinguished himself still more, by the most heroic of all Virtues, that passive courage under great Distresses, which provided equally for personal, as well as national Security; so far as it was possible to obtain either.[28]

Soldier and administrator, Malsechlin rules in adversity to achieve victory over both foreign and domestic enemies. To a Castle supporter, this could well have been seen as the situation of a viceroy in the 1770s. Patriot opposition and public revolt in the American colonies combined to threaten Irish stability. Even if Howard had enemies in Townshend's administration, his political ties were still to the government. Moreover, support for the English administration was not limited to government placeholders and could be found among the indigenous population, with whom Howard sympathized. The Catholics of Ireland knew they were more likely to receive lenience from the Crown and its Dublin administration than they were from the Irish Parliament. As John Curry puts it, "As the case stands in Ireland, at present, with the Papists, who are loyal to their King, and from a sense of religious duty, would be so, even without experience of the royal mercy, to which alone, not the laws of their country, they owe their present quiet existence in these Islands."[29]

Howard was a major proponent of elimination of the penal laws, was recognized as such by Irish Catholics, and was proud of the engraved epergne with which they presented him: "This EPERGNE was presented to Gorges Edmond

Howard, Esq; by the Catholics of Ireland, for his Candour and Humanity, in endeavouring to obtain a Relaxation of the Popery Laws" (*Works*, 1, lii). C. D. A. Leighton argues that Howard's opposition indicates a lawyer's impatience with the penal laws as useless but not very important disabilities.[30] Certainly, however, Howard's rhetoric is much stronger than that. In *Observations and Queries on the Present Laws of this Kingdom Relative to Persons of the Popish Religion*, he declaims,

> These laws are, as they now stand, a reproach to a civilized nation, and an affront to christianity; as they are the cause of promoting idleness, poverty and wickedness, and the emigration of numbers of its inhabitants: That they are against common right, and, several of them totally opposite to the principles of a free constitution, wherefore, however fit they might have been when made, they ought now to be relaxed. (*Works*, 2, 294)

Condemning the penal laws as contrary to the constitution, civilization, and Christianity seems a fairly comprehensive charge. Moreover, Howard insists that the nation includes all its inhabitants, including Catholics, and that the emigration of Catholics is a blow to the national economy and pride.

One of Howard's arguments for relaxation of the penal laws is that the Catholics are no longer dangerous because the Stuarts have ceased to be a credible threat: "Is there not really and truly as much chance now, that the great Mogul shall ever gain the British throne, as one of that secluded family?" (*Works*, 2, 308). Howard's more central argument for Catholics involves an appeal to sympathy, compatible with his conception of how drama involves the audience (discussed in the introduction):

> But the true way of judging in every case in life is to change sides. Suppose then that a protestant was to be this instant removed with all his effects to a popish country, and that the laws were the same against protestants there, as they are against papists here, and the method of conforming the same; could any honest-hearted protestant repair to the place of public worship, and solemnly declare what I have before mentioned, and in the manner wherein these people here are required to declare? (*Works*, 2, 305)

Oaths of Catholic loyalty are not only contrary to Catholic religious obligations; they are a blow to the pride of gentleman. A member of the Protestant upper classes should understand how his social equal cannot humble himself in the manner the law prescribes. Howard's appeal fails, of course, but it also shows how his sympathy to the Catholics places him closer to Castle administrators than to the anti-Catholic patriots, and a sympathetic dramatic treatment of Irish history allies Howard with the native Irish.

Malsechlin, as leader, listens to his subjects but also must reject their advice, thus showing the necessity of administrative independence from popular tumult. The citizens of Dublin wish to speak to the king that they may urge him to surrender to the Danes:

Malsechlin	So let it be. The ears, the hearts of kings
	Be ever free and open to their people.
	The power heav'n gives us, is to guard their
	rights,
	Redress their wrongs, and make subjection happy.
Donnal	But, through impatient fears, should they demand
	Instant compliance with the proffer'd terms,
	(For such the rumor was, as I pass'd hither)
	Say, would, my liege, the city then surrender?
Malsechlin	Should it be aught that reason must not yield,
	And that our gentle counsel cannot sooth them,
	Then must stern fortitude oppose the torrent:
	The public trust, the public safety claims it.

(Works, 1, 188)

Popular opinion is no way to run a kingdom. Wiser than the mob, Malsechlin must act against the citizens' desires for their benefit. The subjection of the citizens ought to make them happy. In short, the role of king (or viceroy) is to reason gently with the deluded subjects but, when that fails, sternly to command. Malsechlin talks them into continued resistance with reference to their ancestors, and all resolve to fight the Dane: "Come, bloody Dane! come, learn our fix'd resolve;/Iërne scorns thy pow'r, and will be free" (*Works,* 1, 191). This, it seems to me, is a far cry from patriot nationalism. The citizens, prompted by wisdom, choose to defend their king in order to retain the status quo.

In contrast to patriot reformers (such as Dobbs), Howard is anxious to stress the opposition between private and public obligations that leadership requires. Turgesius makes the traditional demand for Malsechlin's daughter, which almost drives the king mad. All Malsechlin can do, however, is give his daughter a dagger to take her own life at the last resort. The king's sacrifice inspires wonder:

Donnal	Why then comply? why yield to the fell terms
	Of this insulting Dane? not heav'n itself
	More trial claims, than mortals can endure.
	A father! —
Siorna	True—but of his people first.
	Such his exalted sentiment of soul,
	And such the patriot flame that conquers nature,
	And mortals make immortal.

(Works, 1, 218)

Here we have the seventeenth-century sense of patriot as a father of his country. Under such circumstances, only the king can be the true patriot. Patriot flames have been borrowed to illuminate administration souls. The studied invocation of pathos characteristic of eighteenth-century tragedy and present in this passage has, with surprising deftness, been used to portray sympathetically an ultimately victorious king:

2d Bard   Hear the royal father sue,
                Father of his people too!
                Lo! his great, his patriot soul
                Offers one to save the whole.
                See his tears! O! hear his sighs!
                His only child's the sacrifice.

                                        (*Works*, 1, 227)

It is lonely at the top but surely some consolation to have Irish bards sing of you.

As in the traditional story, Irish men disguised as maidens eliminate the Danes. Here it is Niall who achieves the victory and is rewarded with Eernestha and the kingship, thus representing an Ireland united by shared hardship, victory, and marriage between the north and the high king. (I will discuss in the epilogue Howard's alternate ending of eight years later.) In disguise, Niall pledges to fight for Malsechlin and Ireland:

                My sword, my life,
        I hold devoted to my country's service;
        For her I conquer, or for her I fall.
        Beneath Ïërne's banners here I stand
        Her listed champion.—Here, in her defence,
        Will shed each drop of blood that warms my heart,
        And in the agonies of death lament,
        I had no more to lose in such a cause.
                                        (*Works*, 1, 205)

The last line's echo of Addison's *Cato* no longer carries the signification of patriot opposition (after all, when the Whigs took power, Addison became an important Whig statesman). Niall redeems the betrayals of his treacherous father, earns his reward as Malsechlin's savior, and creates a united Ireland with the antebellum hierarchy restored.

Nevertheless, Howard's choice of Irish history to defend the Castle resonated with patriot audiences. Henry Brooke wrote an epilogue for the play:

        A country by a single wench retriev'd!
        Her country! yes, her country—we are told,
        A country was a precious thing of old;
        Though now—
        Of no use in the world—but to be sold.
                                        (*Works*, 1, 170)

Though Brooke's patriot spin reinterprets Howard's condemnation of place seekers, Brooke is in agreement with the efficacy of applying native Irish history to contemporary Irish problems. Eernestha, Malsechlin, and Niall are all Brooke's and Howard's countrymen.

Charles Macklin, whose political sympathies were also with the patriots, wrote to Howard in February 1773 praising *The Siege of Tamor:* "Upon the whole, Sir, you have not only left your Contemporaries behind in the tragic course, but I really think you have surpassed yourself in *The Siege of Tamor.*" Macklin recognizes the political difficulties from which Howard constructs the plot:

> In the choice of your subject, you are, in my opinion, peculiarly happy; for sure, amongst the infinity of vicissitudes that prove man's constancy, the Patriot and the Father, the dearest relations in life (you may except the Lover if you will) could not have fallen into a greater dilemma, than that of being obliged to surrender his religion, his country, and its liberties, to the cruelty of a Tyrant.[31]

The dilemma makes an impact on Macklin perhaps because he too had sacrificed his religion, country, and language for success. He reaffirms, however, the necessity of liberty from tyrants; the only ones available for that role, from the view of an Irish Protestant like Macklin, were corrupt government ministers. Castle supporter or patriot opponent, Dublin alderman or gentlemanly author (Brooke), all could participate in Irish nationalism.

II

Francis Dobbs represents the mixing of Irish and English heritage, as well as the synthesis of Enlightenment and millenarian tendencies. *The Patriot King; or Irish Chief* (the 1774 version) dramatizes an Irish victory over the Danes as a vehicle for promoting national unity and the application of private moral standards to public issues. All the characters feel moral sentiments, most are directed by them, and the ones who are not feel suitably guilty for their failings and suffer the consequences of poetic justice. In the epilogue I will discuss the 1788 version of *The Patriot King*, in which Dobbs's idealism is tempered with tragic overtones. However, the 1774 version ends in triumphant Irish victory.

Francis Dobbs had as much right as any to claim membership in a new Ireland of mingled blood and heritage: "His ancestor came from England in the reign of Queen Elizabeth, an officer in the army, and by a marriage with the great grand daughter of, Hugh, Earl of Tyrone, he got the estate of *Castle Dobbs*, with other estates in the Country of Antrim." Dobbs's great-grandfather "was mayor of Carrickfergus at the time King William landed, and was the first subject in Ireland who paid his allegiance." The family continued to be of some importance, as Francis's uncle, Arthur Dobbs, was governor of North Carolina.[32] From this genealogy Dobbs could claim descent from the ancient kings of Ireland, and the defenders of the Protestant religion, as well as kinship with the restive colonies challenging England's imperial power.

One of the early founders of the Volunteers, Dobbs, who had previously been an ensign and lieutenant in the Sixty-third Regiment of the English army, was lieutenant to the Second Belfast Company, captain of the Acton Company in Armagh, and major of the Armagh battalions. He was also in favor of a standing army made up exclusively of Irishmen, "born amongst you, and attached by the love implanted in us of our native soil, connected by every tie of marriage, children, friendship and of property, and then doubt if you can, which army it is, that is to assist Irish freedom."[33] The term *freedom* recurs throughout Dobbs's work, as he was an avowed nationalist. In a speech to the Irish Parliament attacking the Act of Union in 1800, he says, "I tell the Noble Lord, I tell you Sir, and this House—and I proclaim it to the British and Irish nations, that the Independence of Ireland is written in the immutable records of Heaven."[34]

Patriot nationalism, while assuredly intending benefit to the commonwealth, had a specific political agenda for Dobbs. In the latter part of the 1760s, Sir William Blackstone's *Commentaries* repeated the old argument that the English Parliament's authority over Ireland was absolute because of the right of conquest.[35] Dobbs repeatedly denied this premise. In his open letter to Lord North he warned the British to treat Ireland as a sister-kingdom:

> If we are deemed a conquered nation, and as such to hold every thing we possess at the will of the English, our conquerors; if we are in all things subject to their caprice; still, my Lord, there is one right I almost blush to mention; it is the right of vanquished; the right of regaining our Freedom, whenever we are able to throw off your yoke.[36]

Blush does not seem quite adequate to the occasion. An argument that if England's right to govern Ireland is founded in force, then that right ceases as soon as the Irish have the force to repel the English, might, to some, have sounded treasonable. Elsewhere Dobbs argues Irish independence on the same Enlightenment grounds of inalienable rights that form the preamble of the Declaration of Independence: "Whether we were, or were not, a conquered nation, is, in my opinion, no way material: We were men, and as such had a right to be free."[37] General rights lead to a specific conclusion in the Irish context.

Like Howard, Dobbs was in favor of eliminating the penal laws: "That the Penal Laws of this country are too bloody,—and punishments and offences, in no wise proportioned, is self-evident.—The best writers on the subject agree, that severe laws will ever defeat their own purpose" (*Principles*, 25). As a general program of reform, Dobbs proposed triennial parliaments, and a payment of a hearth tax on two or more hearths as the only requirement for voting in Ireland:

> As I can conceive Ireland can never be either a great or happy country, till her inhabitants are united by mutual and common interest; I give to every denomination who pay hearth-money, the right of voting for members of parliament: the

> very lowest orders of Roman Catholics may still retain prejudices against protes-
> tants, but I am satisfied among her higher orders, no such prejudice now exists. . . .
> In every thing but sitting in the House of Commons, Protestants and Roman
> Catholics are put on an exact footing; and I am persuaded every liberal Protestant
> will approve of it; and as to the illiberal, I neither write nor act to please them.
> (*Principles,* 3)

Prejudice exists among both Protestants and Catholics and must be overcome
in each, but, fortunately, the illiberal do not represent important parts of
the population. A united Ireland must contain both groups, and a recognition
of common interests—even if Catholics are *still* not allowed a position in Parliament.

Dobbs had a series of proposals (along with an Irish standing army) to increase acceptance of common interests, including government support for the
clergy of all denominations who were willing to agree on the divine inspiration of the Ten Commandments, the Lord's Prayer, and the Sermon on the
Mount (*Principles,* 58–63). Furthermore, he advocated that Trinity and all public schools be open to students of every religious denomination (*Principles,* 64);
Dobbs appears not to have considered the question of whether Catholic bishops
would have been in favor of this provision. Probably few were willing to go as
far as Dobbs, and most desired a much more moderate program of continued
alliance with Great Britain with moderate reform in Irish society.[38] The radical
nature of Dobbs's program, however, shows the synthesis of various forces in
his character and environment: personal idealism, Enlightenment conceptions
of government, and millenarian tendencies.

Dobbs's idealism is apparent in his treatment of marriage. In his poem
"Modern Matrimony" he attacks marriages of economic convenience:

> Oh! what I feel to see thy rites betrayed:
> Thy joys all barter'd for a mammon trade,
> That gives to age, the blooming virgin's charms—
> The pride of youth to antient maidens arms.[39]

The egalitarian impulse here (it is equally immoral for a young man to marry
an old woman as for a young woman to marry an old man) carries over into
The Patriot King. Sitric proposes to trap Ceallachan by offering his sister, Stira,
in marriage and killing Ceallachan when he arrives. Ceallachan, having fallen
in love with Stira at first sight, remains commendably concerned that she
not marry him out of political necessity. Ceallachan sends his friend Duncan
ahead to Sitric's court to allow Stira a chance to back out, and Duncan recounts
Ceallachan's charge:

Duncan   But, Oh! my Duncan, tell the beauteous maid,
                    If in her breast a dearer object lives,
                    Or should a brother's will her hand direct
                    Where inclination does not prompt its course—

Oh! tell her, I resign these promised rites,
And singly wretched to my throne return.
Stira   Go tell the gen'rous prince from whom you came,
(For Stira's soul disdains her sex's arts)
That every future bliss on him depends—[40]

Dobbs's unfortunate tendency to indicate emotional tumult with "Oh!" conceals the radical linkage of private and public morality. Where Malsechlin sees a conflict between his roles as father and as king, Ceallachan subordinates political obligation to private virtue. Because Ceallachan loves Stira he will not marry her without assurance that she loves him; the political alliance between Sitric and Ceallachan that the marriage would secure is a secondary consideration. In a sense the triumph here of romantic love represents a triumph of bourgeois sensibility. The companionate marriage should be based on mutual affection, even if the couple is made up of a king and the daughter of a king.

The Danes are aware of how they ought to feel about love. Pharon, one of Sitric's generals, also loves Stira and hopes to achieve her, first contemplating kidnapping Stira, and then aiding in the capture of Ceallachan. The noble Cleones, Pharon's closest friend, chastises him for his lubricious ambition:

Think'st thou Love's holy raptures can be thine?
When, not the soft murmurs of the yielding maid,
Nor yet the sweet resistance beauty gives,
But tears and harsh complaints assail thine ears,
Pierce thro' thy heart, and load thee with remorse:
Then Pharon wilt thou curse this hateful day,
And damn that hour which gave thee being.

(18)

This works. Pharon, basically good natured, is recalled to virtue, although eventually killed in battle. There is a common moral sense that tells characters when they are behaving badly. Ambition and the desire for revenge can frustrate the moral sense, but they cannot eradicate it. Even Sitric is gnawed by doubt temporarily, as he reflects not only on what the world will say, but on an internal arbiter: "Now conscience too uplifts her awful head,/And in the midst of all my triumphs/Stings my bosom with remorse" (37). Unlike the characters in Howard's play, Dobbs's characters are drawn naturally to virtue. It follows then that no deference to the status quo is necessary, and, indeed, vice may be a function of the existing, corrupt social order, rather than inevitable in self-interested nature.

Cleones opposes to social degradation a pastoral ideal:

Oh! Pharon, what a foe to man is man?
When, from the peaceful shade of rural life,
They crowd together, corruption flows apace;

> Unheard of crimes arise to curse the world,
> And punish men, for violated laws.
>
> (47)

There is a political element to this claim about the origins of evil. Agrarian democracy is preferable to a centralized administration, because wherever urban concentration occurs, "corruption" (with its clear political overtones) arises. The crimes that punish the world are a consequence of transgression against laws, whether natural or divine, that are antecedent to human society. Even Ceallachan would prefer a sylvan nuclear family with Stira to his kingship:

> Had Fortune plac'd me in an humbler sphere,
> How eagerly I'd seek some rural spot,
> Far from the noise and bustle of the world,
> By woods emburied, and by rocks begirt:
> There would I taste true happiness with thee.
>
> (54)

Not wanting the job partially signifies Ceallachan's worthiness, and his decided preference for the countryside suggests that virtue is more easily achieved away from society.

Hierarchy is a function of the world, not nature. Cleones assures Pharon that even if Ceallachan were not his rival, Sitric would not match his sister to less than a king:

Pharon	Where is the mighty merit to descend
	From kings, who trace their boasted ancestry
	Even from the fabled Deities of Heav'n?
	Flows there a richer current thro' the veins?
	Pants in the breast a more exalted worth?
	Doth clay ennobled, purify the soul,
	Or give a virtue humble birth denies?—
Cleones	No, Pharon; but the world is here the judge;
	We may condemn, not alter its decree.

> (17)

Error and hubris are social constructs. Pharon's enlightened attitude toward rank as inferior to virtue contrasts with the false, yet potent, judgments of the world. Beda, Sitric's wife, who also loves Ceallachan, was ensnared by worldly glory when she married Sitric:

> Ah, why!
> Allur'd by title and the farce of state,
> Will woman throw her happiness away?
> I knew this Sitric well, nay, loath'd him;
> Yet caught by grandeur, gave my plighted faith.
>
> (23)

Private judgment (and attraction) ought to rule behavior. Prudence may require acknowledgment of public evaluations of actions, but the individual errs when he or she chooses what society values over individual desires. Pharon is the victim of a corrupt social order in that even if Stira returned his affection, she would be unachievable, while Beda has victimized herself by accepting social rank at society's valuation. Cleones sums up the deleterious influence of society on the moral sensibility: "Each finer feeling is by custom drown'd;/We catch the reigning manners of the age,/And lose abhorrence for the worst of crimes" (51). This attitude toward custom is profoundly radical. If human nature is naturally virtuous, and social custom the source of evil, society must be changed at its foundations to allow the flowering of innate goodness.

Dobbs's play also attacks the notion that affairs of state justify what would be crimes in an individual. Pharon tells Cleones of the plot against Ceallachan and invokes moral relativism: "When policy requires a hidden act,/The very colour of the deed is chang'd" (48). Cleones retorts that crime remains crime under any circumstances:

> Oh, Heav'n! where will mankind's presumption end?
> When thus they dare to alter thy decrees,
> To change those laws their great Creator fram'd,
> And give to villainy the praise of virtue.
> If the assassin, for the price of blood,
> Stab in the dark, and give the hired blow;
> If from revenge the poniard be unsheath'd,
> And buried in the heart for which 'tis drawn;
> You call it murder; and as such you punish.
> But when the statesman acts beneath the mask
> Of seeming peace, and fictitious treaty,
> 'Till he with safety can destroy a foe;
> Both wealth and honours crown the very act
> For which a less exalted villain bleeds!
>
> (49)

Dobbs's characteristic "Oh" shows the close relation between passion and moral judgment; the virtuous Cleones feels vice as much as recognizes it. The text for Cleones' sermon is murder, but the lesson is equally applicable to political corruption. An individual who performs an act that would be wrong in a private capacity is equally culpable in a public one. Sitric, a politician, will use murder and his sister to conquer Ireland. Ceallachan preserves Ireland while suitably valuing love and conscience.

Ceallachan embodies the patriot king who practices private virtues for the public good. Bolingbroke's *Idea of a Patriot King* (1738) in places sounds like a traditional formulation of family as microcosm and kingdom as macrocosm: "The true image of a free people, governed by a Patriot King, is that of a patriarchal family, where the head and all the members are united by one common interest and animated by one common spirit." Despite this, Bolingbroke, writing in opposition to Walpole and in hopes that Prince Frederick will throw the Whigs out, intends a kingdom ruled as an egalitarian family, where pre-eminence is a function not just of heredity, but of virtue:

> What spectacle can be presented to the view of the mind so rare, so nearly divine, as a king possessed of absolute power, neither usurped by fraud, nor maintained by force, but the genuine effect of esteem, of confidence, and affection; the free gift of liberty, who finds her greatest security in this power, and would desire no other if the prince on the throne could be, what his people wish him to be, immortal.[41]

Bolingbroke emphasizes affection over authority, and the subjects' liberty over their duty. The patriot king is loved as a father, not obeyed as a disciplinarian.

Sitric is the king as a politician. Beda, in love with Ceallachan and unaware of Sitric's plan, seeks to dissuade him from allowing the marriage to Stira:

Beda	Trust not, my Lord, to such uncertain hopes,
	Nor think to lead the mean, ignoble crowd,
	By Reason's force. In vain doth wisdom try
	To calm their passions, and their wrath restrain:
	When thoughtless fury spurs, away they run,
	And ev'ry step leaves judgment more behind.
Sitric	Fear not the prudent conduct of thy Lord;
	Well skill'd, I hold the reins of sov'reign pow'r,
	Know when to treat men with an easy hand,
	And how to curb them in their mad career.

(21)

Beda's contempt for the people is matched by Sitric's conception of rule. He is a charioteer driving a balky team. Moreover, Sitric rules by policy, concealing executive decisions even from his wife.

Duncan praises Ceallachan's magnanimity: "E'en Nature form'd thee for a king, and gave/A soul exalted as the rank you bear" (31). Selflessness, Duncan says, is Ceallachan's most kingly virtue: "Munster, what happy days for thee's in store;/Whose monarch thus, in all his schemes, pursues,/His country's welfare and his people's good!" (31). Ceallachan's concern that Stira not be made a pawn of policy is of a piece with his concern for his subjects. In both cases, self-interest is subordinate to sympathy. The king is an affectionate father looking after a family.

When Sitric captures Ceallachan, he demands the surrender of Munster, promising in return that he will even consider letting Ceallachan marry Stira. The alternative of torture and death is scornfully treated by Ceallachan:

> —Think'st thou my soul
> So little knows the firmness of a man,

That poorly frighted by the trick of woe,
Shock'd by a mere parade, I could resign,
A loyal nation to tyrannic sway?
Had you e'er felt the flame of patriot fire,
Whose purifying blaze ennobles man,
And banishes each base, each selfish thought,
Far from the breast wherein it deigns to dwell,
You then would know a monarch's fix'd resolve;
Would know, I court the terrors you display,
And for my country's welfare, long to die!

(41)

Self-abnegation can go no further. Ireland deserves preservation because of loyalty not possession; ultimately, an emotive virtue ("the breast") banishes "selfish thought," the only kind Sitric seems to possess. The prudent calculations of placeholders and pensioners are banished from the temple of patriotism. Even Stira must be refused when she begs Ceallachan to yield: "Would she embrace the king, whose selfish soul/Could meanly practice on a people's love?/Could thus assassinate the public weal!" (55). The most private of relations must reflect public obligations, or rather, a selfish king cannot possibly be a good lover and husband.

A happy ending is achieved. The valiant Fingal (a character whom the audience never meets) kills Sitric by seizing him and leaping with him over a cliff, and another chief serves out Pharon the same way. Beda substitutes a sleeping potion for the poison Stira attempts to drink, and then devotes herself to good works. Most importantly, Cleones, ordered to execute Ceallachan in prison, refuses to "execute a tyrant's fell command" (69) and frees Ceallachan, who makes Cleones the lord of the Danes after the victory. Cleones too deserves approbation, since he attempts to atone for his act of treason by dying in battle against the Irish, although the generous Irish decline to kill him. The plays ends with Ceallachan reciting sentenciously, "Success indeed our admiration draws;/But 'tis Humanity deserves applause" (77). Central to this happy ending is an optimistic conception of national enmity. Irish and Danes are both natively virtuous, and, consequently, peace can be made between them. The marriage of Ceallachan and Stira creates a new Irish race of mixed blood. Their new Ireland parallels Dobbs's idealist vision of a united Ireland in the 1770s, where Catholics and Protestants, Gael and Saxon, would share Irish identity in an independent kingdom.

Howard and Dobbs differ in allegiance, attitude toward the role of a ruler, and conception of human nature. This is not just a matter of party. Howard was an elderly administrator when he wrote *The Siege of Tamor,* and Dobbs was a passionate young radical when he wrote *The Patriot King.* The aphorism sometimes ascribed to Winston Churchill defines the inevitable political disagreements of youth and age: he who is not a socialist at twenty has no heart; he who is not a conservative at forty has no head. Howard is an elderly conservative and Dobbs a young radical. Yet despite their enormous philosophical differences, Howard and Dobbs share a self-identification as Irishmen. That identification determines their use of Irish history for differing purposes. Together they participate in an emergent mythos of a potentially united Ireland where Protestants of English descent claim Irish history as their own.

Epilogue

In 1784 Robert Owenson, an Irishman of Gaelic descent (originally he was named MacOwen), took over Fishamble-street Theater, with the avowed purpose of creating a national theater.[1] His daughter, Lady Sydney Morgan, recalled the event:

> The first performance was to be altogether national, that is Irish, and *very* Irish it was. The play chosen was *The Carmelite,* by Captain Jephson, with an interlude from Macklin's farce of *The Brave Irishman,* and a farce of O'Keefe's *The Poor Soldier.* The overture consisted of Irish airs ending with the Volunteer's March, which was chorused by the gallery to the accompaniment of drums and fifes. . . . My father wrote and spoke the prologue in his own character of an "Irish Volunteer."[2]

The venture came to nothing, as long-term efforts to limit dramatic performances in Dublin to theaters holding a patent finally succeeded in 1786. Still, the identification of "Irishness" had become broadly inclusive, stretching to Protestant convert of Gaelic descent and Catholic Gaelic. The Irish nation was no longer limited to the voting ascendancy. In short, there was in place the opportunity for an Irish theater—an opportunity that rapidly faded, so that, while some avowedly "Irish" drama continued to be written and produced in Dublin, Dion Boucicault would end up writing his plays on Irish subjects in the mid-nineteenth century for London and New York audiences. Even Owenson's daughter, Lady Sydney Morgan, would achieve her literary reputation through novels and biography.

Strikingly, Morgan misidentifies Richard Cumberland's *The Carmelite* as by Robert Jephson, the Irish M.P., in her recollection about the Irish theater, an error that partially delineates the problem of why Irish drama never developed. London of course never lost its attraction for young playwrights. Robert Jephson, as a friend of David Garrick, could get his plays produced there, and he therefore had no need to write on Irish subjects, which, excluding stage Irishmen, had limited appeal for an English audience. Jephson's tragedies are most notable for dramatic engagement with the rising genre of the gothic.[3] The Englishman Richard Cumberland (Ulster secretary under Lord Halifax) was rather more associated with Irish characters than Jephson, as his comedy *The West Indian* (1771) features a sympathetic Irishman, Major O'Flaherty. (The misidentification of *The Brave Irishman* with *Love à la Mode* is not significant, as the plays are very similar in content and humor.)

The ground for Irish dramatic production had never been particularly fertile. While, I have argued, there was always some incipient nationalism in Irish drama and politics from the 1720s, the widespread indifference to the creation of a new Irish culture cannot be denied. An English immigrant, Thomas Marryat puzzled over the widespread emigration from Ireland:

> The Laplander and Hottentot,
> The Welch, the Swiss, nay ev'n the Scot,
> Find in their hearts sensations move
> Of their respective country's love
>   Feel not the Irish such emotion
> Tow'rd the best island in the ocean.[4]

However savage or uncouth, natives typically feel a love of country. The Irish are alone in preferring less favored climates to the "indulgent nature" of Ireland.

In 1763 the English historian Ferdinando Warner also comments on the indifference of the Anglo-Irish to their own country:

> The people of English extraction, though their ancestors have been in possession of it [Ireland] almost six hundred years, yet, by a strange kind of reasoning, don't look upon Ireland as their country; and therefore pay no more regard to its antiquities, than they do those of China or Japan.[5]

Despite the diplomatic phrasing, there is no doubt in the passage that Warner regards the Anglo-Irish as not English, whatever they may think. By 1768, Warner has ceased to be diplomatic. Warner believed that he had been promised parliamentary support for a two-volume history of Ireland. After he published the first volume, the subsidy was not forthcoming, and the second volume was never written:

> Though this application had the favor and concurrence of the Lord Lieutenant, and it was referred to the consideration of a Committee, yet no report was made and it went no further. . . . It shall suffice only to say, that if the General History of the laws and constitution, of the commerce and civil affairs of any Country, is not a work of a Publick Nature, it will be difficult to find what is so; and all other states have been in great error.[6]

Warner is quite confident that he knows what Ireland is; it is a "Country" among other "states." Unfortunately, Ireland happens to be an unusually benighted country, without the recognition of what states need, a knowledge of their own history for the sake of the public good.

Specific circumstances combined with indifference to Irish culture to chill any Irish theatrical endeavor. The patent act of 1786 probably had some adverse impact on Irish drama. From 1660 on, both in England and in Ireland, there had been various controversies over patents, most importantly in the Licensing Act of 1737, which limited the risks theater managers were prepared to run and tamed political satire on the English stage. Moreover, Henry Brooke's *Jack the Giant Quellar* was suppressed in Dublin after one performance in 1749 by the lord justices because "satirical hints were thrown out against bad governors, lord mayors, and alderman."[7] Nervous playwrights and theater managers had good reason to fear closure of controversial plays. As we have seen, however, Macklin was still able to write political satire and on Irish subjects. Moreover, the other Irish playwrights I have examined were more inclined to comedy free of personal reflections and historical subjects, and these should not have been eliminated by the restriction of patents.

The Act of Union certainly played a role as it reduced Dublin from a parliamentary center to a provincial administrative post. The gradual loss of peers from the city had widespread effects,[8] and its consequences for the theater, while impossible to measure, could not have been good. The theatrical tradition in Ireland, as in England, was a commercial one; playwrights who could not find an audience needed to find another line of work. Patronage, however, has always played a role in dramatic production. Aside from occasional gifts for clothes and scenery to mount a new production, the presents given to authors for a dedication were a not unimportant part of the return a playwright could expect on a play. In the absence of an aristocracy, that potential remuneration for a play celebrating the Irish peerage disappears. It has always been easier to revive an old play than to mount a new one. Patrons made it possible for writers and managers to gamble on original work.

John O'Keeffe represents the exception to the claim that Irish drama, never very vital, dies out and, at the same time, represents one of the reasons why a national theater did not develop. O'Keeffe wrote for the London and Dublin stages sympathetic plays about Irish life that admonish an irresponsible gentry. Jonah Barrington, who must have been in complete agreement about the problems of absentee landlords, remembered him as "justly the delight of Dublin."[9] O'Keeffe's most important patron, however, was George IV, and his loyalty to the Crown was never in doubt throughout his career. He wrote that "affection to their monarch was, is, and ever will be native Irish."[10] There is no irony in the closing speech of *Patrick in Prussia*, when Patrick leaves the service of the king of Prussia for "the service of our gracious sovereign, whose life is a blessing to his people,"[11] and this despite the fact that Patrick presumably serves in Prussia because he is more welcome there than in the British army.

O'Keeffe fundamentally has little sympathy with the aristocracy and gentry of Protestant Ireland. His memoirs recall a melancholy trip taken with his parents when a boy:

He and my mother and I went to Knock-drin, near Edenderry, where my father with pride, not unmixed with dejection, led me over tracts of fine lands, once the property of his ancestors: my mother had much the same remark to make of her family losses in the county of Wexford. (*Recollections*, 1, 8)

As a Catholic, O'Keeffe must have been aware that the Irish of his religion could expect more relief from England than from the ascendancy, at least up until 1795.[12] And O'Keeffe is conservative as a matter of temperament. Even in painting, O'Keeffe draws a political application from the principle of teaching painting by "rule" as he was taught: "Genius may step over wall, and scale window, but RULE, established by success is the surest and safest portal. . . . France once tried the slap-dash, short-cut, of doing without rule or order, and what was the result?" (*Recollections*, 1, 124). A rejection of Romanticism and the French Revolution, with its enmity to the Catholic Church, places O'Keeffe at odds with those forces most in favor of Irish nationalism.

Where a conservative Catholic like O'Keeffe preferred monarchy to revolution, elements of the United Irishmen had no interest whatsoever in preserving Gaelic culture. Nancy J. Curtin argues that the United Irishmen, unlike English and Scottish radicals, were antihistorical:

Applauding the intellectual achievements of the Scottish nation, the Dublin United Irishmen suggested that the genius which had been applied to the writing of history should now be engaged in the making of it. The United Irishmen thus eschewed arguments from history as compelling reasons for the introduction of radical reform in Ireland. Rather than calling for a return to an idealized golden age of Irish liberty, Irish radicals drew inspiration from innovative concepts of reform, based on reason and justice rather than tradition.[13]

The United Irishmen were willing to use popular drama and music to advance political goals.[14] They were not, however, interested in historical justifications for Enlightenment political theories—indeed, that would represent a contradiction in terms, as the political reforms espoused by French and Irish radicals were supposed to be demonstrable to the reasonable and unprejudiced observer. Far from appealing to a golden age of liberty, the radical goal was to sweep away the superstition that accorded veneration to corrupt social institutions merely because of their antiquity.

This attitude toward history does not affect comedy, because comedy typically concerns itself with contemporary society. But the materials for eighteenth-century tragedy were usually historical. The United Irishmen's lack of interest in Irish historical topics may well have discouraged talented Irish men and women from writing serious drama. And it was simply a bad time for serious drama in the English language. The Romantic emphasis on the individual makes it difficult to write drama in any case, as drama is about people in conflict with others, not themselves. The Germans were able to write great drama, because classical literature still served as a counterbalance to Romantic impulses, but classical models had been a going concern on the English stage from the Restoration and had long since lost any artistic vitality.

If the United Irishmen were not terribly interested in history, others regarded it with active trepidation. John Fitzgibbon, earl of Clare, used history to remind his fellow members of the ascendancy of the threat Catholic emancipation represented to their vested interests: "The ancient nobility and gentry of this Kingdom have been hardly treated: that Act by which most of us hold our estates was an Act of violence."[15] If the United Irishmen rejected history because it offered no solution to contemporary problems, Fitzgibbon reminds others that it did hold the roots of contemporary difficulties. From that perspective history becomes a divisive force, not the unifying narrative that Howard and Dobbs attempted to make of it. In either case, history is barred as a dramatic subject.

Yet perhaps the chief difficulty for the development of an Irish national drama at the end of the eighteenth century was the failure of Grattan's Parliament to achieve either the incorporation of Catholics into the body politic, or even the more modest goals of true parliamentary independence. According to James Kelly, "Britain remained in control of the destiny of the kingdom of Ireland, and as determined as ever to perpetuate this condition."[16] Consequently, a political playwright like Mary O'Brien in 1790 is still fighting the battles of the 1770s over government corruption and free trade. *The Fallen Patriot* targets Sir Richard Greyley for having sold his conscience to the Castle in order to become a baronet. Greyley is contrasted with his nephew, Freeport, who enters wearing the uniform of a Volunteer.

The funniest scene of the play, however, raises troubling issues. Lady Greyley rather likes the title, but changes the name:

Lady Greyley	Very well, Sir Richard O'Greyley.
Sir Richard	Hey, day! What now?—Sir Richard O'Greyley—Who the devil is he?
Lady Greyley	You, my dear—what! won't you put an O to your title and be a Milesian? Who can dispute it, now that you are a Baronet? Besides, there's the O'Callaghan's—the O'Donovan's, all put O's to their names, that I am sure have no more right than we have.[17]

Lady Greyley wants two honorifics: the English title and the *O* of ancient Irish aristocracy. Political bribery and false pretensions of descent are thus equated. To be Irish has become fashionable, and the referentiality of names obscured by widespread social decay and political malfeasance. A baronetcy was a hereditary knighthood. The Irish kings were supposed to protect their people. Greyley can have only the names, not what they represent.

A real Milesian could not be bought, and what little honor Greyley has left resists the attempts to dress him in false glories:

Lady Greyley	Lord, Sir Richard, you are so nice; why it's all the ton in this country—there are the Keelys, that never had an O in their generation, yet many of them now stile themselves O'Keelys.
Sir Richard	Very likely, Lady Greyley; and if, through your fashionable ton, you should think proper to decorate my head with *the additions of horns,* I will never consent to asses ears.—No— no—woman, I will have no O's of admiration before my name, to lead me like the forehorse in a cart; and whenever I chanc'd to trip, exposing me to ridicule. (9)

The disruption of primogeniture is beyond Sir Richard's control, but he will not claim Irish descent for himself. Legitimacy is threatened in family life by the degeneration of social and political life, while Irishness appears to represent a kind of purity. In a sense, the implication is that any honest patriot counts as Irish. Freeport's Irishness, for instance, is never in doubt, despite his obviously Protestant identity.

The problem is that national identity is contingent only upon political authority; Irish identity is reduced to whether one supports parliamentary independence and reform (Freeport), as opposed to Sir Richard's support for the British administration. Underlying issues of culture, religion, and class are ignored, just as the falsifications of Irish and English titles of honor are treated as equal and identical misuses of language. Grattan himself was for Catholic civil rights, but the ascendancy remained blind to the fundamental fault lines of their society. Roy Foster sums up the political glaucoma of the ascendancy: "'Patriot' nationalism remained exclusive: the rule of an enlightened elite, rather than the broadening of national interests that was so important to the self-image of the American revolutionaries."[18] Irish theater failed to develop during the period of Grattan's Parliament because no one, neither conservatives like Fitzgibbon, nor radicals like William Drennan, nor patriots like Mary O'Brien, could conceive of the problems of Irish society in broad enough terms; that is, as involving questions of culture, politics, and historical relations. The search for common ground comes to a close because most were not looking for it, and some, like the United Irishmen, suffered from the same inability as French "reformers" to see that a society constructed over centuries could not simply be leveled and restarted from scratch.

Howard and Dobbs both revised their plays in the 1780s. I discussed in the introduction the curious Irish tendency to avoid unhappy endings in their tragedies. Howard in 1782 offers an alternate ending to *The Siege of Tamor:*

> And after my tragedy of the SIEGE OF TAMOR had been printed for these works, upon well considering one of Mr. ADDISON's letters in the Spectators, on dramatic writing, I composed an alternative for the last scene of it, so as to make the catastrophe unhappy, which is inserted at the end of the third volume; so that, should it ever be thought worthy of representation, the *Theatric rulers* may choose

whichever of the conclusions they may conceive will better answer their purposes.[19]

The explicit justifications for the revision are aesthetic and pragmatic. In no. 40
of *The Spectator* Addison argues that the happy endings required by the doc-
trine of poetic justice make "small impression" on the audience because they
are counterproductive of the tragic emotions: "We find that Good and Evil
happen alike to all Men on this Side the Grave; and as the principal Design of
Tragedy is to raise Commiseration and Terror in the Minds of the Audience,
we shall defeat this great End, if we always make Virtue and Innocence happy
and successful."[20] Addison then suggests that most of the great classic, French,
and English dramas have ended in catastrophe. Howard is also being practical.
If theater managers would prefer an unhappy ending, and that will increase the
chances of production for his play, then Howard has provided one.

In the revision, Eernestha, instead of being rescued by Niall, is killed by
Turgesius:

Malsechlin	(*Starts.*) Alas! alas! she bleeds.
Eernestha	I do, apace, thank heav'n!—As the Dane sunk,
	All over gor'd with wounds, reeling he plung'd
	The poniard which he just had wrested from me,
	Your last best gift, deep into my bosom.
	All gracious pow'r, whose will doom'd these disasters,
	Save! save my sire!—and take! oh take my spirit!
	[*Dies.*

(*He moves apart, and after some pause raising his eyes to heaven*)

Malsechlin	No more—she's spotless—and my country's free'd.—
	Yet may one moment's loss reverse our triumph.
	For these fell ravagers, this night subdued,
	Let none, in justice to the world, escape.

(*Works,* 3, 355–56)

There are two crucial points here. The first is the consignment of the Danes to
slaughter. In the original version, Niall reports that two-thirds of the Danes
have been killed, but no energy is wasted on the remainder. In the 1782 version,
no mercy is possible; all the invaders must be dispatched. The original play did
not offer much hope for conciliation between native Irish and murderous foreigners, but the later version ends grimly with ethnic cleansing. No Danes will
be left around to intermingle with Irish society. Second, the marriage of Niall
and Eernestha in the original version was, I have argued, an emblem of Irish
unity; enemies come together in an alliance that assures the future tranquility
and independence of Ireland. With the death of Eernestha, the revised version ends with a childless Malsechlin and a bereft Niall. There is no woman

to exchange and create a kinship alliance. Thus both of Howard's significant changes reduce the chances of any kind of complex social union. Ireland at the end of the play is united under Malsechlin through victory, but there is no promise of marriage to ensure future concord between north and south, and the Danes are simply dead invaders.

The Dobbs revision is not so grim but still represents a movement toward greater pessimism. The version of *The Patriot King* in Dobbs's 1788 poetical works is problematic in terms of authorial revision, as it may represent an acting version. The play is 25 percent shorter, with most of the cuts from sententious moralizing, and consequently offers a swifter narrative line. Moreover, Ceallachan has been renamed Cealla "to make it easier to the pronunciation,"[21] a change that seems to make sense only for production. Nevertheless, there is no evidence that anyone else in 1788 would have been revising Dobbs's play, so the changes must be assumed to be authorial.

The most noticeable change involves Sitric's wife, named Beda in the 1774 version, and renamed Melissa in the 1788 text. In each version, the wife loves Cealla/Ceallachan, saves Stira from poisoning herself, and resolves to devote herself to good works. But Melissa has two extra scenes in the later version, despite the much shorter text as a whole. The reason for the change may be that Dobbs had read or reread Dermod O'Connor's translation of Geoffrey Keating, or some other history of Ireland in which Sitric's wife is Irish.[22] In O'Connor's translation, "It happen'd that *Sitric* the *Danish* General had married an *Irish* Lady, whose name was *Morling*," who "had entertain'd a very tender esteem for that Prince [Ceallachan], and was perfectly in Love with him from the Time she by chance saw him at *Waterford*." Morling even warns Ceallachan of Sitric's intended treachery, a scene that Dobbs adds to the play.[23]

Although the name *Melissa* has Greek roots, Dobbs may be attempting to anglicize *Morling,* and the name and warning scene may suggest that Melissa has become Irish in the later version. It is also possible that Dobbs was anglicizing the Irish name *Maoilíosa,* which sounds much like *Melissa.* While Maoilíosa is a male name, the terminal *a* may have confused Dobbs into thinking it was feminine. Alternately, if Dobbs knew some Irish, the name means "tonsured follower of Jesus"—i.e., a monk—and Melissa disguises herself twice in the play as a monk. If Dobbs does intend the character to be regarded as Irish, Melissa's unhappy marriage undercuts the possibility of a happy marriage between the Danes and the Irish, affirmed in both versions through the marriage of Ceallachan and Stira. On the other hand, Melissa never states her nation.

The other scene that Dobbs added occurs when Melissa confronts the captive Ceallachan in jail and offers to escape with him; he declines to commit adultery, and she rages at him about double standards:

> What then,
> Have I for thee, broke thro' all female ties—

For thee, disguis'd my sex, and in this garb,
Pronounc'd my shame; that thou should'st thus insult
   me!
Thus talk to me, of ties that bind thy sex—
When e'en the world, scarce censures man for what,
It ne'er forgives in ours—Then die, Cealla—
For as thou seek'st, I'll leave thee to thy fate.

                       (60)

Melissa's rage accords with Dobbs's idealism in that while Cealla must not commit sin, the worldly judgment that condemns unchastity in women and ignores it in men is at fault. Her desire for liberty from her unhappy marriage resonates with the laudable Irish desire for liberty from the Danes. The trouble is that some mistakes cannot be corrected. A faulty alliance leaves no room for recovery. The greater role for Melissa may suggest that the Irish alliance with England may be inescapable, not a happy union of equals, but a political prison from which there is no release.

Even Ceallachan has been darkened by self-doubt. In both plays, the Irish chief is tricked into coming to the Danish camp with insufficient forces. In the 1774 version, Ceallachan reproaches the Danes for their violation of honor. In the revision, Cealla reproaches himself: "Why did I leave my camp? Why thus confide,/Where confidence was folly? Too late I feel it,/And must bear my fortune" (39). In the earlier version, the blame attaches to the perfidious Danes precisely because they should know how to behave better. In the latter version, Cealla blames himself because he should have realized that the Danes, for the most part, are inherently untrustworthy. Human nature in the rapacious foreigners will probably lead to treachery on their part, a much more pessimistic view than Dobbs's play portrays in 1774, and perhaps a consequence of the darkening of patriot hopes after 1782 and the failure of the Irish Parliament to achieve most of the reforms Dobbs favored.

By the early 1780s, Dobbs became a millenarian predicting Armageddon in Armagh and the Second Coming in Ireland. Indeed, in the Irish Parliament his religious speeches were "by some Members treated with apparent levity."[24] In 1798, Dobbs mediated between imprisoned United Irishmen and Dublin Castle. Denis Carroll, Thomas Russell's biographer, in a section called "The mysterious Francis Dobbs," first misidentifies him as "a former governor of North Carolina," and then describes him as "at best, a meddlesome interferer or, at worst, a duplicitous agent of Dublin Castle."[25] Carroll does not attempt to explain why either the Castle or Russell would think mediation from the contemptible figure he describes would be useful. The situation of course was quite different from what Carroll supposes. From a good family, a founder of the Volunteers, a member of Parliament, devoutly religious (as was Russell), and a reformer who believed in peaceful resolution of sectarian conflicts, Dobbs was one of the few men in Ireland in 1798 who could speak to both sides, the revolutionaries and the government.

Dobbs succeeded in persuading Russell to agree to leave Ireland and thus gained Russell's freedom—an ultimately meaningless event, as Russell returned to participate in Emmet's rising and was executed. Ultimately Dobbs failed, as the Irish Protestant drama of the eighteenth century failed, because he sought a common ground between opposing forces that were not interested in conciliation or compromise, but only in victory and dominance. Dobbs could well be castigated as a trimmer, ignoring the necessity of resolution, or as a peacemaker with an insufficient sense of reality. Some kinds of condemnation should be regarded as more complimentary than praise.

The Protestant drama of the Restoration and eighteenth century in Ireland is not, by contemporary standards, aesthetically compelling, and only the comedies are still producible (virtually none of the serious drama in English of the period is still producible, whatever the country of origin). Still, the playwrights attempted to grapple with the political and cultural issues that affected Irish life in the seventeenth and eighteenth centuries. Their efforts to make sense out of the disparate elements in Irish society, and to create a theatrical community that appealed to as many members of that society as possible are worth trying to understand if only because that kind of endeavor is fundamentally heroic, even if the motive is to generate good box office receipts. Drama domesticates conflict and out of it brings harmony through dramatic structure. The harmony is temporary, lasting only so long as the play is allowed to run, and an angry audience can stop the show anytime it wants. Although the playwrights of Ireland in the Restoration and eighteenth century have not received the attention lavished (rightly) on Synge and O'Casey, they are part of the same tradition: writers who tried to depict a complex society and present it on stage. To some extent, I believe, they succeeded, and that makes them worth reading.

NOTES

INTRODUCTION

1. *Modern Irish Literature, Sources and Founders,* ed. Eilís Dillon (Oxford: Clarendon Press, 1994), p. 36.

2. "Literature in English, 1691–1800," in *A New History of Ireland,* ed. T. W. Moody and W. E. Vaughan, vol. 4 (Oxford: Clarendon Press, 1986), p. 428.

3. *A Short History of Anglo-Irish Literature from Its Origins to the Present Day* (Dublin: Wolfhound Press, 1982), p. 143.

4. *A Short History of Irish Literature* (London: Hutchinson & Co., 1986), p. 118.

5. "The Strange Death of the Irish Language, 1780–1800," in *Parliament, Politics and People: Essays in Eighteenth-Century Irish History,* ed. Gerard O'Brien (Blackrock, Co. Dublin: Irish Academic Press, 1989), p. 150.

6. For the period 1720–45, see John C. Greene and Gladys H. Clark, *The Dublin Stage 1720–1745* (Bethlehem, Pa.: Lehigh University Press, 1993), which provides as complete a stage calendar as fragmentary records allow. For the periods of 1745–54 and 1756–58, see Esther K. Sheldon, *Thomas Sheridan of Smock Alley* (Princeton: Princeton University Press, 1967). Professor Greene is currently working on a complete calendar of the Irish stage for the entire century.

7. *An Epistle to Henry Mossop, Esq. on the Institution and End of the Drama, and the Present State of the Irish Stage* (Dublin: printed for J. Milliken, n.d.), p. 21.

8. William Smith Clark, *The Early Irish Stage: The Beginnings to 1720* (Oxford: Clarendon Press, 1955), p. 38.

9. (Dublin: 1641), p. 66. All subsequent references are to this edition.

10. "To the Reader," *The Faithful Shepherdess,* in *The Dramatic Works in the Beaumont and Fletcher Canon,* vol. 3, gen. ed. Fredson Bowers (Cambridge: Cambridge University Press, 1976), p. 497.

11. For the conventions of English tragicomedy, see Eugene M. Waith, *The Pattern of Tragicomedy in Beaumont and Fletcher* (New Haven: Yale University Press, 1952), pp. 36–40.

12. For instance, it is quite clear to the twentieth century that Molière is a master of high comedy and Thomas Corneille is the author of amusing but inconsequential farces. That was by no means clear to English audiences of the seventeenth century, at least, as there are almost as many adaptations of Corneille as Molière on the Restoration stage.

13. "*Landgartha* and the Irish Dilemma," *Éire-Ireland* 13 (Spring 1978): 26–39.

14. Clark, Shaw, and Murray all refer to the character as "Marsisa," but despite the similarity between the character *f* and the elongated *s* in seventeenth-century typography, a closer look at the 1641 quarto shows that the disputed letter in this character's name in *Landgartha* is clearly an *f*.

15. Clark, *The Early Irish Stage,* p. 206.

16. This does not contradict what I argued about tragic death above. Cothurnus is not the protagonist of *Rotherick O'Connor*, Strongbow is.

17. *The Work of Mr. Charles Shadwell*, vol. 2 (Dublin: 1720), p. 275.

18. See Robert Hume, *The Rakish Stage: Studies in English Drama, 1660–1800* (Carbondale: Southern Illinois University Press, 1983), pp. 214–44, and Richard Bevis, *The Laughing Tradition: Stage Comedy in Garrick's Day* (London: George Prior Publishers, 1980), p. 63.

19. (Dublin: 1790), p. 6.

20. *The Miscellaneous Works, in Verse and Prose, of Gorges Edmond Howard*, vol. 1 (Dublin: 1782), p. 205.

21. *The London Stage, 1660–1800; Part Two, 1700–1729*, vol. 2, ed. Emmett L. Avery (Carbondale: Southern Illinois University Press, 1960), p. 663.

22. (Dublin: 1720), p. 9.

23. *An Answer to the Proposal for the Universal Use of Irish Manufactures* (Dublin: 1720), p. 6.

24. *Hibernia Freed. A Tragedy* (London: 1722), p. 30.

25. *Four Comedies by Charles Macklin*, ed. J. O. Bartley (Hamden, Conn.: Archon Books, 1968), p. 23.

26. See Joseph T. Leerssen, *Mere Irish & Fíor-Ghael: Studies in the Idea of Irish Nationality, Its Development and Literary Expression Prior to the Nineteenth Century* (Philadelphia: John Benjamins, 1986), p. 140.

27. Francis Aspry Congreve, *Authentic Memoirs of the Late Mr. Charles Macklin, Comedian* (London: 1798), pp. 39–40.

28. William W. Appleton, *Charles Macklin, an Actor's Life* (Cambridge: Harvard University Press, 1960), pp. 211–13.

29. William Cooke, *Memoirs of Charles Macklin, Comedian* (London: 1804), p. 304.

30. See Bartley, p. 26.

31. Bartley, pp. 111–12.

32. James Thomas Kirkman, *Memoirs of the Life of Charles Macklin, Esq.*, vol. 2 (London: 1799), p. 2.

33. (Dublin: 1728), prologue.

34. *The Life of William Carleton*, vol. 1 (New York: Garland Press, 1979), p. 27.

35. Piers Wauchope, *Patrick Sarsfield and the Williamite War* (Blackrock, Co. Dublin: Irish Academic Press, 1992), p. 230.

36. *Irish Hospitality, or Virtue Rewarded* (Dublin: 1720), p. 205.

37. I have borrowed this wonderfully spurious etymology from *The Irish Hudibras, or Fingallian Prince*: "*And, first, for the title* Fingallian. Fingaul, *i.e.* Finis Galliae, *viz. the Confines, Bounds and Limits of the* Gauls *in Ireland*"; (London: 1689), "To the Reader."

38. *Hibernia Anglicana: or, the History of Ireland from the Conquest thereof by the English to the Present Time*, pt. 1 (London: 1689), "To the Reader."

39. "Paddy's Opinion. An Irish Ballad," in *The Political Monitor; or Regent's Friend. Being a Collection of Poems Published in England During the Agitation of the Regency* (Dublin: 1790), p. 32.

40. (London: 1774), p. [9].

41. *A Concise View from History and Prophecy, of the Great Predictions in the Sacred Writings, that have been fulfilled; also of those that remain to be accomplished* (London: 1800), pp. 108, 106.

42. *Mere Irish & Fíor-Ghael*, p. 430.

43. *The Miscellaneous Works in Verse and Prose, of Gorges Edmond Howard, ESQ*, vol. 1, p. 37.

44. "'George My Belov'd King, and Ireland My Honour'd Country': John O'Keeffe and Ireland," *Irish University Review* 22 (1992): 54.

45. "John O'Keeffe as an Irish Playwright within the Theatrical, Social and Economic Context of His Time," *Éire-Ireland* 22 (1987): 42.

46. *The Hidden Ireland: A Study of Gaelic Munster in the Eighteenth Century* (1924; reprint, Dublin: Gill and Macmillan, 1967), p. 9.

47. *King of the Beggars* (1938; reprint, Swords, Co. Dublin: Poolbeg Press, 1995), pp. 14–38.

48. *The Harp Re-strung: The United Irishmen and the Rise of Irish Literary Nationalism* (Syracuse, N.Y.: Syracuse University Press, 1994), pp. 17–63.

49. *An Duanaire 1600–1900: Poems of the Dispossessed*, curtha i láthair ag Seán Ó Tuama, trans. Thomas Kinsella (n.p.: Dolmen Press, 1981), p. 197.

I. DUBLIN AS UTOPIA

1. In *Famous Utopias*, intro. by Charles M. Andrews (New York: Tudor Publishing, n.d.), p. 155.

2. Richard Head, *Hic et Ubique; or, the Humours of Dublin* (London: printed by R. D. for the Author, 1663). All subsequent references are to this edition. La Tourette Stockwell suggests that "it is not improbable that it was also acted 'publicly' at Smock-Alley"; *Dublin Theatres and Theatre Customs, 1637–1820* (1938; reprint, New York: Benjamin Blom, 1968), p. 30. There is, however, no evidence of a public production.

3. *Teague, Shenkin and Sawney: Being an Historical Study of the Earliest Irish, Welsh, and Scottish Characters in English Plays* (Cork: Cork University Press, 1954), p. 104.

4. *Mere Irish & Fíor Ghael: Studies in the Idea of Irish Nationality, Its Development and Literary Expression Prior to the Nineteenth Century* (Philadelphia: John Benjamins, 1986), p. 484 n. 390.

5. See Robert D. Hume, *The Development of English Drama in the Late Seventeenth Century* (Oxford: Clarendon Press, 1976), p. 235.

6. *Utopics: The Semiological Play of Textual Spaces*, trans. Robert A. Vollrath (Atlantic Highlands, N.J.: Humanities Press International, 1984), p. 57. All subsequent references are to this edition. This is, of course, not the common definition of *utopia*, which William Nelson sums up as "the imagination of a 'best state of commonwealth' and the report of a wise traveler to strange lands"; introduction, *Twentieth Century Interpretations of Utopia*, ed. William Nelson (Englewood Cliffs, N.J.: Prentice-Hall, 1968), p. 8. However, as Northrop Frye points out, utopic literature always involves a satirical element: "The desirable society, or the utopia proper, is essentially the writer's own society with its unconscious ritual habits transposed into their conscious equivalents. The contrast in value between the two societies implies a satire on the writer's own society, and the basis for the satire is the unconsciousness or inconsistency in the social behavior he observes around him"; "Varieties of Literary Utopias," in *Utopias and Utopian Thought*, ed. Frank E. Manuel (Boston: Beacon Press, 1966), p. 27. Marin's theory of how utopic literature functions provides a coherent vision of how the satire Frye describes works and is applicable therefore to Head's sardonic comedy.

7. (London: 1665), p. 7. All subsequent references are to this edition and are indicated in the text by *Rogue*.

8. *Proteus Redivivus: or the Art of Wheedling* (London: 1679), pp. 16–17. All subsequent references are to this edition and are referred to in the text by *Proteus*.

9. For instance, Sir John Davies, writing in 1612, claims about the Irish gentry, "And though their portions were never so small, and themselves never so poor (*For Gavel-kind must needs in the end make a poor Gentility*) yet did they scorn to descend to Husbandry, or Merchandize, or to learn any mechanical Act or Science"; *Historical Relations: or, a Discovery of the true Causes why Ireland was never entirely Subdued, Nor brought under Obedience of the Crown of England until the Beginning of the Reign of King James I* (Dublin: 1704), p. 37.

10. See Louis M. Cullen, *The Emergence of Modern Ireland 1600–1900* (New York: Holmes and Meier, 1981), p. 84.

11. *A Treatise of Taxes & Contributions . . . the Same being frequently applied to the present State and Affairs of Ireland* (London: 1662), preface.

12. As quoted in Kathleen Lynch, *Roger Boyle, First Earl of Orrery* (Knoxville: University of Tennessee Press, 1965), p. 114. For a succinct expression of the difficulties in terms of land settlements, see Edmund Curtis, *A History of Ireland* (London: Methuen, 1936), pp. 256–59.

13. Vincent Gookin, *The Great Case of Transplantation in Ireland Discussed* (London: 1663), pp. 3, 13, 22.

14. Amy Boesky, "Nation, Miscegenation: Membering Utopia in Henry Neville's *The Isle of the Pines*," *Texas Studies in Language and Literature* 37 (1995): 165–84.

15. Martin G. Plattel argues that utopic literature is partially a consequence of the Scientific Revolution in the Renaissance in *Utopian and Critical Thinking* (Pittsburgh: Duquesne University Press, 1972), pp. 30–31.

16. J. C. Davis, *Utopia and the Ideal Society: A Study of English Utopian Writing 1516–1700* (Cambridge: Cambridge University Press, 1981), p. 103.

17. T. C. Barnard, *Cromwellian Ireland: English Government and Reform in Ireland, 1649–1660* (Oxford: Oxford University Press, 1975), pp. 229–30.

18. *The Complaisant Companion, or new Jests; witty Reparties; Bulls; Rhodomontados; and pleasant Novels* (London: 1674), p. 78.

19. In *The Floating Island: or, a New Discovery, relating the strange Adventure on a late Voyage from Lambethana to Villa Franca alias Ramallia, to the Eastward of Terra del Templo: by three Ships, Viz. the Pay-naught, Excuse, Least-in-sight, Under the Conduct of Captain* Robert Owe-much: *Describing the Nature of the Inhabitants, their Religion, Laws and Customs. Published by* Frank Careless, *one of the Discovers* (n.p.: 1673), debtors seek through London and its suburbs for the utopic liberties where "he that by specious pretences and subtle perswasions hath gotten largely into a Vintner's score, and for some special kindnesses hath borrowed so much money of his wife to cancel the debt, without the least mistrust of an overflowing familiarity, is a *Merchant Adventurer,* and a singular good *Accountant*" (31). The key phrase here is *merchant adventurer,* which was also used to describe those who subsidized Cromwell's Irish invasion in return for promises of land.

20. W. S. Clark, *The Early Irish Stage: The Beginnings to 1720* (Oxford: Clarendon Press, 1955), p. 56.

21. (London: 1673), p. 25.

22. Kiltory's misogyny marks him as comic. In Head's *Jackson's Recantation or, the*

Life and Death of the Notorious High-Way-Man now hanging in Chains at Hampstead (London: 1674), Jackson voices similar sentiments about the mistress who turned him to crime, ending with, "She resolved to desert me when I least dreamed thereof; and now I cannot choose but rail at her whole sex, for her sake, rewarding my kindness with so much baseness and ingratitude; for as she carried away all I had left, so she left me something that was none of my own, a swingeing clap, which laid me up in a pickle above six week before I was cured"; reprinted in *Miscellanea Antiqua Anglicana* 3:31 (London: 1873): 23.

23. David Dickson, *New Foundations: Ireland 1660–1800* (Dublin: Criterion Press, 1987), p. 8.

24. J. C. Beckett, *The Making of Modern Ireland 1603–1923* (London: Faber and Faber, 1981), pp. 127–28.

25. Thomas Bartlett, "Army and Society in Eighteenth-Century Ireland," in *Kings in Conflict: The Revolutionary War in Ireland and Its Aftermath 1689–1750*, ed. W. A. Maguire (Belfast: Blackstaff Press, 1990), p. 175.

26. *English Money and Irish Land: The "Adventurers" in the Cromwellian Settlement of Ireland* (Oxford: Clarendon Press, 1971), p. 142. S. J. Connolly indicates that in the Parliament of 1661 only sixteen of the members were adventurers and fewer than fifty were members of the parliamentary armies; *Religion, Law and Power: The Making of Protestant Ireland 1660–1760* (Oxford: Clarendon Press, 1992), p. 16.

27. S. J. Connolly points to William Conolly as an example of the rise of self-made families in the Restoration; *Religion, Law and Power*, p. 64.

28. *Tricksters & Estates: On the Ideology of Restoration Comedy* (Lexington: University Press of Kentucky, 1997), p. 172.

29. See Bartley, *Teague, Shenkin and Sawney*, p. 274, and Alan Bliss, *Spoken English in Ireland 1600–1740* (Dublin: Cadenus Press, 1979), pp. 332–34.

30. *The Impartial History of Ireland* (1695; reprint, London: 1762), p. 32.

31. R. F. Foster, *Modern Ireland 1600–1972* (London: Penguin Books, 1989), p. 115.

32. *The Speech of Sir Audley Mervyn Knight . . . 13 February 1662* (London: 1662), p. 19.

33. A. T. Lucas discusses the use of the dummy calf in *Cattle in Ancient Ireland* (Kilkenny: Boethius Press, 1989), pp. 51–55.

34. *Cambrensis Refuted by Gratianus Lucius*, trans. Theophilus O'Flanagan (Dublin: 1795), pp. xxxv–xxxvi.

35. *The Answer of a Person of Quality to a Scandalous Letter Lately Printed and Subscribed by P.W.* (Dublin: 1662), p. 14.

36. *The Irish Colours Folded, or the Irish Roman Catholicks Reply to the (pretended) English Protestants Answer to the Letter desiring a just and merciful regard of the Roman Catholicks of Ireland (Which Answer is entitled the Irish Colours Displayed)* (London: 1662), p. 11. Thomas D'Arcy M'Gee attributes *The Irish Colours Displayed* to Roger Boyle, earl of Orrery; *The Irish Writers of the Seventeenth Century* (Dublin: 1846), p. 128.

2. "I'VE SAVED YOUR COUNTRY."

1. Ben Ross Schneider, Jr., *Index to the London Stage 1660–1800*. (Carbondale: Southern Illinois University Press, 1979), p. 758.

2. *The Fair Quaker of Deal, or, the Humours of the Navy* (London: 1710).

3. *Teague, Shenkin and Sawney* (Cork: Cork University Press, 1954), p. 113.

4. *The Field Day Anthology of Irish Writing,* vol. 1, gen. ed. Seamus Deane (Derry: Field Day Publications, 1991), p. 501.

5. *Dublin Theatres and Theatre Customs, 1637–1820* (1938; reprint, New York: Benjamin Blom, 1968), p. 57.

6. *The Early Irish Stage: The Beginnings to 1720* (Oxford: Clarendon Press, 1955), p. 174. All dates for Dublin premieres are from Clark.

7. *Mere Irish & Fíor-Ghael: Studies in the Idea of Irish Nationality, Its Development and Literary Expression Prior to the Nineteenth Century* (Philadelphia: John Benjamins, 1986), p. 381.

8. Some sections of *Hibernia Anglicana* are simply transposed into blank verse. Compare, for instance, the following passages where Cox explains how Dermond found himself needing help with Rotherick's self-justification in *Rotherick O'Connor:*

> For *Dermond MacMurrough* King of *Leinster,* having forced *O Neale, O Mlaghlin* and *O Caroll,* to give him Hostages, grew so insolent at these successes, that he became oppressive to his Subjects, and injurious to his Neighbors, more especially by the Rape of the Wife of *Orourk* King of *Brehny, who was Daughter of O Mlaghlin* King of *Meath;* whereupon he was invaded by his enemies, and abandoned by his Subjects and Tributaries, particularly by *Morough O Borne, Hasculphus Mac Turkil* Governor of *Dublin,* and *Daniel,* Prince of *Ossory.*

Source: vol. 1 (London: 1689), p. 11. All subsequent references are to this edition. Rotherick's self-justification:

> Thy Father it is true, was King of *Leinster,*
> And had he govern'd well, might still have reigned;
> But you forget he ravished *O Rourk*'s Wife,
> Who was the Daughter of the King of *Meath;*
> Know you, that he plunder'd all the Country round,
> And forc'd *O Neale, O Carroll* and *McLoughlin,*
> To give him Hostages, which he destroy'd;
> Whilst *O Borne* and *Daniel* Prince of *Ossory*
> Amazed at all his horrid Villanies,
> As all good Men should do, deser[t]ed him.

Source: vol. 2 (Dublin: 1720), p. 283. All subsequent references are to this edition.

Cox's history includes a lengthy introduction without page numbers. When citing the introduction "To the Reader," I have included in roman numerals and in square brackets my own page count of where the quotation occurs.

9. *Colonial Evangelism: A Socio-Historical Study of an East African Mission at the Grassroots* (Bloomington: Indiana University Press, 1982), pp. 127–28.

10. For instance, for Emily Lennox, daughter of the second duke of Richmond, to marry James Fitzgerald, twentieth earl of Kildare (and subsequently first duke of Leinster), and for her sister, Louisa, to marry Thomas Conolly, great-nephew of William Conolly and the wealthiest man in Ireland, the grooms had to accept disadvantageous marriage settlements because of their Irish extraction; see Stella Tillyard, *Aristocrats* (New York: Farrar Straus Giroux, 1994), pp. 51–53, 96.

11. J. C. Beckett, *The Making of Modern Ireland, 1603–1923* (London: Faber and Faber, 1981), p. 191. See also J. L. McCracken, "The Political Structure, 1714–60," in *A*

New History of Ireland, vol. 4, *1691–1800,* ed. T. W. Moody and W. E. Vaughan (Oxford: Clarendon Press, 1986), pp. 58–59.

12. See Montague Summers's introduction to *The Complete Works of Thomas Shadwell,* vol. 1, ed. Montague Summers (London: Fortune Press, 1927), pp. xxi–xxiii.

13. As quoted in Clark, *The Early Irish Stage,* pp. 157–58.

14. Dryden, for instance, in "Absalom and Achitophel," names him "Barzillai, crowned with honor and with years:/Long since, the rising rebels he withstood/In regions waste, beyond the Jordan's flood" (ll. 818–20).

15. Irvin Ehrenpreis, *Swift; the Man, His Works, and the Age,* vol. 3 (London: Methuen, 1983), p. 7.

16. (London: 1713). All subsequent references are to this edition.

17. For the importance of "conquest myths" as justification for aristocratic privilege in Irish and European history, see C. D. A. Leighton, *Catholicism in a Protestant Kingdom: A Study of the Irish Ancien Régime* (Dublin: Gill and Macmillan, 1994), pp. 36–37.

18. Ian Montgomery, "An Entire and Coherent History of Ireland, Richard Cox's *Hibernia Anglicana,*" *The Linen Hall Review* 12:1 (Spring 1995): 9.

19. *Writing Ireland: Colonialism, Nationalism, and Culture* (Manchester: Manchester University Press, 1988), p. 10.

20. *Leviathan,* ed. C. B. Macpherson (Harmondsworth, Middlesex, England: Penguin, 1981), p. 188.

21. In *Five New Plays* (London: 1720), p. 114.

22. In *Five New Plays,* p. 295. Interestingly, in this play the Cornishman is the buffoon while the Dubliners are portrayed as urban sophisticates.

23. Robert Shepherd, *Ireland's Fate: The Boyne and After* (London: Aurum Press, 1990), pp. 192, 196.

24. *A Rational and Historical Account of the Principles which Gave Birth to the Late Rebellion* (reprint, Dublin: 1718), p. 32.

25. *Secret Memoirs of Barleduc . . . With an Account of the Late Conspiracies for an Invasion and Rebellion in Great Britain* (Dublin: reprinted by T. Humes for P. Campbell, 1715), p. 3. All subsequent references are to this edition.

26. *A Modest Apology for Priestcraft by a Christian* (London: 1720), p. 9.

27. *An Argument to Prove the Affections of the People of England to be the best Security of the Government* (London: 1716), p. 8.

28. Moses Lowman, *The Mercy of the Government Vindicated* (London: 1716), p. 21.

29. *A Faithful Register of the Late Rebellion* (London: 1718), p. 196.

30. *The History of Ireland Collected by Three Learned Authors Viz. Meredith Hanmer Edmund Campion and Edmund Spenser* (Dublin: 1633), p. 115.

31. Robert E. Burns, *Irish Parliamentary Politics in the Eighteenth Century,* vol. 1 (Washington: Catholic University of America Press, 1989), p. 69.

32. In *Five New Plays,* n.p.

33. *Modern Ireland, 1600–1972* (London: Penguin, 1989), pp. 162–63.

34. *A Letter from a Member of the House of Commons of Ireland to a Gentleman of the Long Robe in Great-Britain: Containing an Answer to some Objections made against the Judicatory Power of the Parliament of Ireland* (Dublin: 1719), p. 18.

35. *Religion, Law and Power: The Making of Protestant Ireland 1660–1760* (Oxford: Clarendon Press, 1992), p. 111.

36. *A Brief Discourse in Vindication of the Antiquity of Ireland* (Dublin: 1717), p. 144.

37. *Historical Relations: or, a Discovery of the true Causes why Ireland was never entirely Subdued, Nor brought under Obedience of the Crown of England until the Beginning of the Reign of James I* (reprint, Dublin: 1704), p. 9.

38. *A brief Discourse in Vindication of the Antiquity of Ireland*, p. 64.

39. See Louis C. Cullen, *The Emergence of Modern Ireland, 1600–1900* (New York: Holmes and Meier, 1981), p. 173.

40. See Kevin Whelan, "An Underground Gentry? Catholic Middlemen in Eighteenth-Century Ireland," *Eighteenth-Century Ireland* 10 (1995): 26–28.

41. Shadwell is eulogized in a broadsheet as "Constant in Friendship, in his Love sincere,/Prudently Gay, and Virtuously severe"; *Myrtillo. A Pastoral Poem, Lamenting the Death of Mr. Charles Shadwell, Gratefully inscrib'd to all his Friends* (Dublin: 1726).

3. "AND MIX THEIR BLOOD WITH OURS"

1. The Saint Patrick's Day showing is probably not an accident. The printed text of Henry Burnell's *Landgartha* ends with "This Play was first Acted on *S. Patrick's* day, 1639, with the allowance of the Master of Revels," thus showing an earlier example of an association of Saint Patrick with dramatic depictions of Irish nationalism (Dublin: 1641).

2. For performance records, see *The London Stage 1660–1800; Part Two, 1700–1729*, vol. 2, ed. Emmett L. Avery (Carbondale: Southern Illinois University Press, 1960), pp. 665–69. Except for this night, the play did not do particularly well. On opening night, the gate took in £57, 10s. 6d.; on 15 February, for Philips's first benefit, the gate was only £51, 4s. (or, after house charges, £11 for Philips); on 19 February the company presumably lost money, as the gate receipts were only £38, 15s., and the company took an absolute bath on 20 February when the take was £19, 8s. Surprisingly, Philips was given a third benefit on 22 February and approximately broke even, as gate receipts were £38, 11s., 6d., with ticket sales of two and a half pounds. The Saint Patrick's Day showing made a small profit as combined ticket sales and receipts came to approximately £48. For a discussion of the benefit system in the period, see *The London Stage 1660–1800; Part Two, 1700–1729*, vol. 1, pp. xcvi–cii.

3. As quoted in *The London Stage 1660–1800; Part Two, 1700–1729*, vol. 1, p. clxiv.

4. The play conflates the victory of Mael Sechnaill I over Turgesius in approximately 845 with Brian Boruma's victories over the Danes in the early tenth century.

5. See Christopher Murray's introduction to *St. Stephen's Green, or, the Generous Lovers* (Dublin: Cadenus Press, 1979), pp. 8–17.

6. *Hibernia Freed. A Tragedy* (London: 1722), p. [2]. All subsequent references are to this edition.

7. Louis M. Cullen, *An Economic History of Ireland Since 1660*, 2nd ed. (London: B. T. Batsford, 1987), pp. 36–37.

8. J. C. Beckett, *The Making of Modern Ireland, 1603–1923*, rev. ed. (London: Faber and Faber, 1981), p. 164.

9. R. F. Foster, *Modern Ireland, 1600–1972* (London: Penguin, 1989), p. 178.

10. *Irish Tracts 1720–1723*, ed. Herbert Davis, and *Sermons*, ed. Louis Landa (Oxford: Basil Blackwell, 1963), p. 17.

11. See Carol Fabricant, *Swift's Landscape*, rev. ed. (Notre Dame, Ind.: University of Notre Dame Press, 1995), pp. xxvi–xxvii.

12. Irvin Ehrenpreis, *Swift; the Man, His Works, and the Age,* vol. 3 (London: Methuen, 1983), p. 128.

13. *An Act for the better Securing the Dependency of Ireland upon the Crown of Great-Britain to which is Added, J——n T——d, Esq; His Reasons Why the Bill for the Better Securing the Dependency of, should not Pass* (London: 1720), p. 12.

14. Ian Campbell Ross has discussed the Jacobite sensibilities of this work and the probable misunderstanding of these sensibilities by most members of an English reading public in "'One of the Principal Nations of Europe': The Representation of Ireland in Sarah Butler's *Irish Tales,*" *Eighteenth-Century Fiction* 7 (1994): 1–16.

15. Diarmid Ó Catháin, "Dermot O'Connor, Translator of Keating," *Eighteenth-Century Ireland* 2 (1987): 86. The view that "there was no significant cultural intercourse between the two sides" is expressed by Declan Kiberd in "Irish Literature and Irish History," in *The Oxford History of Ireland,* ed. R. F. Foster (Oxford: Oxford University Press, 1989), p. 249.

16. Patrick Fagan, *The Second City: Portrait of Dublin 1700–1760* (Dublin: Branar, 1986), p. 207.

17. "Walpole and Ireland," in *Britain in the Age of Walpole,* ed. Jeremy Black (London: Macmillan, 1984), p. 98.

18. *St. Stephen's Green,* p. 111.

19. Dermo'd O'Connor, *The General History of Ireland . . . Collected by the Learned Jeoffrey Keating, D.D.* (London: 1723), n.p.

20. "Popery and Protestantism, Civil and Religious Liberty: The Disputed Lessons of Irish History 1690–1812," *Past and Present* 118 (1988): 102.

21. As quoted in J. L. McCracken, "The Political Structure, 1714–60," in *A New History of Ireland,* vol. 4, *Eighteenth-Century Ireland 1691–1800,* ed. T. W. Moody and W. E. Vaughan (Oxford: Clarendon Press, 1986), p. 64. Thomond is listed as a member of the privy council in *Hiberniae Notitia* (Dublin: 1723), n.p.

22. Gerard O'Brien, *Anglo-Irish Politics in the Age of Grattan and Pitt* (Blackrock, Co. Dublin: Irish Academic Press, 1987), p. 19.

23. Somerset led a group of Whigs against the repeal of the Triennial Act; see I. S. Leadam, *The History of England from the Accession of Anne to the Death of George II* (1912; reprint, New York: Greenwood Press, 1969), p. 268.

24. For instance, "A Lover of Truth" praises the O'Briens shortly after the Restoration and indicates that they had been acceptable in the highest circles since Elizabeth: "Alexander Fitton, who was a Captain there in Queen *Elizabeth's* Wars, and marryed indeed an *Irish* Woman, but of such extraction, as he did not thereby discredit his Family, but added to it a Nobler Allyance. She was of the Family of the *O'Briens,* Earls of *Thomond,* whose *Stem* is well known in that Kingdom to be so Noble, that divers of their Ancestors are said to have been Kings of *Ireland*"; *A True Narrative of the Proceedings in the severall Suits in Law that have been between the Right Honourable Charl[e]s Lord Gerard of Brandon, and Alexander Fitton, Esq.* (The Hague: 1663), p. 4.

25. Donough O'Brien, *History of the O'Briens* (London: B. T. Batsford, 1949), p. 76.

26. Maureen Wall, *Catholic Ireland in the Eighteenth Century,* ed. Gerard O'Brien (Dublin: Geography Publications, 1989), p. 40.

27. *The Revengeful Queen* (London: 1698), n.p.

28. *The Fall and Rise of the Irish Nation* (Dublin: Gill and Macmillan, 1992), p. 24.

29. Charles Chenevix Trench, *Grace's Card: Irish Catholic Landlords 1690–1800* (Cork and Dublin: Mercier Press, 1997), pp. 67–68.

30. D. W. Hayton, "Ireland and the English Ministers 1707–1716" (D.Phil. thesis, Oxford University, 1975), p. 337.

31. James Macpherson, *Original Papers; containing the Secret History of Great Britain, from the Restoration, to the accession of the House of Hannover*, vol. 2 (London: 1775), pp. 378, 379.

32. *Irish Tracts and Sermons*, p. 18.

33. Beckett, *Making of Modern Ireland*, p. 156.

34. Thomas Bartlett, "The Rise and Fall of the Protestant Nation, 1690–1800," *Éire-Ireland* 26 (Summer 1991): 10–12.

35. Louis M. Cullen, *The Emergence of Modern Ireland, 1600–1900* (New York: Holmes and Meier, 1981), p. 147.

36. *Irish Tracts and Sermons*, p. 18.

37. Geoffrey Holmes, *British Politics in the Age of Anne*, rev. ed. (London: Hambledon Press, 1987), p. 117.

38. (London: 1724), p. 40. All subsequent references are to this edition.

39. *A Prospect of the State of Ireland, from the Year of the World 1756 to the Year of Christ 1652* (London: 1682), pp. 76, 148.

40. (Dublin: 1717), p. 180. This volume was also dedicated to William O Brien, earl of Inchiquin, and Thomond was again one of the subscribers.

41. *The General History of Ireland*, p. 421.

42. *Historical Relations or, a Discovery of the true Causes why Ireland Was never entirely Subdued, Nor brought under Obediance of the Crown of England until the Beginning of the Reign of King James I* (Dublin: 1704), p. 3.

43. *Hibernia Anglicana*, p. 8.

44. I am indebted to Helen Burke for this point, made in an unpublished paper, "Charles Shadwell and Irish Patriot Politics: The Case of *Rotherick O'Connor*."

45. There may be a pun involved here on the name *Agnes*, as the Irish woolen trade was greatly afflicted by English commercial legislation. On the other hand, Sabina is also an object of desire, and both women may simply represent Ireland.

4. ROBERT ASHTON'S HEROIC PALIMPSEST

1. *New Selected Poems* (London: Faber and Faber, 1989), p. 55.

2. *Seventeenth-Century Ireland: The War of Religions* (Dublin: Gill and Macmillan, 1988), p. 254. Fitzpatrick is, however, mistaken in thinking the Irish foot soldiers were not fighting as Catholics, despite lack of pontifical approval. John Davis, writing to John Michelburne from Dublin Castle on 15 July 1691, draws attention to the fact that "on their side, it's said, their General St. Ruth is killed, who speech't them greatly in the Morning, animating them to Fight, as did the Priests, the Common Soldiers, who also gave them Absolution"; *An Account of the Transactions in the North of Ireland, Anno Domini, 1691* (London: 1692), p. 11. Other early accounts such as Story's *Impartial History* also call attention to the sectarian nature of the conflict.

3. *The Printed Word and the Common Man: Popular Culture in Ulster 1700–1900* (Belfast: Institute of Irish Studies, 1987), p. 70. The 1728 edition was identified as the earliest in *The Irish Book Lover* 10 (Jan.–March, 1919): 65–66.

4. *Irish Literature, a Social History* (Oxford: Basil Blackwell, 1990), p. 66.

5. *A Biographical Dictionary of Irish Writers* (Dublin: Lilliput Press, 1985), p. 5.

6. For instance, *Tamerlane* was presented on 5 November 1733 in honor of the an-

niversary of the "horrid Gunpowder Plot." The duke of Dorset, lord lieutenant, was unable to attend the performance because of a meeting of the Boyne Club; consequently, *Tamerlane* was presented again on 12 November, apparently at Dorset's request. See John C. Greene and Gladys L. H. Clark, *The Dublin Stage, 1720–1745* (Bethlehem, Penn.: Lehigh University Press, 1993), p. 156. For the importance of ritual commemorations to Protestants in Ireland, see James Kelly, " 'The Glorious and Immortal Memory': Commemoration and Protestant Identity in Ireland 1660–1800," *Proceedings of the Royal Irish Academy* 94C (1994): 25–52.

7. Nicholas Rowe, *Tamerlane*, ed. Landon C. Burnes, Jr. (Philadelphia: University of Pennsylvania Press, 1966), pp. 22–23.

8. *A History of the City of Dublin*, vol. 1 (Dublin: 1861), p. 70. The Gilbert collection in the Dublin City Library does not contain this broadside, nor was I able to locate it at the Royal Irish Academy, where Gilbert was librarian for many years.

9. *Alumni Dublinenses* (Dublin: 1935).

10. The Reverend Wm. Ball Wright, *The Ussher Memoirs* (Dublin: 1889), p. 166.

11. *The Battle of Aughrim: or, the Fall of St. Ruth. A Tragedy* (Dublin: printed by S. Powell for Richard Norris, at the corner of Crane-Lane, Essex Street, 1728). All subsequent references are to this edition.

12. Piers Wauchope, *Patrick Sarsfield and the Williamite War* (Blackrock, Co. Dublin: Irish Academic Press, 1992), p. 230.

13. Robert Munter, *A Dictionary of the Print Trade in Ireland* (New York: Fordham University Press, 1988), pp. 217–18, 198.

14. Vol. 1 (Dublin: 1804), p. 279.

15. *Ireland's Mirror: or, a Chronicle of the Times* (Dublin: 1805), 138–39.

16. In *An Answer to the Paper Delivered by Mr. Ashton at his Execution to Sir Francis Child: Sheriff of London, &c. Together with the Paper it self* (London: 1690), Ashton claims he was arrested because he was a believer in passive obedience.

17. (Dublin: 1841), p. vii.

18. *The Irish Sketchbook* (Dublin: Gill and Macmillan, 1990), pp. 156, 181–82.

19. *My Life in Two Hemispheres*, vol. 1 (New York: Macmillan, 1898), p. 11.

20. See Nancy J. Curtin, *The United Irishmen: Popular Politics in Ulster and Dublin 1791–1798* (Oxford: Clarendon Press, 1994), pp. 185–87.

21. *The Life of William Carleton*, vol. 1 (London: Downey & Co., 1896), pp. 26–27.

22. The war was largely a consequence of Austrian annoyance at the treaty of Hanover and Spain's desire to regain Gibraltar. See Basil Williams, *The Whig Supremacy, 1714–1760* (Oxford: Clarendon Press, 1942), pp. 189–92. The death of George I and the possibility therefore of dynastic strife may also have contributed to Spanish perceptions of English vulnerability; I. S. Leadam, *The History of England from the Accession of Anne to the Death of George II* (1912; reprint, New York: Greenwood Press, 1969), p. 337.

23. *An Enquiry into the Reasons of the Conduct of Great Britain with Relation to the Present State of Affairs in Europe* (Dublin: 1727), p. 27.

24. *True Interest of the Hanover Treaty Considered by a Lover of His Country* (Dublin: 1727), p. 10.

25. *A Letter to the Right Honourable Sir Robert Sutton For Disbanding the Irish Regiments in the Service of France and Spain by CH. Forman, Gent.* (Dublin: 1728), pp. 20–21.

26. *A Preservation Against Popery* (Dublin: 1728), p. 45.

27. (Dublin: printed by S. Powell, 1727), p. 4.

28. Wauchope, *Patrick Sarsfield and the Williamite War*, p. 198.

29. *An Impartial History of the Wars of Ireland With a Continuation thereof. In Two Parts* (London: 1693), p. 135.

30. Catherine Cole Mambretti, "Orinda on the Restoration Stage," *Comparative Literature* 37 (1985): 233–51.

31. For performance calendars, see *The London Stage 1660–1800; Part Two, 1700–1729*, ed. Emmett L. Avery (Carbondale: Southern Illinois University Press, 1960).

32. Greene and Clark, *The Dublin Stage*, pp. 125, 13.

33. *An Essay of Dramatic Poesie* in *The Works of John Dryden*, vol. 17, ed. Samuel Holt Monk, et al. (Berkeley: University of California Press, 1971), p. 74.

34. *A Vindication of his Excellency John, Lord Cartaret From the Charge of favouring none but Tories, High-Churchmen, and Jacobites*, in *Irish Tracts and Sermons*, ed. Herbert Davis (Oxford: Basil Blackwell, 1964), p. 155.

35. (Dublin: 1728), n.p.

36. See D. W. Hayton, "From Barbarian to Burlesque: English Images of the Irish c. 1660–1750," *Irish Economic and Social History* 15 (1988): 5–31. For further evidence of increasing Protestant indifference to the possibility of a return by the Stuarts, see Thomas Bartlett, *The Fall and Rise of the Irish Nation: The Catholic Question 1690–1830* (Dublin: Gill and Macmillan, 1992), p. 29.

37. Vincent Morley, "Hugh MacCurtin: An Irish Poet in the French Army," *Eighteenth-Century Ireland* 8 (1993): 57.

38. Thomas Bartlett points out that "in 1728 a number of officers were suspended for attempting to enlist Irish recruits"; "'A Weapon of War yet Untried': Irish Catholics and the Armed Forces of the Crown, 1760–1830," in *Men, Women and War*, ed. T. G. Fraser and Keith Jeffery (Dublin: Lilliput Press, 1993), p. 69.

39. Louis M. Cullen, "Catholic Social Classes under the Penal Laws," in *Endurance and Emergence: Catholics in Ireland in the Eighteenth Century*, ed. T. P. Power and Kevin Whelan (Dublin: Irish Academic Press, 1990), p. 75.

40. *Amiable Renegade: The Memoirs of Captain Peter Drake, 1671–1753* (Stanford: Stanford University Press, 1960).

41. Jeremy Black, *Eighteenth-Century Europe, 1700–1789* (New York: St. Martin's Press, 1990), p. 315.

42. See Louis M. Cullen, *The Emergence of Modern Ireland, 1600–1900* (New York: Holmes and Meier, 1981), p. 117.

43. As quoted in Robert Shepherd, *Ireland's Fate* (London: Aurum Press, 1990), p. 394.

44. *The Correspondence of Jonathan Swift*, vol. 4, rev. ed., ed. Harold Williams (Oxford: Clarendon Press, 1972), p. 51.

45. *Nationalism in Ireland*, 2nd ed. (New York: Routledge, 1991), p. 101.

46. *A History of Ireland* (London: Methuen, 1936), p. 297.

47. See J. C. Beckett, *The Making of Modern Ireland, 1603–1923* (London: Faber and Faber, 1981), p. 189.

48. *The Case of John Browne, Esq.* (London: 1725), p. 16.

49. [William Dunkin], *ΤΕΧΝΗΘΥΡΑΜΒΕΙΑ* [*Technethyrambeia*] *or a Poem upon Paddy Murphy, Porter of Trin. Coll. Dublin. Translated from the Latin Original* [by Joseph Cowper] (Dublin: 1728), pp. 10–11.

50. *Remonstrance in the Name of the Lads in all the Schools of Ireland* (Dublin: 1727–28), p. 15.

51. (Dublin: 1728), p. 3.

52. La Tourette Stockwell, *Dublin Theaters and Theater Customs, 1637–1820* (1938; reprint, New York: Benjamin Blom, 1968), p. 60, and Greene and Clark, *The Dublin Stage, 1720–1745*, p. 123. It was also revived frequently in London, three times in 1727 alone.

53. *Eighteenth-Century Plays*, ed. Ricardo Quintana (New York: Modern Library, 1952), p. 8. All subsequent references are to this edition.

54. James McGuire, "James II and Ireland, 1685–90," in *Kings in Conflict: The Revolutionary War in Ireland and Its Aftermath, 1689–1750*, ed. W. A. Maguire (Belfast: Blackstaff Press, 1990), p. 46. Moreover, Story lists a Colonel James Talbot as among the Irish dead (138).

55. John Michelburne has "wicked *Will* Talbot . . . a near relation to *Tyrconnel*," carried on wounded in *Ireland Preserv'd; or the Siege of Londonderry. A Tragi-Comedy* (1705; reprint, Belfast: 1744), p. 56.

56. *An Impartial History*, p. 142.

5. "OUR OWN GOOD, PLAIN, OLD IRISH ENGLISH"

1. James Thomas Kirkman, *Memoirs of the Life of Charles Macklin, Esq.*, vol. 1 (London: 1799), p. 165. All subsequent references to this biography are parenthetical and indicated by "Kirkman."

2. *Obituaries of Remarkable Persons; with Biographical Anecdotes*, July 1797, p. 622.

3. J. L. McCracken, "The Social Structure and Social Life, 1714–60," in *A New History of Ireland*, vol. 4, *Eighteenth-Century Ireland, 1691–1800*, ed. T. W. Moody and W. E. Vaughan (Oxford: Clarendon Press, 1986), p. 38.

4. Thomas Bartlett, *The Fall and Rise of the Irish Nation: The Catholic Question, 1690–1830* (Dublin: Gill and Macmillan, 1992), pp. 24–27.

5. Louis M. Cullen, *The Emergence of Modern Ireland, 1600–1900* (New York: Holmes and Meier, 1981), pp. 114–15.

6. *The Emergence of Modern Ireland*, pp. 115, 125.

7. "An Underground Gentry? Catholic Middlemen in Eighteenth-Century Ireland," *Eighteenth-Century Ireland* 10 (1995): 10.

8. *Journals and Memoirs of Thomas Russell*, ed. C. J. Woods (Blackrock, Co. Dublin: Irish Academic Press, 1991), p. 90.

9. Conor Cruise O'Brien, *The Great Melody: A Thematic Biography and Commented Anthology of Edmund Burke* (London: Minerva, 1993), pp. 3–4.

10. Quoted in Edmund Burke, *Irish Affairs*, intro. by Conor Cruise O'Brien (London: Cresset Library, 1988), p. xxviii.

11. *Amelia*, ed. David Blewett (New York: Penguin, 1987), p. 17.

12. *The History of Tom Jones*, ed. R. P. C. Mutter (New York: Penguin, 1989), p. 536.

13. *Ireland in the Age of Imperialism and Revolution, 1760–1801* (Oxford: Clarendon Press, 1979), p. 142.

14. William Cooke, *Memoirs of Charles Macklin, Comedian* (London: 1804), pp. 208–9. Subsequently cited parenthetically in the text.

15. "Poor *Sam* died last Night at his House in the *Hay-market:* In that House where he has been labouring Night after Night to serve me and my Family—by hurting us as far as in him lay; Excuse that Sentence from the Orator—consider it as from the *Irishman*—Oh! My Country!"; (London: 1755), pp. 3–4.

16. *An Epistle from Tully in the Shades to Orator Ma——n in Covent Garden* (London: 1755), p. 10.

17. *A Will and No Will, or a Bone for the Lawyers* and *The New Play Criticiʒ'd, or the Plague of Envy*, intro. by Jean B. Kern, Augustan Reprint Series, 127–28 (Los Angeles: William Andrews Clark Memorial Library, 1967), pp. 54, 65–66.

18. *A Sixteenth Address to the Free Citiʒens and Free-Holders of the City of Dublin* (Dublin: 1748), pp. 31–32.

19. Esther Sheldon describes the incidents of the riot and subsequent controversy in *Thomas Sheridan of Smock Alley* (Princeton: Princeton University Press, 1967), pp. 82–99.

20. *The Book of the Prophecies of the Prophet L——S* (Dublin: 1748), p. 7.

21. *The Tickler Nº I. II. III. IV. V. VI and VII. The Second Edition* (Dublin: 1748), p. 12.

22. Neil Longley York, *Neither Kingdom nor Nation: The Irish Quest for Constitutional Rights, 1698–1800* (Washington: Catholic University of America Press, 1994), p. 72.

23. Seán Murphy, "Charles Lucas, Catholicism and Nationalism," *Eighteenth-Century Ireland* 8 (1993): 86.

24. *An Apology for the Civil Rights and Liberties of the Commons and Citiʒens of Dublin* (Dublin: 1748–49), p. 5.

25. The Viking conquest of Ireland could be appropriated by government supporters as well. In 1753 an anonymous pamphlet comically equates Norway and England: "Anno T MXXXXXII (for their History begins,) *Magnus* King of *Norway* was in Possession of *Ireland* and the *British* Isles. . . . He had the love of his *British* Subjects, but the Adoration of his *Irish*, who had prospered more under his equal Government in a few Years, than in any Century before"; *Hibernia Pacata: or, a Narrative of the Affairs of Ireland, from the Famous Battle of Clontarf, where Brian Boirom defeated the Norwegians, till the Settlement under Henry II. Written originally in Irish and now First Translated by Father Neri of Tuam, and Adorned with Notes by several Hands* (n.p.: 1753), pp. 6–7. This reversal of the metaphoric identification of England with Viking oppression indicates the author's awareness of the increasing use of the trope by the patriot opposition.

26. *An Eleventh Address to the Free Citiʒens, and Free-Holders of the City of Dublin* (Dublin: 1749), pp. 8, 11.

27. *The Farmers Letter to the Protestants of Ireland* [1–6] (Dublin: 1745), no. 2: 8.

28. Thomas Bartlett, *The Fall and Rise of the Irish Nation*, p. 54.

29. The best discussion of Henry Brooke's "colonial nationalism" is Kevin Donovan's "*Jack the Giant Quellar:* Political Theater in Ascendancy Dublin," *Éire-Ireland* 30 (1995): 70–88.

30. *Brookiana*, vol. 1 (London: 1804), p. 86.

31. Robert E. Burns, *Irish Parliamentary Politics in the Eighteenth-Century*, vol. 2 (Washington: Catholic University of America Press, 1990), p. 125.

32. William W. Appleton, *Charles Macklin, an Actor's Life* (Cambridge: Harvard University Press, 1960), p. 209.

33. *Four Comedies by Charles Macklin*, ed. J. O. Bartley (Hamden, Conn.: Archon Books, 1968), pp. 58–59. All subsequent references to *Love à la Mode, The True-Born Irishman, The School for Husbands*, and *The Man of the World* are to this edition and are indicated by parenthetical reference in the text.

34. In the catalogue are the following titles that indicate Macklin's interest in Irish history: *Laws of Ireland* (1678); Davis, *on Ireland* (1747); *Hibernia Curiosa* (1769); *English Rogue* (1680); Crawford's *History of Ireland* (1783); O'Connor's *History of Ireland* (1766);

Vallancey, *Collecteana de Rebus Hibernicis* (1770); Smith, *Cork, Waterford, and Kerry* (1784); Wynne's *History of Ireland* (1773); Twif's *Tour in Ireland* (1775), Folger Shakespeare Library catalogue number Pn 2598 M2 A3. The relatively late date of most of these books is a function of the fact that Macklin's first library was sunk in an unfortunate crossing of the Irish Sea.

35. As quoted in Appleton, *Charles Macklin*, p. 198. Mark Scowcroft suggests that the passage attempts to anglicize "Ach níl an dídean an bhannsach agan bó agan bhóithrín," which might mean "the pen [roof, shelter] is no protection to the cow on the road." Seamus Ó Maoláin offers the emmendation "Ach ní haon dídean an bhannsach don bhó agan bhóithrín" as more idiomatic. In fairness to both Dr. Scowcroft and Dr. Ó Maoláin, it must be added that both suggestions are very tentative as neither is familiar with the expression.

36. Seán Murphy, "Burke and Lucas: An Authorship Problem Re-examined," *Eighteenth-Century Ireland* 1 (1986): 156.

37. (London: 1746), p. 3.

38. I am indebted to Thomas Bartlett for this point.

39. *The Impartial History of Ireland* (London: 1762), p. 19.

40. *The Monthly Visitor*, 5 August 1797, p. 132.

41. *A Biographical Dictionary of Actors, Actresses, Musicians, Dancers, Managers & Other Stage Personnel in London 1660–1800*, vol. 10 (Carbondale: Southern Illinois University Press, 1984), p. 24.

42. Francis Aspry Congreve, *Authentic Memoirs of the Late Mr. Charles Macklin, Comedian* (London: 1798), p. 11.

43. *The London Stage, 1660–1800; Part Three, 1729–1747*, ed. A. H. Scouten (Carbondale: Southern Illinois University Press, 1961), p. 1235.

44. *A Scotsman's Remarks on the Farce of Love A La Mode* (London: 1760), pp. 5–6. Not all the Scots reacted this way, as a later edition makes clear: "It is singular that it has always been acted with more *eclat* in Scotland than anywhere else; which is a proof that the satire concentrated in the person of Sir Archy does not tell upon the consciences of the natives, and that the national lineaments of the part are true to nature"; (Edinburgh: 1829), p. iv.

45. *An Account of the Life and Genius of Mr. Charles Macklin, Comedian*, in *Mackliana*, vol. 2 (n.p.: n.d.), p. 37. Folger Shakespeare Library Catalogue number PN 2598 M2 A3 Cage.

46. J. O. Bartley discusses Macklin's hostility to Bute's administration in the introduction to *Four Comedies by Charles Macklin*, pp. 29–30.

47. Joseph T. Leerssen, *Mere Irish & Fíor-Ghael: Studies in the Idea of Irish Nationality, Its Development and Literary Expression Prior to the Nineteenth Century* (Philadelphia: John Benjamins, 1986), p. 140.

48. William Appleton, *Charles Macklin*, p. 130.

6. "BENEATH IËRNE'S BANNERS"

1. See J. G. Simms, *Colonial Nationalism 1698–1776* (Cork: Mercier Press, 1976), p. 62.

2. (London: 1770), pp. xv–xvi.

3. *An Introduction to the Study of the History and Antiquities of Ireland* (Dublin: 1772), p. xviii.

4. John Greene, who has in preparation a calendar of the Irish stage from 1720 to 1820, informs me that *The Siege of Tamor* was produced at Smock Alley on 26 April 1774 as a benefit for "Mr. Wilder."

5. W. S. Clark, *The Irish Stage in the Country Towns, 1720 to 1800* (Oxford: Clarendon Press, 1965), p. 235.

6. See W. J. McCormack, *Ascendancy and Tradition in Anglo-Irish Literary History from 1789 to 1939* (Oxford: Clarendon Press, 1985), pp. 71–75. James Kelly, however, argues that the use of the term was much more widespread than McCormack believes in "The Genesis of 'Protestant Ascendancy': The Rightboy Disturbances of the 1780s and Their Impact upon Protestant Opinion," in *Parliament, Politics and People: Essays in Eighteenth-Century Irish History,* ed. Gerard O'Brien (Blackrock, Co. Dublin: Irish Academic Press, 1989), pp. 93–127.

7. *The Miscellaneous Works, in Verse and Prose, of Gorges Edmond Howard, Esq.,* vol. 1 (Dublin: 1782), pp. xli–xlii. All subsequent references to this edition are identified in the text as *Works.*

8. "Anglo-Irish Patriotism and Its European Context: Notes toward a Reassessment," *Eighteenth-Century Ireland* 3 (1988): 15.

9. Christopher J. Wheatley, "Thomas Shadwell's *The Volunteers* and the Rhetoric of Honor and Patriotism," *ELH* 60 (1993): 397–418.

10. (reprint, Dublin: 1747), pp. 11–12.

11. *Britannia's Issue: The Rise of British Literature from Dryden to Ossian* (Cambridge: Cambridge University Press, 1993).

12. *The Antiquities and History of Ireland* (London: 1705), p. 6.

13. *Hibernia Anglicana: or, the History of Ireland from the Conquest thereof by the English, to the present Time,* Part One (London: 1689), "To the Reader," [iv].

14. *An Introduction to the Study of the History and Antiquities of Ireland,* p. i.

15. *Ierne Defended: or, a Candid Refutation of such Passages in the Rev. Dr. Leland's and the Rev. Mr. Whitaker's Works, as seem to affect the Authenticity and validity of Antient Irish History* (Dublin: 1774), p. 10.

16. Robert E. Ward, *Prince of Dublin Printers: The Letters of George Faulkner* (Lexington: University Press of Kentucky, 1972), pp. 32–33.

17. *An Epistle from G—— E—— H——RD, Esq. to Alderman George Faulkner with Notes Explanatory, Critical, and Historical by the Alderman and other Learned Authors* (Barataria: printed by Andrew Ferrara, at the Sign of Sancho's Head, Bribery Lane, 1772), p. 11.

18. *A Candid Appeal to the Public, on the Subject of a late Epistle, by Gorges Edmond Howard* (Dublin: 1771), p. 7.

19. *A Letter to Sir L——s O——n on the Late Prorogation and in Answer to his Letter to Mr. Faulkner, on the Subject of the rejected Money-Bill* (Dublin: 1770), p. 6.

20. *Some Questions upon the Legislative Constitution of Ireland* (Dublin: 1770), p. 4.

21. (Dublin: 1770), p. 20.

22. *The Policy of Poynings Law Fairly Explained and Considered: with Seasonable Advice to the People of Ireland* (Dublin: 1770), p. 15.

23. As quoted in R. B. McDowell, *Ireland in the Age of Imperialism and Revolution, 1760–1801* (Oxford: Clarendon Press, 1979), p. 226.

24. J. C. Beckett, *The Making of Modern Ireland, 1603–1923* (London: Faber and Faber, 1981), p. 204.

25. *A Comparative State of the Two Rejected Money Bills by a Barrister* (Dublin: 1770),

pp. 3–4. The Royal Irish Academy copy has a note suggesting that the pamphlet is by Ridley Powes.

26. C.f. *Some Questions upon the Legislative Constitution of Ireland*, p. 18, and "Posthumus," *A Letter to the People of Ireland*, 3rd ed. (London: 1770), p. 15.

27. *Dissertations on the History of Ireland* (Dublin: 1766), pp. 5, 276–77.

28. Ibid., pp. 236–37.

29. *An Historical and Critical Review of the Civil Wars in Ireland, from the Reign of Queen Elizabeth, to the Settlement under King William* (Dublin: 1775), pp. v–vi.

30. *Catholicism in a Protestant Kingdom: A Study of the Irish Ancien Régime* (Dublin: Gill and Macmillan, 1994), p. 14.

31. In James Thomas Kirkman, *Memoirs of the Life of Charles Macklin, Esq.*, vol. 2 (London: 1799), pp. 55, 50–51.

32. *By Authority. Memoirs of Francis Dobbs, Esq. also Genuine Reports of his Speeches in Parliament on the Subject of an Union, and his Prediction of the Second Coming of the Messiah; with extracts from his Poem on the Millenium* (Dublin: 1800), p. 6.

33. *The True Principles of Government applied to the Irish Constitution in a Code of Laws* (Dublin: 1783), p. 47. Subsequently cited in the text as *Principles*.

34. *Memoirs of Francis Dobbs*, p. 34.

35. Neil Longley York, *Neither Kingdom nor Nation: The Irish Quest for Constitutional Rights, 1698–1800* (Washington: Catholic University of America Press, 1994), pp. 84–85.

36. *A Letter to the Right Honourable Lord North on his Propositions in Favour of Ireland* (Dublin: 1780), p. 8.

37. *A History of Irish Affairs from the 12th of October, 1779, to the 15th September, 1782, the Day of Lord Temple's Arrival* (Dublin: 1782), p. [7].

38. McDowell, *Ireland in the Age of Imperialism and Revolution*, pp. 297–98.

39. *Poems by Francis Dobbs* (Dublin: 1788), p. 11.

40. *The Patriot King; or Irish Chief* (London: 1774), p. 15. All subsequent references are to this edition.

41. Henry St. John, Viscount Bolingbroke, *Political Writings*, ed. Isaac Kramnick (New York: Meredith Corp., 1970), pp. 76, 78.

EPILOGUE

1. In an undated pamphlet from around 1758, an anonymous commentator also calls for a nationalized, if not national, theater: "I could wish, for the Good of the State, and the Honour of the Stage, that our Theatre was put on the same Footing as that of *Holland* is; where the Government undertaking the Management of it, pays the best performers but 300 £ per Annum, and the worst 100 £: and the Overplus of the Profits is appropriated to public Uses. This would produce a great Revenue to the State; confine the Luxury of the Capital players within the proper Bounds; relieve the Necessities of the inferior Ones; render such huge Numbers of Performers, as our *Irish* Stage is loaded with, unnecessary; and save them the disagreeable and disgraceful Task of forcing their Tickets on their Creditors for, what is *called*, Benefits"; *An Epistle to Henry Mossop, Esq. on the Institution and End of the Drama, and the Present State of the Irish Stage* (Dublin: printed for J. Milliken, n.d.), p. 41.

2. As quoted in La Tourette Stockwell, *Dublin Theatres and Theatre Customs, 1637–1820* (1938; reprint, New York: Benjamin Blom, 1968), pp. 154–56.

3. Martin Severin Peterson, "Robert Jephson (1736–1803): A Study of His Life and Works," *Language, Literature, and Criticism* 11 (Lincoln: University of Nebraska Press, 1930): 1–45.

4. "The Turtle and the Epicure/To an Irish Nobleman," in *Sentimental Fables* (Belfast: 1771), p. 202.

5. *The History of Ireland* (London: 1763), pp. v–vi.

6. *The History of the Rebellion and Civil-War in Ireland* (Dublin: 1768), p. x.

7. Robert Hitchcock, *An Historical View of the Irish Stage from the Earliest Period down to the close of the Season 1788*, vol. 1 (Dublin: 1788), p. 197.

8. Maurice Craig, *Dublin 1660–1860* (London: Penguin, 1992), p. 274.

9. *The Ireland of Sir Jonah Barrington, Selections from His Personal Sketches*, ed. Hugh B. Staples (Seattle: University of Washington Press, 1967), p. 202.

10. *Recollections of the Life of John O'Keeffe*, vol. 1 (London: 1826), p. 47. Subsequently cited in the text as *Recollections*.

11. *Patrick in Prussia, or, Love in a Camp* (Dublin: 1786), p. 34.

12. Thomas Bartlett, *The Fall and Rise of the Irish Nation: The Catholic Question, 1690–1830* (Dublin: Gill and Macmillan, 1992), pp. 98, 201.

13. *The United Irishmen: Popular Politics in Ulster and Dublin, 1791–1798* (Oxford: Clarendon Press, 1994), p. 21.

14. For example, Allan Ramsay's *Gentle Shepherd*, John Michelburne's *Ireland Preserved; or, the Siege of Londonderry*, and Ashton's *The Battle of Aughrim* were apparently popular with United Irishmen in Belfast; Mary Helen Thuente, *The Harp Restrung: The United Irishmen and the Rise of Literary Nationalism* (Syracuse, N.Y.: Syracuse University Press, 1994), pp. 69–73.

15. As quoted in D. George Boyce, *Nationalism in Ireland*, 2nd ed. (London: Routledge, 1991), p. 125.

16. *Prelude to Union: Anglo-Irish Politics in the 1780s* (Cork: Cork University Press, 1992), p. 1.

17. *The Fallen Patriot* (Dublin: 1790), p. 8. All subsequent references are to this text.

18. *Modern Ireland, 1600–1972* (London: Penguin Books, 1989), p. 252.

19. *The Miscellaneous Works, in Verse and Prose, of Gorges Edmond Howard, Esq.*, vol. 1 (Dublin: 1782), p. ix. Subsequently cited in the text as *Works*.

20. *Selections from the Tatler and the Spectator*, ed. Angus Ross (Harmondsworth, Middlesex, England: Penguin, 1982), p. 322.

21. *Poems by Francis Dobbs* (Dublin: 1788), p. [22]. All subsequent references are to this edition.

22. Warner's *History of Ireland* (1763) mentions that Sitric's wife was Irish, although he does not name her (see pages 383–84). Moreover, William Crawford's *A History of Ireland. From the Earliest Period to the Present Time*, to which Francis Dobbs was a subscriber, also claims Sitric's wife was Irish: vol. 1 (Strabane: 1783), p. 77.

23. *The General History of Ireland* (London: 1723), pp. 467, 468.

24. *By Authority. Memoirs of Francis Dobbs, Esq. also Genuine Reports of his Speeches in Parliament on the Subject of an Union, and His Prediction of the Second Coming of the Messiah; with Extracts from his Poem on the Millenium* (Dublin: 1800), p. 11.

25. *The Man from God Knows Where* (Blackrock, Co. Dublin: Tartan, 1995), p. 149.

BIBLIOGRAPHY

Adams, J. R. R. *The Printed Word and the Common Man: Popular Culture in Ulster 1700–1900.* Belfast: Institute of Irish Studies, 1987.

Addison, Joseph. *Cato.* In *Eighteenth-Century Plays.* Ed. Ricardo Quintana. New York: Modern Library, 1952.

Addison, Joseph, and Sir Richard Steele. *Selections from the Tatler and the Spectator.* Ed. Angus Ross. Harmondsworth, Middlesex, England: Penguin: 1982.

Almon, John. Introduction to *The Case of Ireland Being Bound by Acts of Parliament in England Stated.* London: 1770.

Alumni Dublinenses. Dublin: 1935.

The Answer of a Person of Quality to a Scandalous Letter Lately Printed and Subscribed by P.W. Dublin: 1662.

An Answer to the Paper Delivered by Mr. Ashton at his Execution to Sir Francis Child: Sheriff of London, &c. Together with the Paper it self. London: 1690.

An Answer to the Proposal for the Universal Use of Irish Manufactures. Dublin: 1720.

Appleton, William W. *Charles Macklin, an Actor's Life.* Cambridge: Harvard University Press, 1960.

Ashton, Robert. *The Battle of Aughrim: or the Fall of St. Ruth.* Dublin: 1728.

[Atterbury, Francis]. *An Argument to Prove the Affections of the People of England to be the Best Security of the Government.* London: 1716.

Avery, Emmett L., ed. *The London Stage, 1660–1800; Part Two, 1700–1729.* 2 vols. Carbondale: Southern Illinois University Press, 1960.

Barnard, T. C. *Cromwellian Ireland: English Government and Reform in Ireland 1649–1660.* Oxford: Oxford University Press, 1975.

Barrington, Jonah. *The Ireland of Sir Jonah Barrington: Selections from His Personal Sketches.* Ed. Hugh B. Staples. Seattle: University of Washington Press, 1967.

Bartlett, Thomas. "Army and Society in Eighteenth-Century Ireland." In *Kings in Conflict: The Revolutionary War in Ireland and Its Aftermath 1689–1750,* ed. W. A. Maguire, 173–84. Belfast: Blackstaff Press, 1990.

———. "The Rise and Fall of the Protestant Nation, 1690–1800," *Éire-Ireland* 26 (1991): 7–18.

———. *The Fall and Rise of the Irish Nation: The Catholic Question, 1690–1830.* Dublin: Gill and Macmillan, 1992.

———. "'A Weapon of War yet Untried': Irish Catholics and the Armed Forces of the Crown, 1760–1830." In *Men, Women and War,* ed. T. G. Fraser and Keith Jeffery, 66–85. Dublin: Lilliput Press, 1993.

Bartley, J. O. *Teague, Shenkin and Sawney: Being an Historical Study of the Earliest Irish, Welsh, and Scottish Characters in English Plays.* Cork: Cork University Press, 1954.

Beckett, J. C. *The Making of Modern Ireland, 1603–1923.* Rev. ed. London: Faber and Faber, 1981.

———. "Literature in English, 1691–1800." In *A New History of Ireland,* vol. 4. Ed. T. W. Moody and W. E. Vaughan, 424–70. Oxford: Clarendon Press, 1986.

Beidelman, T. O. *Colonial Evangelism: A Socio-Historical Study of an East African Mission at the Grassroots.* Bloomington: Indiana University Press, 1982.

Bevis, Richard. *The Laughing Tradition: Stage Comedy in Garrick's Day.* London: George Prior Publishers, 1980.

Black, Jeremy. *Eighteenth-Century Europe, 1700–1789.* New York: St. Martin's Press, 1990.

Bliss, Alan. *Spoken English in Ireland 1600–1740.* Dublin: Cadenus Press, 1979.

Boesky, Amy. "Nation, Miscegenation: Membering Utopia in Henry Neville's *The Isle of the Pines.*" *Texas Studies in Language and Literature* 37 (1995): 165–84.

Bolingbroke, Henry St. John. *Political Writings.* Ed. Isaac Kramnick. New York: Meredith Corp., 1970.

Book of the Prophecies of the Prophet L——s. Dublin: 1748.

Bottigheimer, Karl S. *English Money and Irish Land: The "Adventurers" in the Cromwellian Settlement of Ireland.* Oxford: Clarendon Press, 1971.

Boyce, D. George. *Nationalism in Ireland.* 2nd ed. London: Routledge, 1991.

Brady, Anne M., and Brian Cleeve. *A Biographical Dictionary of Irish Writers.* Dublin: Lilliput Press, 1985.

[Brooke, Henry]. *The Farmers Letter[s] to the Protestants of Ireland [1–6].* Dublin: 1745.

Brookiana. 2 vols. London: 1804.

Browne, John. *The Case of John Browne, Esq.* London: 1725.

Burke, Edmund. *Irish Affairs.* Intro. by Conor Cruise O'Brien. London: Cresset Library, 1988.

Burnell, Henry. *Landgartha.* Dublin: 1641.

Burns, Robert E. *Irish Parliamentary Politics in the Eighteenth Century.* 2 vols. Washington: Catholic University of America Press, 1989–90.

Butler, Sarah. *Irish Tales: or, Instructive Histories for the Conduct of Life.* London: 1716.

Cairns, David, and Shaun Richards. *Writing Ireland: Colonialism, Nationalism, and Culture.* Manchester: Manchester University Press, 1988.

Canfield, J. Douglas. *Tricksters & Estates: On the Ideology of Restoration Comedy.* Lexington: University Press of Kentucky, 1997.

Carleton, William. *The Life of William Carleton.* New York: Garland Press, 1979.

Carroll, Denis. *The Man from God Knows Where.* Blackrock, Co. Dublin: Tartan, 1995.

C.J. *Irelands Mirror: or, a Chronicle of the Times.* 2 vols. Dublin: 1804–5.

Clark, William Smith. *The Early Irish Stage: The Beginnings to 1720.* Oxford: Clarendon Press, 1955.

———. *The Irish Stage in the County Towns, 1720–1800.* Oxford: Clarendon Press, 1965.

A Comparative State of the Two Rejected Money Bills, by a Barrister. Dublin: 1770.

Congreve, Francis Aspry. *Authentic Memoirs of the Late Mr. Charles Macklin, Comedian.* London: 1798.

Connolly, S. J. *Religion, Law and Power: The Making of Protestant Ireland 1660–1760.* Oxford: Clarendon Press, 1992.

Cooke, William. *Memoirs of Charles Macklin, Comedian.* London: 1804.

Corkery, Daniel. *The Hidden Ireland: A Study of Gaelic Munster in the Eighteenth Century.* 1924. Reprint, Dublin: Gill and Macmillan, 1967.

Cox, Richard. *Hibernia Anglicana: or, the History of Ireland from the Conquest thereof by the English to the Present Time.* Part One, London: 1689. Part Two, London: 1690.

Crawford, William. *A History of Ireland. From the Earliest Period to the Present Time.* Vol. 1. Strabane: 1783.

Cullen, Louis M. *The Emergence of Modern Ireland, 1600–1900*. New York: Holmes and Meier, 1981.

——. *An Economic History of Ireland Since 1660*. 2nd ed. London: B. T. Batsford, 1987.

——. "Catholic Social Classes under the Penal Laws." In *Endurance and Emergence: Catholics in Ireland in the Eighteenth Century*, ed. T. P. Power and Kevin Whelan, 57–84. Dublin: Irish Academic Press, 1990.

Curry, John. *An Historical and Critical Review of the Civil Wars in Ireland, from the Reign of Queen Elizabeth, to the Settlement under King William*. Dublin: 1775.

Curtin, Nancy J. *The United Irishmen: Popular Politics in Ulster and Dublin 1791–1798*. Oxford: Clarendon Press, 1994.

Curtis, Edmund. *A History of Ireland*. London: Methuen, 1936.

Craig, Maurice. *Dublin 1660–1860*. London: Penguin, 1992.

Davies, John. *Historical Relations: or, a Discovery of the True Causes why Ireland was never entirely Subdued, Nor brought under Obediance of the Crown of England until the Beginning of the Reign of King James I*. Dublin: 1704.

Davis, J. C. *Utopia and the Ideal Society: A Study of English Utopian Writing 1516–1700*. Cambridge: Cambridge University Press, 1981.

Deane, Seamus. *A Short History of Irish Literature*. London: Hutchinson & Co., 1986.

Dickson, David. *New Foundations: Ireland 1660–1800*. Dublin: Criterion Press, 1987.

Dobbs, Francis. *The Patriot King; or Irish Chief*. London: 1774.

——. *A Letter to the Right Honourable Lord North on his Propositions in Favour of Ireland*. Dublin: 1780.

——. *A History of Irish Affairs from the 12th of October, 1779, to the 15th September, 1782, the Day of Lord Temple's Arrival*. Dublin: 1782.

——. *The True Principles of Government applied to the Irish Constitution in a Code of Laws*. Dublin: 1783.

——. *Poems by Francis Dobbs*. Dublin: 1788.

——. *By Authority. Memoirs of Francis Dobbs, Esq. also Genuine Reports of his Speeches in Parliament on the Subject of an Union, and his Prediction of the Second Coming of the Messiah; with extracts from his Poem on the Millenium*. Dublin: 1800.

——. *A Concise View from History and Prophecy, of the Great Predictions in the Sacred Writings, that have been fulfilled; also of those that remain to be accomplished*. London: 1800.

Donovan, Kevin. "*Jack the Giant Quellar:* Political Theater in Ascendancy Dublin." *Éire-Ireland* 30 (1995): 70–88.

Drake, Peter. *Amiable Renegade: The Memoirs of Captain Peter Drake, 1671–1753*. Stanford: Stanford University Press, 1960.

Dryden, John. *The Works of John Dryden*. Vol 17. Ed. Samuel Holt Monk, A. E. Wallace Maurer, Vinton A. Dearing, R. V. LeClerq, and Maximillian E. Novak. Berkeley: University of California Press, 1971.

Duffy, Charles Gavan. *My Life in Two Hemispheres*. New York: Macmillan, 1898.

[Dunkin, William]. *TEXNHΘYPAMBEIA* [*Technethyrambeia*] *or a Poem upon Paddy Murphy, Porter of Trin. Coll. Dublin. Translated from the Latin Original* [by Joseph Cowper]. Dublin: 1728.

Ehrenpreis, Irvin. *Swift; the Man, His Works, and the Age*. Vol. 3. London: Methuen, 1983.

An Epistle from Tully in the Shades to Orator Ma——n in Covent Garden. London: 1755.

An Epistle to Henry Mossop, Esq. on the Institution and End of the Drama, and the Present State of the Irish Stage. Dublin: n.d.

An Exact Journal of the Victorious Progress of their Majesties forces under the Command of General Ginckle, This Summer in Ireland. London: 1691.

Fabricant, Carol. *Swift's Landscape.* Rev. ed. Notre Dame, Ind.: University of Notre Dame Press, 1995.

Fagan, Patrick. *The Second City: Portrait of Dublin 1700–1760.* Dublin: Branar, 1986.

Fitzpatrick, Brendan. *Seventeenth-Century Ireland: The War of Religions.* Dublin: Gill and Macmillan, 1988.

Fielding, Henry. *Amelia.* Ed. David Blewett. New York: Penguin, 1987.

———. *The History of Tom Jones, a Foundling.* Ed. R. P. C. Mutter. New York: Penguin, 1989.

Fletcher, John. *The Faithful Shepherdess.* In *The Dramatic Works of the Beaumont and Fletcher Canon,* vol. 3, gen. ed. Fredson Bowers. Cambridge: Cambridge University Press, 1976.

Forman, Charles. *A Letter to the Right Honourable Sir Robert Sutton for Disbanding the Irish Regiments in the Service of France and Spain.* Dublin: 1728.

Foster, R. F. *Modern Ireland 1600–1972.* London: Penguin, 1989.

Frye, Northrop. "Varieties of Literary Utopias." In *Utopias and Utopian Thought,* ed. Frank E. Manuel, 25–49. Boston: Beacon Press, 1966.

Gilbert, J. T. *A History of Dublin.* Vol. 1. Dublin: 1861.

[Good, Benjamin]. *True Interest of the Hanover Treaty Considered by a Lover of His Country.* Dublin: 1727.

Gookin, Vincent. *The Great Case of Transplantation in Ireland Discussed.* London: 1663.

Graham, John, ed. *Ireland Preserved; or, the Siege of Londonderry and The Battle of Aughrim,* by John Michelburne and Robert Ashton. Dublin: 1841.

Greene, John C., and Gladys L. H. Clark. *The Dublin Stage, 1720–1745.* Bethlehem, Penn.: Lehigh University Press, 1993.

Hanmer, Meredith. *The History of Ireland Collected by Three Learned Authors Viz. Meredith Hanmer Edmund Campion and Edmund Spenser.* Dublin: 1633.

Harvey, Karen J., and Kevin B. Pry. "John O'Keefe as an Irish Playwright within the Theatrical, Social and Economic Context of His Time." *Éire-Ireland* 22 (1987): 19–43.

Hayton, D. W. "Ireland and the English Ministers 1707–16." D.Phil. thesis, Oxford University, 1975.

———. "Walpole and Ireland." In *Britain in the Age of Walpole.* 95–120. London: Macmillan, 1984.

———. "From Barbarian to Burlesque: English Images of the Irish c. 1660–1750." *Irish Economic and Social History* 15 (1988): 5–31.

Head, Richard. *Hic et Ubique; or, the Humours of Dublin.* London: 1663.

———. *The English Rogue.* London: 1665.

———. *The Floating Island: or, a New Discovery, relating the strange Adventure on a late Voyage from Lambethana to Villa Franca alias Ramallia, to the Eastward of Terra del Templo.* n.p.: 1673.

———. *The Western Wonder: or, O Brazeel.* London: 1673.

———. *The Complaisant Companion, or new Jests; witty Reparties; Bulls; Rhodomontados; and pleasant Novels.* London: 1674.

———. *Jackson's Recantation or, the Life and Death of the Notorious High-Way-Man now hanging in Chains at Hampstead.* 1674. Reprint, *Miscellanea Antiqua Anglicana* 3:31. London: 1873.

———. *Proteus Redivivus: or the Art of Wheedling.* London: 1679.

Hibernia Notitia. Dublin: 1723.

Hibernia Pacata: or, a Narrative of the Affairs of Ireland, from the Famous Battle of Clontarf, where Brian Boirom defeated the Norwegians, till the Settlement under Henry II. Written originally in Irish and now First Translated by Father Neri of Tuam, and Adorned with Notes by several Hands. N.p.: 1753.

[Hiffernan, Paul]. *The Tickler Nº I. II. III. IV. V. VI and VII. The Second Edition.* Dublin: 1748.

Highfill, Philip, Jr., Kalman A. Burnim, and Edward Langhams. *Biographical Dictionary of Actors, Actresses, Musicians, Dancers, Managers & Other Stage Personnel in London 1660–1800.* Vol. 10. Carbondale: Southern Illinois University Press, 1984.

Hill, Jacqueline R. "Popery and Protestantism, Civil and Religious Liberty: The Disputed Lessons of Irish History 1690–1812." *Past and Present* 118 (1988): 96–129.

The History of the Rise, Progress, and Tendency of Patriotism by a Freeholder. The Third Edition. Dublin: 1747.

Hitchcock, Robert. *An Historical View of the Irish Stage from the Earliest Period down to the close of the Season 1788.* 2 vols. Dublin: 1788.

Hobbes, Thomas. *Leviathan.* Ed. C. B. Macpherson. Harmondsworth, Middlesex, England: Penguin, 1981.

Holinshead, Raphael, and John Hooker. *The Second Volume of Chronicles: Conteining the description, conquest, inhabitation, and troublesome state of Ireland.* n.p.: 1586.

Holmes, Geoffrey. *British Politics in the Age of Anne.* Rev. ed. London: Hambledon Press, 1987.

Howard, Gorges Edmond. *Some Questions upon the Legislative Constitution of Ireland.* Dublin: 1770.

———. *The Miscellaneous Works, in Verse and Prose, of Gorges Edmond Howard.* 3 vols. Dublin: 1782.

Hume, Robert D. *The Development of English Drama in the Late Seventeenth Century.* Oxford: Clarendon Press, 1976.

———. *The Rakish Stage: Studies in English Drama, 1660–1800.* Carbondale: Southern Illinois University Press, 1983.

Irish Book Lover. 10 (1919): 65–66.

The Irish Hudibras or Fingallian Prince. London: 1689.

Jephson, Robert. *A Candid Appeal to the Public, on the Subject of a Late Epistle, by Gorges Edmond Howard.* Dublin: 1771.

———. *An Epistle from G—— E—— H——RD, Esq. to Alderman George Faulkner with Notes Explanatory, Critical, and Historical by the Alderman and other Learned Authors.* Barataria: printed by Andrew Ferrara, at the Sign of Sancho's Head, Bribery Lane, 1772.

Kelly, James. "The Genesis of 'Protestant Ascendancy': The Rightboy Disturbances of the 1780s and Their Impact upon Protestant Opinion." In *Parliament, Politics and People: Essays in Eighteenth-Century Irish History,* ed. Gerard O'Brien, 93–127. Blackrock, Co. Dublin: Irish Academic Press, 1989.

———. *Prelude to Union: Anglo-Irish Politics in the 1780s.* Cork: Cork University Press, 1992.

———. " 'The Glorious and Immortal Memory': Commemoration and Protestant Identity in Ireland 1660–1800." *Proceedings of the Royal Irish Academy* 94C (1994): 25–52.

Kiberd, Declan. "Irish Literature and Irish History." In *The Oxford History of Ireland*, ed. R. F. Foster, 230–81. Oxford: Oxford University Press, 1989.

Kirkman, James Thomas. *Memoirs of the Life of Charles Macklin, Esq.* 2 vols. London: 1799.

Kosok, Heinz. "'George My Belov'd King, and Ireland My Honour'd Country': John O'Keeffe and Ireland." *Irish University Review* 22 (1992): 40–54.

Leadam, I. S. *The History of England from the Accession of Anne to the Death of George II.* 1912. Reprint, New York: Greenwood Press, 1969.

Leerssen, Joseph T. [Joep]. *Mere Irish & Fíor Ghael: Studies in the Idea of Irish Nationality, Its Development and Literary Expression Prior to the Nineteenth Century.* Philadelphia: John Benjamins, 1986.

———. "Anglo-Irish Patriotism and Its European Context: Notes toward a Reassessment." *Eighteenth-Century Ireland* 3 (1988): 7–24.

Leighton, C. D. A. *Catholicism in a Protestant Kingdom: A Study of the Irish Ancien Régime.* Dublin: Gill and Macmillan, 1994.

A Letter from a Member of the House of Commons in Ireland to a Gentleman of the Long Robe in Great-Britain: Containing an Answer to some Objections made against the Judicatory Power of the Parliament of Ireland. Dublin: 1719.

A Letter to Sir L——s O——n on the Late Prorogation and in Answer to his Letter to Mr. Faulkner, on the Subject of the rejected Money-Bill. Dublin: 1770.

[Lowman, Moses]. *The Mercy of the Government Vindicated.* London: 1716.

Lucas, A. T. *Cattle in Ancient Ireland.* Kilkenny: Boethius Press, 1989.

Lucas, Charles. *An Apology for the Civil Rights and Liberties of the Common and Citizens of Dublin.* Dublin: 1748–49.

———. *A Sixteenth Address to the Free Citizens and Free-holders of the City of Dublin.* Dublin: 1748.

———. *An Eleventh Address to the Free Citizens, and Free-Holders of the City of Dublin.* Dublin: 1749.

Lynch, John. *Cambrensis Refuted by Gratianus Lucius.* Trans. by Theophilus O'Flanagan. Dublin: 1795.

Lynch, Kathleen. *Roger Boyle, First Earl of Orrery.* Knoxville: University of Tennessee Press, 1965.

MacCurtin, Hugh. *A Brief Discourse in Vindication of the Antiquity of Ireland.* Dublin: 1717.

McDowell, R. B. *Ireland in the Age of Imperialism and Revolution, 1760–1801.* Oxford: Clarendon Press, 1979.

Mackliana. 2 vols. N.p.: n.d. Folger Shakespeare Library Catalogue number PN 2598 M2 A3 Cage.

Macklin, Charles. *King Henry the VII, or the Popish Impostor.* London: 1746.

———. *Love à la Mode.* Edinburgh: 1829.

———. *A Will and no Will, or a Bone for the Lawyers and The New Play Criticiz'd, or the Plague of Envy.* Intro. by Jean B. Kern. Augustan Reprint Series 127–8. Los Angeles: William Andrews Clark Memorial Library, 1967.

———. *Four Comedies by Charles Macklin.* Ed. J. O. Bartley. Hamden, Conn.: Archon Books, 1968.

M——ckl——n's Answer to Tully. London: 1755.

Macpherson, James. *Original Papers; containing the Secret History of Great Britain, from the Restoration, to the accession of the House of Hannover.* London: 1775.

Mambretti, Catherine Cole. "Orinda on the Restoration Stage." *Comparative Literature* 37 (1985): 233–51.

Marin, Louis. *Utopics: The Semiological Play of Textual Spaces*. Trans. by Robert A. Vollrath. Atlantic Highlands, N.J.: Humanities Press International, 1984.

Marryat, Thomas. *Sentimental Fables*. Belfast: 1771.

McCormack, W. J. *Ascendancy and Tradition in Anglo-Irish Literary History from 1789 to 1939*. Oxford: Clarendon Press, 1985.

McCracken, J. L. "The Political Structure, 1714–60." In *A New History of Ireland*, vol. 4, ed. T. W. Moody and W. E. Vaughan, 57–83. Oxford: Clarendon Press, 1986.

———. "The Social Structure and Social Life." In *A New History of Ireland*, vol. 4, *Eighteenth Century Ireland, 1691–1800*, ed. T. W. Moody and W. E. Vaughn, 31–56. Oxford: Clarendon Press, 1986.

McGuire, James. "James II and Ireland, 1685–90." In *Kings in Conflict: The Revolutionary War in Ireland and Its Aftermath, 1689–1750*, ed. W. A. Maguire, 45–60. Belfast: Blackstaff Press, 1990.

McHugh, Roger, and Maurice Harmon. *A Short History of Anglo-Irish Literature from Its Origins to the Present Day*. Dublin: Wolfhound Press, 1982.

Mercier, Vivian. *Modern Irish Literature, Sources and Founders*. Ed. Eilís Dillon. Oxford: Clarendon Press, 1994.

Mervyn, Audley. *The Speech of Sir Audley Mervyn Knight*. London: 1662.

M'Gee, Thomas D'Arcy. *The Irish Writers of the Seventeenth Century*. Dublin: 1846.

Michelburne, John. *Ireland Preserv'd; or the Siege of Londonderry*. 1705. Reprint, Belfast: 1744.

A Modest Apology for Priestcraft. London: 1720.

Montgomery, Ian. "An Entire and Coherent History of Ireland, Richard Cox's *Hibernia Anglicana*." *The Linen Hall Review* 12 (1995): 9–11.

More, Thomas. *Utopia*. In *Famous Utopias*, intro. by Charles M. Andrews. New York: Tudor Publishing, n.d.

Morley, Vincent. "Hugh MacCurtin: An Irish Poet in the French Army." *Eighteenth-Century Ireland* 8 (1993): 49–59.

Munter, Robert. *A Dictionary of the Print Trade in Ireland*. New York: Fordham University Press, 1988.

Murphy, Richard. *New Selected Poems*. London: Faber and Faber, 1989.

Murphy, Seán. "Burke and Lucas: An Authorship Problem Re-examined." *Eighteenth-Century Ireland* 1 (1986): 143–76.

———. "Charles Lucas, Catholicism and Nationalism." *Eighteenth-Century Ireland* 8 (1993): 83–102.

Murray, Christopher. "Drama 1690–1800." In *The Field Day Anthology of Irish Writing*, vol. 1, gen. ed. Seamus Deane, 500–657. Derry: Field Day Publications, 1991.

Myrtillo. A Pastoral Poem, Lamenting the Death of Mr. Charles Shadwell, Gratefully inscrib'd to all his Friends. Dublin: 1726.

Nelson, William. Intro. to *Twentieth-Century Interpretations of Utopia*. Englewood Cliffs, N.J.: Prentice-Hall, 1968.

Obituaries of Remarkable Persons; with Biographical Anecdotes. (n.p.: n.p., July 1791), p. 622.

O'Brien, Conor Cruise. *The Great Melody: A Thematic Biography and Commented Anthology of Edmund Burke*. London: Minerva, 1993.

O'Brien, Donough. *History of the O'Briens*. London: B. T. Batsford, 1949.

O'Brien, Gerard. *Anglo-Irish Politics in the Age of Grattan and Pitt*. Blackrock, Co. Dublin: Irish Academic Press, 1987.

———. "The Strange Death of the Irish Language, 1780–1800." In *Parliament, Politics and People: Essays in Eighteenth-Century Irish History*, ed. Gerard O'Brien, 149–70. Blackrock, Co. Dublin: Irish Academic Press, 1989.

O'Brien, Mary. *The Fallen Patriot*. Dublin: 1790.

———. *The Political Monitor; or Regent's Friend. Being a Collection of Poems Published in England During the Agitation of the Regency*. Dublin: 1790.

Ó Catháin, Diarmid. "Dermot O'Connor, Translator of Keating." *Eighteenth-Century Ireland* 2 (1987): 67–87.

O'Connor, Dermo'd. *The General History of Ireland . . . Collected by the Learned Jeoffrey Keating D.D.* London: 1723.

O'Conor [or O'Connor], Charles. *Dissertations on the History of Ireland*. Dublin: 1766.

O'Faolain, Sean. *King of the Beggars: A Life of Daniel O'Connor*. 1938. Reprint, Swords, Co. Dublin: Poolbeg Press, 1995.

O'Halloran, Sylvester. *An Introduction to the Study of the History and Antiquities of Ireland*. Dublin: 1772.

———. *Ierne Defended: or, a Candid Refutation of Such Passages in the Rev. Dr. Leland's and the Rev. Mr. Whitaker's Works, as seem to affect the Authenticity and validity of Antient Irish History*. Dublin: 1774.

O'Keeffe, John. *Patrick in Prussia, or, Love in a Camp*. Dublin: 1786.

———. *Recollections of the Life of John O'Keeffe*. Vol 1. London: 1826.

Ó Tuama, Seán, ed. *An Duanaire 1600–1900: Poems of the Dispossessed*. Trans. Thomas Kinsella. n.p.: Dolmen Press, 1981.

Peterson, Martin Severin. "Robert Jephson (1736–1803): A Study of His Life and Works." *Language, Literature, and Criticism* 11. Lincoln: University of Nebraska Press, 1930. 1–45.

Philips, William. *The Revengeful Queen*. London: 1698.

———. *Hibernia Freed*. London: 1722.

———. *Belisarius*. London: 1724.

———. *St. Stephen's Green, or, the Generous Lovers*. Ed. Christopher Murray. Dublin: Cadenus Press, 1979.

Plattel, Martin G. *Utopian and Critical Thinking*. Pittsburgh: Duquesne University Press, 1972.

The Policy of Poynings Law Fairly Explained and Considered: with Seasonable Advice to the People of Ireland. Dublin: 1770.

"Posthumus." *A Letter to the People of Ireland*. 3rd ed. London: 1770.

A Preservative Against Popery. Dublin: 1728.

Reily, Hugh. *The Impartial History of Ireland*. London: 1762.

Remonstrance in the Name of the Lads in all the Schools of Ireland. Dublin: 1727–28.

Ross, Ian Campbell. "'One of the Principal Nations of Europe': The Representation of Ireland in Sarah Butler's *Irish Tales*." *Eighteenth-Century Fiction* 7 (1994): 1–16.

Rowe, Nicholas. *Tamerlane*. Ed. Landon C. Burnes, Jr. Philadelphia: University of Pennsylvania Press, 1966.

Russell, Thomas. *Journals and Memoirs of Thomas Russell*. Ed. C. J. Woods. Blackrock, Co. Dublin: Irish Academic Press, 1991.

Schneider, Ben Ross, Jr. *Index to the London Stage 1660–1800*. Carbondale: Southern Illinois University Press, 1979.

A Scotsman's Remarks on the Farce of Love A La Mode. London: 1760.

Scouten, A. H., ed. *The London Stage 1660–1800; Part Three, 1729–1747.* Carbondale: Southern Illinois University Press, 1961.

Secret Memoirs of Barleduc . . . With an Account of the Late Conspiracies for an Invasion and Rebellion in Great Britain. Dublin: 1715.

Shadwell, Charles. *The Fair Quaker of Deal, or, the Humours of the Navy.* London: 1710.

——. *The Humours of the Army.* London: 1713.

——. *Five New Plays.* London: 1720.

——. *The Work of Mr. Charles Shadwell.* 2 vols. Dublin: 1720.

Shaw, Catherine. "*Landgartha* and the Irish Dilemma." *Éire-Ireland* 13 (1978): 26–39.

Sheldon, Esther K. *Thomas Sheridan of Smock Alley.* Princeton: Princeton University Press, 1967.

Shepherd, Robert. *Ireland's Fate: The Boyne and After.* London: Aurum Press, 1990.

Sheridan, Thomas. *The Intelligencer.* No 6. Dublin: 1728.

Simms, J. G. *Colonial Nationalism 1698–1776.* Cork: Mercier Press, 1976.

Smedley, Jonathan. *A Rational and Historical Account of the Principles which Gave Birth to the Late Rebellion.* Dublin: 1718.

"Society of Gentlemen." *Monthly Visitor,* 5 August 1797, p. 132.

Stockwell, La Tourette. *Dublin Theatres and Theatre Customs, 1637–1820.* 1938. Reprint, New York: Benjamin Blom, 1968.

Story, George. *An Impartial History of the Wars of Ireland with a Continuation thereof. In Two Parts.* London: 1693.

A Stricture upon Observations on a Speech by an Impartial Observer. Dublin: 1770.

Summers, Montague. Introduction to *The Complete Works of Thomas Shadwell.* London: Fortune Press, 1927.

Sutherland, Robert. *An Enquiry into the Reasons of the Conduct of Great Britain with Relation to the Present State of Affairs in Europe.* Dublin: 1727.

Swift, Jonathan. *A Proposal for the Universal Use of Irish Manufacture.* Dublin: 1720.

——. "Dialogue between Mad Mullinix and Trim." In *The Intelligencer,* no. 8. Dublin: 1728.

——. *Irish Tracts and Sermons.* Ed. Herbert Davis and Louis Landa. Oxford: Basil Blackwell, 1963.

——. *The Correspondence of Jonathan Swift.* Vol. 4. Rev. ed. Ed. Harold Williams. Oxford: Clarendon Press, 1972.

The Tallies of War and Peace. Dublin: 1724.

Thackeray, William. *The Irish Sketchbook.* Dublin: Gill and Macmillan, 1990.

Thornton, William. In *A Faithful Register of the Late Rebellion.* London: 1718.

Thuente, Mary Helen. *The Harp Re-strung: The United Irishmen and the Rise of Irish Literary Nationalism.* Syracuse, N.Y.: Syracuse University Press, 1994.

Tillyard, Stella. *Aristocrats: Caroline, Emily, Louisa, and Sarah Lennox 1740–1832.* New York: Farrar Straus Giroux, 1994.

[Toland, John]. *An Act for the better Securing the Dependency of Ireland upon the Crown of Great-Britain to which is Added, J——n T——d, Esq.; His Reasons Why the Bill for the Better Securing the Dependency of, should not Pass.* London: 1720.

A Treatise of Taxes & Contribution . . . the Same being frequently applied to the present State and Affairs of Ireland. London: 1662.

Trench, Charles Chenevix. *Grace's Card: Irish Catholic Landlords 1690–1800.* Cork and Dublin: Mercier Press, 1997.

Bibliography

A True Narrative of the Proceedings in the severall Suits in Law that have been between the Right Honourable Charl[e]s Lord Gerard of Brandon, and Alexander Fitton, Esq. The Hague: 1663.

Vance, Norman. *Irish Literature, a Social History.* Oxford: Basil Blackwell, 1990.

Waith, Eugene M. *The Pattern of Tragicomedy in Beaumont and Fletcher.* New Haven: Yale University Press, 1952.

Wall, Maureen. *Catholic Ireland in the Eighteenth Century.* Ed. Gerard O'Brien. Dublin: Geography Publications, 1989.

Walsh, Peter. *The Irish Colours Folded, or the Irish Roman Catholics Reply to the (pretended) English Protestants Answer to the Letter desiring a just and merciful regard of the Roman Catholics of Ireland (which Answer is entitled the Irish Colours Displayed).* London: 1662.

———. *A Prospect of the State of Ireland, from the year of the World 1756 to the Year of Christ 1652.* London: 1682.

Ward, Robert E. *Prince of Dublin Printers: The Letters of George Faulkner.* Lexington: University Press of Kentucky, 1972.

Ware, James. *The Antiquities and History of Ireland.* London: 1705.

Warner, Ferdinando. *The History of Ireland.* London: 1763.

———. *The History of the Rebellion and Civil-War in Ireland.* Vol. 1. Dublin: 1768.

Wauchope, Piers. *Patrick Sarsfield and the Williamite War.* Blackrock, Co. Dublin: Irish Academic Press, 1992.

Weinbrot, Howard. *Britannia's Issue: The Rise of British Literature from Dryden to Ossian.* Cambridge: Cambridge University Press, 1993.

Wheatley, Christopher J. "Thomas Shadwell's *The Volunteers* and the Rhetoric of Honor and Patriotism." *ELH* 60 (1993): 397–418.

Whelan, Kevin. "An Underground Gentry? Catholic Middlemen in Eighteenth-Century Ireland." *Eighteenth-Century Ireland* 10 (1995): 7–68.

Williams, Basil. *The Whig Supremacy, 1714–1760.* Oxford: Clarendon Press, 1942.

York, Neil Longley. *Neither Kingdom nor Nation: The Irish Quest for Constitutional Rights, 1698–1800.* Washington: Catholic University of America Press, 1994.

INDEX

absentee landlords, 46
Act of Union, 13, 114, 125
Adams, J. R. R., 63
Addison, Joseph, 4, 5, 9, 46, 64, 67, 72, 76–77, 81, 112, 128–29
Adrian IV, 36
aisling poetry, 79
Alexander's Bull, 36
Almon, John, 101
ancien régime, 17
Andrews, Charles M., 135n. 1
Anglo-Irish, 4, 13, 100, 124
Anne, Queen of England, 36, 37
Answer to the Proposal for the Universal Use of Irish Manufacture, An, 51, 53, 55, 56
Antrim, third earl of (Alexander McDonnell), 49
Appleton, William W., 134n. 28, 146n. 32, 147n. 48
Arachne, 53–54
Aristotle, 4
Ashton, John, 66
Ashton, Robert: biography, 65–66; *The Battle of Aughrim*, 8–9, 13, 63–65, 70–72, 76–83, 95
Atterbury, Francis, 30, 37–38
Auden, W. H., 10
Augher, 68
Austria, 68
Avery, Emmett L., 134n. 21

Baldwin, Richard, 75
Bangor Controversy, 36
Barnard, T. C., 136n. 17
Barrington, Jonah, 125
Bartlett, Thomas, 53, 137n. 25, 142n. 34, 144nn. 36, 38; 145n. 4; 146n. 28; 147n. 38; 150n. 12
Bartley, J. O., 15, 29, 134n. 25, 137n. 29, 147n. 46
Beckett, J. C., 1, 137n. 24, 138n. 11, 140n. 8, 144n. 47, 148n. 24
Beidelman, T. O., 30–31
Beowulf, 12
Bermingham, John, 3
Bevis, Richard, 134n. 18

Black, Jeremy, 141n. 17, 144n. 41
Blackstone, William, 114
Blessington, 65
Bliss, Alan, 137n. 29
Boesky, Amy, 136n. 14
Bolingbroke, Henry St. John, 32, 118–19
Bolton, second duke of (Charles Paulet), 39
Bottigheimer, Karl S., 23
Boucicault, Dion, 123
Bowers, Fredson, 133n. 10
Boyce, D. George, 74, 150n. 15
Boyle, Henry, 91
Brady, Anne M., 65
Brecht, Bertolt, 4
British Army, 73
Brooke, Charlotte, 91
Brooke, Henry, 90–91, 92, 112, 125, 146n. 29
Browne, John, 74–75
Burford's, 58
Burke, Edmund, 87, 145nn. 9, 10
Burke, Helen, 142n. 44
Burnell, Henry, 10, 13, 140n. 1; *Landgartha*, 2–4
Burns, Robert E., 139n. 31, 146n. 31
Burton, Robert, 19
Butler, Christopher, 52
Butler, Sarah, 51, 76

Cairns, David, 33
Campion, Edmund, 139n. 30
Canfield, J. Douglas, 24
Canterbury Tales, The, 12
Carleton, William, 9, 67–68
Carroll, Dennis, 131
Cartaret, John, 72–73
Catholic Confederacy, The, 3
Cato. See Addison, Joseph
Charles I, 75
Charles II, 16, 18, 22, 26, 27, 32
Church of Ireland, 42, 86
Cibber, Colley, 2
Clare, first earl of (John Fitzgibbon), 86, 127
Clare, sixth viscount of (Charles O'Brien), 52
Clark, Gladys H., 133n. 6, 143n. 6, 144n. 32, 145n. 52

Clark, W. S., 30, 133nn. 8, 14, 15; 136n. 22; 139n. 13; 148n. 5
Cleeve, Brian, 64
Clonfert, 65
Colum, Padraic, 12
Congreve, Francis Asprey, 96, 134n. 27
Connolly, S. J., 41, 137nn. 26, 27
Conolly, Thomas, 138n. 10
Conolly, William, 137n. 27, 138n. 10
Conrad, Joseph, 10
converts, 13
Cooke, William, 93, 95, 97, 134n. 29
Corkery, Daniel, 13–14
Corneille, Pierre, 4, 71
Corneille, Thomas, 133n. 12
Covent Garden Theatre, 1, 5, 11
Cowley, Hannah, 2
Cowper, Joseph, 144n. 49
Cox, Richard, 5, 10, 30, 32, 33, 41–43, 45, 53, 60, 77, 104
Craig, Maurice, 150n. 8
Crawford, William, 150n. 22
Cromwell, Oliver, 18, 19, 53
Crow Street Theatre, 8
Cullen, L. M., 86, 136n. 10, 140n. 39, 140n. 7, 142n. 35, 144nn. 39, 42; 145n. 5
Cumberland, Richard, 123–24
Curll, Edmund, 51
Curry, John, 109
Curtin, Nancy J., 126, 143n. 20
Curtis, Edmund, 74, 136n. 12

Davies, John, 45, 59, 136n. 9
Davis, Herbert, 140n. 10
Davis, J. C., 136n. 16
Deane, Seamus, 1, 138n. 4
Declaration of Independence, 114
Declaratory Act, The (sixth of George I), 7, 40, 50, 72
Dennis, William, 106
Dickson, David, 137n. 23
Dillon, Eilís, 133n. 1
dissenters, 13
Dobbs, Arthur, 113
Dobbs, Francis, 102; background, 113; mille-narianism, 131–32; opposition to Penal Laws, 114–15; *The Patriot King*, 4, 11, 102, 115–21, 130–31
Doneraile, 53
Donovan, Kevin, 146n. 29
Dorset, first duke of (Lionel Cranvile Sackville), 143n. 6

Drake, Peter, 73
Drennan, William, 128
Drury Lane Theatre, 1, 5, 7, 11
Dryden, John, 29; *Absalom and Achitophel*, 103, 139n. 14; *Aureng-Zebe*, 71; *MacFlecknoe*, 9
Dublin Castle, 39, 73, 105, 109, 127, 131
Dublin Intelligence, 51
Duffy, Charles Gavan, 67
Dunkin, William, 144n. 49
dystopia, 21

Edict of Nantes, 69
Ehrenpreis, Irvin, 139n. 15, 141n. 12
Eliot, T. S., 10
Elizabeth I, 53, 113
Emmet's Rising, 132
Ennis, 67
Ervine, St. John, 12
Exact Journal of the Victorious Progress of their Majesties Forces, An, 69–70
Exclusion Crisis, 32

Fabricant, Carol, 140n. 11
faction, 103, 105–8
Fagan, Patrick, 141n. 16
Farquhar, George, 2
Faulkner, George, 105
feudal society, 16
Field Day Anthology of Irish Literature, 1
Fielding, Henry, 87–88
Fishamble-Street Theatre, 123
Fitzpatrick, Brendan, 63
Fletcher, John, 3, 15, 22
Flood, Henry, 106–7
Foote, Samuel, 86
Forde, Arthur, 75
Forman, Charles, 69, 73–74
Foster, R. F., 40, 128, 137n. 31, 140n. 9
Four Masters, 10
Fraser, T. G., 144n. 38
Frederick, Prince of Wales, 119
Freeholder's Journal, The, 49
Freeman's Journal, 91
Frye, Northrup, 135n. 6

Galway, 67
Garrick, David, 8, 123
George I, 5, 33, 52, 57, 143n. 22
George II, 7, 77
George IV, 125
Germany, 11
Gilbert, J. T., 65

Glorious Revolution, the, 28, 33, 35
Godfrey, Edmund Berry, 81–82
Goethe, Johann Wolfgang von, 11
Good, Benjamin, 68
Gookin, Vincent, 136n. 13
Graham, John, 66
Grattan, Henry, 74
Grattan's Parliament, 102, 127
Greene, John C., 133n. 6, 143n. 6, 144n. 32, 145n. 52, 148n. 4
Gunpowder Plot, 64

Hale, Nathan, 76
Halifax, second earl of (George Montague Dunk), 93, 124
Hamilton, William Gerard, 93
Hanmer, Meredith, 38, 139n. 30
Hanmer, Thomas, 50, 53, 57
Hanoverian succession, 53
Harmon, Maurice, 1
Hartlib, Samuel, 19
Harvey, Karen J., 12
Hayton, D. W., 51–52, 142n. 30, 144n. 36
Head, Richard, 29, 47; *The Complaisant Companion*, 19; *The English Rogue*, 17; *Hic et Ubique*, 15–16, 20–22, 23–26; *Proteus Redivivus*, 18; *The Western Wonder: or, O Brazeel*, 22
Henry II, 59
Henry V, 70
Hiffernan, Paul, 89
Hill, Jacqueline R., 52
History of the Rise, Progress, and Tendency of Patriotism by a Freeholder, 103
Hitchcock, Robert, 150n. 7
Hobbes, Thomas, 34–35
Holinshead, Raphael, 45
Holmes, Geoffrey, 142n. 37
Home, John, 4, 6
Homer, 17
Hooker, John, 45
Howard, Gorges Edmond, 114; *Apothegms and Maxims on Various Subjects, for the Good Conduct of Life*, 105, 107; background, 102; government allegiance, 105–6; *His Majesty's Revenues*, 102; *Observations and Queries on the Present Laws of this Kingdom Relative to Persons of the Popish Religion*, 110; *The Siege of Tamor*, 4, 6, 11–12, 101, 108–13, 120, 128–30
Howard, Robert, 25
Hume, Robert, 134n. 18, 135n. 5
humours comedy, 15

Iliad, 8, 54
Inchiquin, second earl of (William O'Brien), 32, 52, 142n. 40
India, 11
Ireland's Mirror, 66
Irish Brigades, 52, 68, 73–74, 79, 98
Irish language, 2, 92, 100
Irish literary nationalism, 2, 67, 123–24
Irish Protestant nationalism, 66, 67, 93

Jacobitism, 5, 32, 36, 37, 56, 57, 70, 80, 94
James II, 5, 35, 63, 64, 69, 78
James III, 5, 35, 36, 68, 72
Jeffery, Keith, 144n. 38
Jephson, Robert, 105, 108, 123
Johnson, Samuel, 4, 11, 92
Jonson, Ben, 3

Keating, Geoffrey, 10, 51, 59, 66, 130
Keats, John, 83
Kelly, Hugh, 2
Kelly, James, 127, 143n. 6, 148n. 6
Kelly riots, 89–90
Kern, James B., 146n. 17
Kiberd, Declan, 141n. 15
Kinsella, Thomas, 135n. 49
Kipling, Rudyard, 11
Kirkman, James, 94–96, 97, 99
Kosok, Heinz, 12

Lacy, Peter de, 35
Landa, Louis, 140n. 10
Leadam, I. S., 141n. 23, 143n. 22
Lee, Nathaniel, 71
Leerssen, Joseph (Joep), 12, 15–16, 30, 103, 134n. 26, 147n. 47
Leibnitz, Gottfried Wilhelm, 5
Leighton, C. D. A., 110, 139n. 17
Lennox, Emily, 138n. 10
Lennox, Louisa, 138n. 10
Lessing, Gotthold, 11
Licensing Act (1737), 125
Lillo, George, 4
Louis XIV, 63, 64
Lowman, Moses, 139n. 28
Lucas, A. T., 137n. 33
Lucas, Charles, 89–90, 92, 93
Lynch, John (Gratiano Lucius), 27
Lynch, Kathleen, 136n. 12

macaria, 19
MacCurtin, Hugh, 42, 45, 58–59

MacDowell, R. B., 88, 148n. 23, 149n. 38

Macklin, Charles, 85, 113, 123, 125; background, 94–96; *King Henry the VIII, or the Popish Impostor*, 93; library, 146n. 34; *Love à la Mode*, 7, 91, 96, 97–98, 124; *The Man of the World*, 7–8, 92, 96, 99; *The New Play Criticiz'd*, 88–89; personality, 86; *The School for Husbands*, 92, 93; *The True-born Irishman*, 1, 8, 92

Macpherson, C. B., 139n. 20

Macpherson, James, 102, 142n. 31

Maguire, W. A., 145n. 54

Malone, Anthony, 91

Malone, Arthur, 106

Mambretti, Catherine Cole, 144n. 30

Manuel, Frank E., 135n. 6

Marin, Louis, 16, 20

Marlborough, first duke of (John Churchill), 32

Marlowe, Christopher, 4, 64

Marryat, Thomas, 124

McCormack, W. J., 148n. 6

McCracken, J. L., 138n. 11, 141n. 21, 145n. 3

McGuiness, Frank, 82

McGuire, James, 145n. 54

McHugh, Roger, 1

M——ckl——n's Answer to Tully, 88

merchant adventurers, 18

Mercier, Vivian, 1

Mervyn, Audley, 27

M'Gee, Thomas D'Arcy, 137n. 36

Michelburne, John, 66, 142n. 2, 145n. 55, 150n. 14

Molière (Jean Baptiste Poquelin), 133n. 12

Molyneux, William, 60, 101

Monmouth, first duke of (James Scott), 22

Montgomery, Ian, 139n. 18

Moody, T. W., 133n. 2, 139n. 11

More, Thomas, 15

Morgan, Lady Sydney, 123

Morley, Vincent, 144n. 37

Mossop, Henry, 133n. 7, 149n. 1

Munter, Robert, 143n. 13

Murphy, Seán, 146n. 23, 147n. 36

Murray, Christopher, 1, 29, 133n. 14, 140n. 5

Muscovy, 35

Nabokov, Vladimir, 10

Navigation Act (1663), 50

Nelson, William, 135n. 6

Neville, Henry, 19

Newcastle, first duke of Newcastle-upon-Tyne (Thomas Pelham-Holles), 53

New English, 4, 40, 44, 45, 47, 49, 64, 74

New Historicism, 13

Newton, Issac, 5

Norman conquest, 5, 32, 42, 44

Norris, Richard, 66

North America, 6

Northern Ireland, 14

O'Brien, Conor Cruise, 145nn. 9, 10

O'Brien, Donough, 141n. 25

O'Brien, Gerard, 2, 141n. 22

O'Brien, Lucius, 105

O'Brien, Mary: *The Fallen Patriot*, 6, 127–28; politics, 10

Ó Bruadair, Dáibhí, 14

O'Casey, Sean, 132

Ó Catháin, Diarmid, 141n. 15

O'Connor, Dermo'd, 51, 59, 66, 130

O'Conor, Charles, 91, 93, 108, 109

O'Faolain, Sean, 14

O'Flanagan, Theophilus, 137n. 34

O'Halloran, Sylvester, 101, 104

O'Keeffe, John, 12, 13, 125–26; *Patrick in Prussia*, 125; *The Poor Soldier*, 1, 123; *The Wicklow Mountains*, 10

Old English, 3–4, 5, 63, 74

Old Historicism, 13

Ó Maoláin, Seamus, 147n. 35

O'Meally, Luke, 95

Ormond, first duke of (James Butler), 18, 22, 23, 32

Ormond, second duke of (James Butler), 32, 35, 53

Orrery, first earl of (Roger Boyle), 71, 137n. 36

Ó Tuama, Seán, 135n. 49

Owenson, Robert, 123

Oxford, first earl of (Robert Harley), 57

Palliser, John, 75

Paradise Lost, 13, 64

Paris, 53

Patrick, Saint, 36

patriotism, 38, 47, 62, 75, 90, 92, 103–4, 106–7, 111–12, 128

patronage, 125

Peter the Great, 35

Peterson, Martin Severin, 150n. 3

Philips, George, 49

Philips, Katherine, 71

Philips, William, 9, 10, 85, 108; *Belisarius*, 57–58; *Hibernia Freed*, 4, 6–7, 11, 49, 53–62, 76, 101; politics, 53; *The Revengeful Queen*, 53; *St. Stephen's Green*, 52

Plattel, Martin G., 136n. 15
Porter, James, 67
Powell, Sylvester, 66, 69
Power, T. P., 144n. 39
Powes, Ridley, 149n. 25
Poynings Law, 93, 106
Protestant ascendancy, 6, 11, 102
Pry, Kevin B., 12

Quin, James, 86

Ramsay, Allen, 150n. 14
rebellion of the earls, 49
Regency crisis, 10
Reily, Hugh, 26, 94
Rhodesia, 74
Richards, Shaun, 33
Ross, Angus, 150n. 20
Ross, Ian Campbell, 141n. 14
Rowe, Nicholas, 4, 64
Russell, Thomas, 86–87, 131–32

Schneider, Ben Ross, Jr., 137n. 1
Scotland, 6
Scott, Walter, 95
Scowcroft, R. Mark, 147n. 35
sentimental comedy, 6, 9
Sequin, Peter, 11
Seven Years' War, 93
Shadwell, Charles, 9, 62, 85; *The Fair Quaker of
    Deal*, 29; *The Hasty Wedding*, 39, 40–41; *The
    Humours of the Army*, 29, 33–34, 96, 99; *Irish
    Hospitality*, 9, 29, 39, 45–47; *The Plotting
    Lovers*, 4, 5–6, 29, 30, 32, 34, 55, 90; *The
    Sham Prince*, 35, 42
Shadwell, John, 31–32
Shadwell, Thomas, 5, 29, 31
Shakespeare, William, 4, 88; *Henry V*, 33, 44;
    Troilus and Cressida, 79
Shaw, Catherine, 3, 133n. 14
Sheldon, Esther K., 133n. 6, 146n. 19
Shepherd, Robert, 139n. 23
Sheridan, Thomas (1678–1738), 75–76
Sheridan, Thomas (1719–1788), 1, 89, 123–24
Sherlock v. Annesley, 50
Simms, J. G., 147n. 1
Smedley, Jonathan, 35
Smock Alley Theatre, 9, 22, 71
Somerset, sixth duke of (Charles Seymour), 52
Spain, 35, 68, 73
Spenser, Edmund, 139n. 30
Staples, Hugh B., 150n. 9
Steele, Richard, 46

Sterne, Laurence, 11
Stockwell, La Tourette, 29, 135n. 2, 145n. 52,
    149n. 2
Stone, George, 91
Story, George, 70, 81
*Strictures upon Observations on a Speech by an
    Impartial Observer*, 106
Summers, Montague, 139n. 12
Sutherland, Robert, 68
Swift, Jonathan, 73, 74; *The Intelligencer*, 73;
    *Proposal for the Universal Use of Irish Manu-
    facture*, 7, 50, 54, 56
Synge, J. M., 132

Talbot, Will, 145n. 55
Tallies of War and Peace, The, 69
Thackeray, William, 67
Thomond, eighth earl of (Henry O'Brien), 10,
    49, 50, 52, 142n. 40
Thornton, William, 37
Thuente, Mary Helen, 14, 150n. 14
Tillyard, Stella, 138n. 10
Toland, John, 51
Tories, 13, 32, 35, 57; High Church, 35–36, 37–
    38; raiders, 19, 23
Townshend, George, 105, 106, 109
tragicomedy, 3
Trench, Charles Chenevix, 141n. 29
Trinity College, Dublin, 65, 75, 96, 115
Tyrconnell, first earl of (Richard Talbot), 78
Tyrone, first earl of (Hugh O'Neil), 113

United Irishmen, 12, 14, 67, 126, 128, 131
Ussher, Adam, 65
Ussher (or Usher), Charles, 65
Ussher, William, 65
utopia, 16–17, 20

Vanbrugh, John, 2
Vance, Norman, 64
Vaughan, W. E., 133n. 2
Vollrath, Robert A., 135n. 6
Voltaire (François-Marie Arouet), 11, 76
Volunteers, the, 113, 123, 127, 131

Waith, Eugene M., 133n. 11
Waiting for Godot, 13
Wall, Maureen, 141n. 26
Walpole, Robert, 103, 119, 141n. 17
Walsh, Peter, 27–28, 58
Ward, Robert E., 148n. 16
Ware, James, 104
Warner, Ferdinando, 124, 150n. 22

Wauchope, Piers, 134n. 35, 143n. 12, 144n. 28
weaving industry, 54
Webb, General John Richmond, 57
Weinbrot, Howard, 104
Whelan, Kevin, 86, 140n. 40, 144n. 39
Whig ideology, 30, 41, 47
Whigs, 5, 13, 32, 55, 58, 103, 112, 119
Wilder, Thornton, 4
Wild Geese, The, 52, 69
Wilkes, John, 87, 97, 101

William III, 5, 29, 32, 53, 64, 66, 77, 113
Williams, Basil, 143n. 22
Wogan, Charles, 74
Woods, C. J., 145n. 8
Wood's halfpence, 50, 72, 74
Woolen Act (1699), 50
Wright, Wm. Ball, 143n. 10
Wyndham, Thomas (Lord Chancellor), 52

York, Neil Longley, 146n. 22, 149n. 35